W9-CRN-072

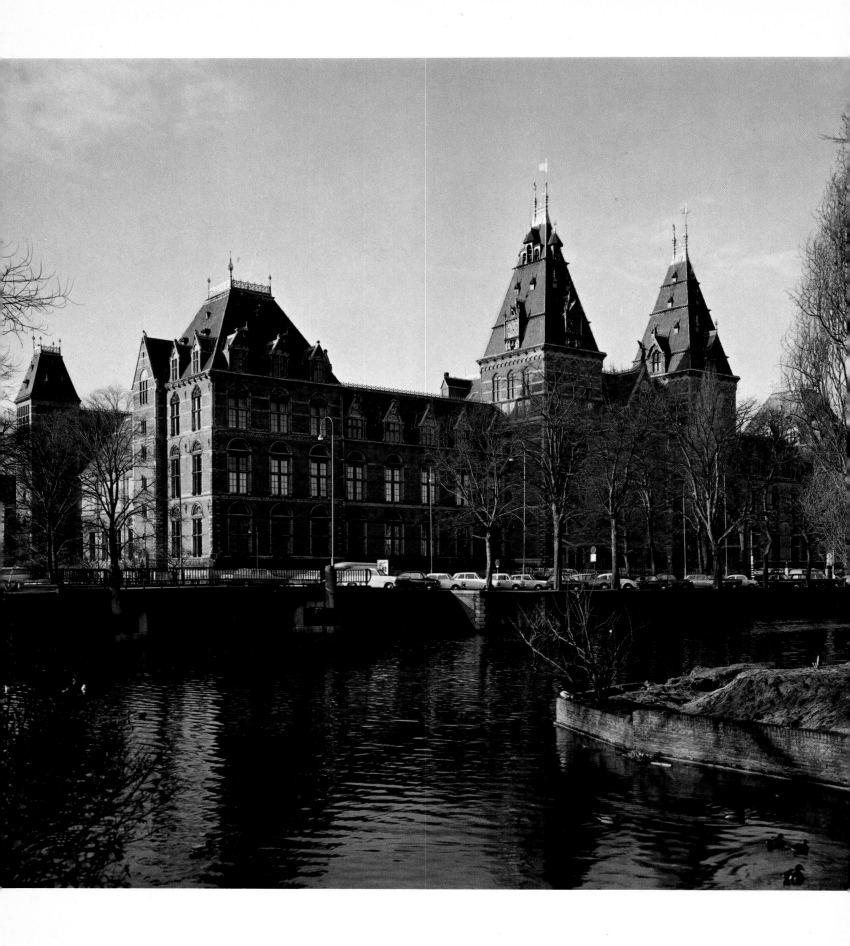

RIJKSMUSEUM
AMSTERDAM PAINTINGS

Newsweek / GREAT MUSEUMS OF THE WORLD

NEW YORK, N.Y.

**GREAT MUSEUMS
OF THE WORLD**

Editorial Director—Carlo Ludovico Ragghianti

Assistant—Giuliana Nannicini

Translation and Editing—Editors of ARTNEWS

RIJKSMUSEUM
AMSTERDAM

Texts by:

Giorgio T. Faggin

Ugo Ruggeri

Raffaele Monti

Design:

Fiorenzo Giorgi

Published by

NEWSWEEK, INC.

& ARNOLDO MONDADORI EDITORE

Library of Congress Catalog Card No. 69-19063

© 1969—Arnoldo Mondadori Editore—CEAM—Milan

© 1969—Photographs Copyright by Kodansha Ltd.—Tokyo

All rights reserved. Printed and bound in Italy.

INTRODUCTION

GERARD VAN DER HOEK
Head of the Educational Section, Rijksmuseum

The visitor who enters the Rijksmuseum in Amsterdam is welcomed by *Architecture* and *Sculpture,* statues of beautiful women standing on either side of one of the two main entrances. At the other entrance he is greeted by similar works, called *Painting* and *Engraving.* Once inside, and having paid for his ticket, he may proceed in any of a number of directions. Most visitors, however, come in at the west entrance and go up the broad stairs to the floor above. There paintings by Rembrandt, Vermeer, Frans Hals and hundreds of other Dutch artists await them. Although the Rijksmuseum includes many other works of art, it is exceptional in offering, on their own ground, so many masterpieces of Dutch painting. This art in particular, which flourished notably in the 17th century, is magnificently represented in the museum.

Art collections are often housed in buildings erected for other purposes — schools, orphanages, etc. — which have been merely adapted to their new function. The Rijksmuseum's building is one of the few, and one of the first in Europe, to have been built expressly as a museum. The collection itself, however, predates the edifice now housing it.

The National Art Gallery, opened to the public in 1800, originally occupied the 150-year-old Huis ten Bos, an unused summer palace near The Hague. Only five years earlier, in 1795, the French Revolution had put an end to the Dutch Republic, the United Provinces of the Netherlands; and the Stadholder, William V, had fled to England. The new Batavian Republic came under French control.

The House of Orange's notable collection of paintings, ethnological specimens and models illustrating physical laws, was moved to Paris and absorbed by the Louvre. Other pieces from the Stadholder's collection were sold at auction by order of the new rulers. About two hundred works, mainly history paintings and objects with historical associations, were saved. These pieces, along with the National Art Gallery that was housed in the Huis ten Bos, formed the basis of the Rijksmuseum collection. The first acquisition, Jan Asselyn's *The Threatened Swan,* was made in the same year of 1800, after which the collection was increased by regular purchases. Shortly thereafter, an official decided that the collection needed a more prestigious setting, and had it moved back to the building at The Hague where, as the property of the prince, it had been displayed originally.

Under foreign occupation the country's government became first the Batavian Republic, then the Kingdom of Holland, with Louis Bonaparte, the brother of the French Emperor, as king. This was a period of intensive growth for the collection. Amsterdam became the capital of the kingdom, and the Town

Hall on the Dam — built by Jacob van Campen in the 17th century — was adapted as the Royal Palace (and such it has remained to the present day).

The new king wanted Amsterdam to become a center of culture as well as the royal residence and governmental center. In 1808 Louis Bonaparte founded what he called the Great Royal Museum and had it arranged in a hall and two smaller rooms on the first floor of the palace on the Dam. This crowded display included, among other things, a selection of works from the House of Orange, which were formerly in the National Art Gallery, and sixty-five paintings acquired immediately after the establishment of the museum. Among the latter were Gerard Dou's then famous *Night School,* a landscape by Potter, two marine views by Willem van de Velde, Geertgen tot Sint Jans' *Adoration of the Magi,* Govert Flinck's *Isaac Blessing Jacob,* Jan van Goyen's *View of the Dordtse Kil Before Dordrecht* and works by Jan Steen. The City of Amsterdam contributed seven important paintings, including Rembrandt's *The Night Watch* and his *Syndics of the Cloth Guild,* Bartholomeus van der Helst's *The Banquet of the Civic Guard* and Willem van de Velde's *The Harbor of Amsterdam.* The king's great interest in the museum is shown by his acquisition within one year of 137 paintings for it. Among them were Gabriel Metsu's *Breakfast* and Jan Steen's *The Feast of St. Nicholas.*

This initial period of prosperity, under the sagacious administration of the museum's director, Cornelis Apostool, was temporarily interrupted when the Emperor Napoleon abolished the Kingdom of Holland and annexed its territory to France. The museum was then renamed the Hollandsch Museum and was scheduled to move out of its building, which had now become the Royal Palace. A change in the political situation altered the program. By 1815, French domination had come to an end and the sixth Prince of Orange had returned to the newly formed United Kingdom of the Netherlands as King William I. The new king also inaugurated an ambitious cultural program, which included the decision that the national museum would continue to be situated in Amsterdam. Shortly afterwards it was given the name which it still bears today: Rijksmuseum, i.e., Museum of the Kingdom.

If there was already concern over the inadequate accommodations under French domination, now the restitution of confiscated works of art from the Louvre made acute the need for additional space. Furthermore, the museum had resumed making acquisitions. Among the first after the liberation were Philips Wouwerman's *The White Horse* and Frans Hals's *The Merry Toper,* to cite two works reproduced in this book. Consequently, the collection was transferred to the Trippenhuis, a building constructed in the 17th century as the residence of Trip, a rich merchant of the Netherlands' Golden Age. The Trippenhuis was opened to the public as a museum in February, 1817. As often happens, it was apparent even at the time of the inauguration of the new museum that its space was still too limited, yet the Trippenhuis was to continue to house the Rijksmuseum for the next seventy years. For some time after moving to the Trippenhuis, the collection was regularly increased by works of such masters as Pieter de Hooch, Ruysdael, Jan Steen, Metsu, Berckheyde, Troost and Nicolaas Maes.

This second period of growth came to an end when the Southern Provinces (united to the Netherlands by the Congress of Vienna) seceded in 1830 to form the separate Kingdom of Belgium. In the resulting depression, fewer works could be acquired for the museum. In fact, two important Rembrandts and a Ruisdael that came up for sale at this time could not be bought, because of lack of funds. Except for some rare purchases, most of the accessions at this time were private donations. Thanks to these, even at such an inauspicious moment in history, the Rijksmuseum became increasingly rich. The number of works continued to grow, but the space available at the Trippenhuis remained the same, lighting was poor and the heating was provided by ordinary stoves. In addition, there was constant danger of fire, because of a kerosene storage depot situated close to the museum.

If only from a practical point of view, the need for a new building was pressing. The right psychological moment arrived in 1862 during the celebrations commemorating the country's liberation from France. It was felt that a new building for the museum would satisfy local nationalistic sentiments. The building would be a national monument, standing in the eyes of the present and future generations as a symbol of the power and splendor of Holland. Twenty-one architects entered the competition for the design of the building, but ten years passed before the plan submitted by P. H. J. Cuypers was selected as the winning design, and construction took another decade. On July 13, 1885, the new Rijksmuseum in Amsterdam was officially inaugurated.

The design of the building was intended to emphasize the museum's function as a temple of art and history. Constructed in a Neo-Gothic style, it sought to carry out its theme by exploiting the materials, forms and decorative motifs of the great periods in Dutch art. Thus there rises before us, between the old city and the new urban expansion of the 19th century, the present red terra-cotta edifice, constructed in accordance with the logic of medieval architecture, on which various Renaissance forms have been grafted. The decorations are in harmony with the architecture; they do not violate the principles of the fundamental structure, but flow from the construction itself. Above and between the windows, porches and entrances, the façade is decorated with statues, reliefs and ceramic plaques. These and the leaded windows exemplify the various eras in Dutch art and history.

Inside the building, art and artists are glorified in mosaic pavements and vaults, decorated pilasters, inscriptions and murals. This plethora of decoration did not aid in viewing the works of art, whose number increased enormously after the inauguration of the new building. Among the most famous of the new acquisitions were Vermeer's *Young Woman Reading a Letter*, Frans Hals's *Self-Portrait* and Vermeer's *Street in Delft*. The works on display now numbered 1,600, and people spoke of the "Rijks Warehouse" rather than the Rijksmuseum.

After World War I a program of thinning out the collection was undertaken, and this involved a radical alteration of the building. In its definitive phase, this program was interrupted by World War II. By "definitive" we mean "definitive for the time," for despite all the criticism of the building, after eighty years it still seems capable of adjusting itself to contemporary needs. Perhaps the future will bring other conceptions of what a museum should be, and there will be attempts to adapt the building to such ideas.

Let us now follow the visitor who at the beginning of our account was walking up the stairs that lead to the painting gallery. From the acquisitions mentioned above, it will be clear that the Rijksmuseum is mainly intended to show the course of Dutch art. For that reason, along with the great masters, the most important works of secondary painters are shown, in order to give a complete picture of what Dutch artists have created from the late Middle Ages to the early 19th century. The paintings are displayed in chronological sequence. A visit to the collection begins in the rooms devoted to late medieval and Renaissance artists. A number of the painters have been identified only recently, thanks to new research in art history; others, who remain anonymous, are identified as the Master of the Virgo inter Virgines, the Master of Alkmaar, etc. Then there are Geertgen tot Sint Jans, Jan Mostaert, Jacob Cornelisz van Oostsanen, Cornelis Engelbrechtsz, Lucas van Leyden, Jan van Scorel and Maerten van Heemskerck, among others.

Many 17th-century Dutch artists were specialists, unequalled in their fields. Frans Hals is the painter of the Dutch character, which he caught on canvas in numerous single and group portraits. Jan Miense Molenaar and Johannes Verspronck also made portraiture a specialty. The Dutch atmosphere becomes tangible in Jan van Goyen's works, and other painters dealt with different aspects of the landscape. Hendrick Avercamp's winter scenes almost reproduce the feeling of frost. Ruisdael is known for his views of placid rivers and majestic forests; Paulus Potter for his soft meadows and flourishing cattle. Adriaen van Ostade painted bucolic scenes, and Jan Steen recorded the daily life of the Dutch in the 17th century. Marine views were very popular in Amsterdam, which was already a busy maritime port, and Willem van de Velde, a master of the genre, portrayed great harbors crowded with imposing frigates and elegant sloops. Jan van de Velde and Pieter Claesz devoted themselves to sumptuous still lifes. A group of artists who had followed an international trend by traveling and studying in the South produced Italianized Dutch landscapes. Impressed by the sunny, romantic atmosphere of the Peninsula, artists like Johannes Both and Adam Pynacker, on their return to Holland, expressed their nostalgia for the blue skies of the idealized Roman landscapes.

What is true in general for the museum, which shows the whole development of Dutch art, is true of Rembrandt in particular. The evolution of his style can nowhere be better followed than in his own country, and the Rijksmuseum has twenty-two of his paintings. Among his youthful works, *Jeremiah Lamenting the Destruction of Jerusalem* and *Rembrandt's Mother* should be mentioned. Belonging to his middle period are *St. Peter's Denial, Self-Portrait as St. Paul, Syndics of the Cloth Guild* and *The Jewish Bride,* also called *The Bridal Couple.* Rembrandt's largest painting, *The Night Watch,* has a room to itself. In composition it is a bold departure from the traditional handling of a common Dutch theme of the time. It would be a mistake, however, to maintain — as some critics have — that Rembrandt's contemporaries were unable to appreciate the painting.

Cabinet — that is, small-sized — pictures are also a special feature of Dutch art. The museum has four of Vermeer's forty known works: *Young Woman Reading a Letter, The Kitchen Maid, Street in Delft* and *The Letter*. All four are painted on wood panels and show the artist's marvelous purity and intensity of light, which calmly illuminates the space and lingers on the objects in it. In the same section of the museum are some particularly fine interiors by Pieter de Hooch, spacious interior views of churches by Emanuel de Witte and small, pleasing portraits by Gerard Ter Borch.

Although less important than the works of the Golden Age, the Neoclassical and Romantic paintings of the 18th century in Holland reveal a mastery of technique of the first order. The artists of this period devoted themselves especially to portraiture, of individuals and groups, and still lifes with flowers. In genre painting, Cornelis Troost's attractive little scenes of daily life are outstanding.

Of a different caliber from the French, impressionism nevertheless had a following in Holland in the schools of The Hague and Amsterdam. Anton Mauve and the Maris brothers rendered the sunlit atmosphere of Dutch meadows and dunes. Breitner taught an entire generation how to see Amsterdam in a new way. With these late 19th-century artists the collection of Dutch painting comes to an end.

The foreign paintings in the museum are few in number, but highly select. They include the Italian primitives, Piero di Cosimo and Carlo Crivelli, the latter represented by a *Mary Magdalene* that is almost Oriental in taste. Then there are a *Crucifixion* by El Greco, a simple but vibrant *Portrait of a Man* by Goya and a cold, aloof male portrait by Anthonis Mor. Among other masters shown are Lorenzo Monaco, the Carracci, Murillo, Rubens, Van Dyck and Liotard.

In addition to its paintings, the museum has other collections, but they are not presented in this book. In sculpture and the decorative arts, the emphasis is on the work of Dutch artists and craftsmen, but there are also a number of displays of French, German and Italian objects. With great sensitivity, an unknown medieval master carved the *Meeting of Joachim and Anna* out of a block of wood. Sculpture in this period was generally carved in wood and also originally polychromed. In late Gothic times, Adriaen van Wesel combined traditional style with realistic elements in his *Angel Musicians*. The museum's sculpture collection continues with works of Quellinus of Antwerp, who executed the decorations for the new Town Hall on the Dam. Then there are Falconet, the distinguished French sculptor of the end of the 18th century, and others.

In the section covering the transition from the Gothic to the Renaissance in the northern and southern Netherlands, the tapestries are particularly important. In theme these are religious, historical (Charles V's coat of arms) and mythological (the *Story of Diana*). The splendid *Diana* tapestry is the work of Frans Spiering, from the southern Netherlands, who like many of his compatriots took refuge in the north from religious persecution. As a result of these disturbances, the art of tapestry weaving was introduced to the north, and in this specific case to Delft.

Furniture is shown in a series of period rooms, that have been reconstructed complete to the last detail. Cabinets, tables and chairs trace the development of furniture as well as various patterns of domestic life. Exquisite doll houses, one of them furnished by the daughter of de Ruyter, the celebrated Dutch admiral, show the interior of 17th-century aristocratic households in miniature, executed with great fidelity.

The Rijksmuseum's silver collection is the richest of its kind. It includes old pieces that belonged to the guilds, such as ceremonial chains and cups used at the banquets held by those corporations. Among the famous Dutch silversmiths, special mention should be made of the van Vianen brothers. Adam van Vianen decorated his cups with such typically baroque motifs as human and animal figures and plant forms variously combined. Johannes Lutma's masterpieces are simple and functional, with sober decoration.

The blue glazed pottery of Delft is famous all over the world. Trade with the Orient familiarized the Dutch gentry of the Golden Age with Chinese porcelain, and many attempts were made to imitate these beautiful but costly wares. The attempts failed, but Delft became one of the great pottery centers of Europe. Along with the effort to reproduce Oriental porcelains, the decorators copied Japanese and Chinese ornamental motifs. Craftsmen at Meissen, in Saxony, succeeded in reproducing porcelain thanks to the availability of the proper raw material, and at Meissen, too, Chinese motifs appeared on fine ornamental vases, trays and plates. When the sculptor Kandler became chief designer there, he also produced amusing polychrome figurines which were inspired by *commedia dell'arte* characters. Italian craftsmen introduced the art of glass blowing into Holland. The ancillary art of engraving on glass with a diamond was then developed by men like Willem van Heemskerck, who was an expert calligrapher. In the display cases devoted to Dutch and foreign glassware, all the various techniques are represented, including carved, engraved and variegated glass, the last being an 18th-century specialty.

The presence in the museum of the little ship's model of *The Seven Provinces* and the stern decoration of the *Royal Charles,* the English flagship captured by Admiral de Ruyter, testify to the fact that the history of the Netherlands is closely connected with the sea. Banners and ships' models, as well as paintings of naval subjects executed by the two van de Veldes, father and son, keep alive the memory of the Netherlands' glorious history. These are not only interesting historical mementos, but often also great artistic creations.

Less well known is the Rijksmuseum's print collection, since — like all such collections — only a part of the prints, drawings, engravings, etc., can be displayed, while the rest is stored away from the dangerous light. The Print

14

Room, however, contains a selection of Dutch drawings in which there is no artist of the Netherlands from the 15th century on who is not represented. A high point of the collection is the group of one hundred drawings by Rembrandt. Thus with some thousand of the master's etchings, which are also in the museum, along with the twenty-two paintings, the Rijksmuseum possesses the most complete repertory of Rembrandt's work. Another high point of the collection is the large number of magnificent etchings by Hercules Seghers. In addition there are notable drawings and graphics by foreign artists, including almost the entire opus of Albrecht Dürer and that of the anonymous 16th-century German graphic artist, known as the Master of the Amsterdam Print Collection.

Since 1952, the Rijksmuseum has housed the collection of the Society of Friends of the Arts of Asia. Previously the museum owned only a small group of Middle Eastern ceramics and carpets. Now, the Asian Art Department includes works from the entire continent of Asia and from the Indonesian archipelago. Since Indonesia was a Dutch colony for centuries, it is natural for the area's bronze and stone sculpture to be represented at the Rijksmuseum. From Japan there is a dancing *Siva* and from China a seated *Buddha*. Although this department is rather small, it contains a number of magnificent works.

Following modern ideas concerning the function of a museum, improvements have been made in the building, and the display collections have been selectively refined. Our imaginary visitor may now pause in his tour at an excellent restaurant on the premises. He may buy publications, reproductions and art books at the counter in the main vestibule, utilize its information service or consult the museum's extensive library on the history of art. These facilities are intended to bring the treasures of the Rijksmuseum within reach of as large a public as possible.

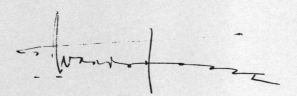

**HOLLAND
FLANDERS**

GEERTGEN TOT SINT JANS. *The Tree of Jesse.*

From the supine body of the aged Jesse, asleep in a walled garden, emerges the trunk of a tree whose branches support the kings of Judah, the progenitors of Jesus. The youth with a harp, seated on the lowest branch, is David; behind him to the right is King Solomon. At the crown of the tree, between two adoring angels, are the Madonna and Child. The two prophets standing on either side of Jesse are probably Isaiah and Jeremiah.

It is difficult to believe that this impressive painting is the work of Geertgen. In all likelihood, Friedländer is right to associate it with the early work of Jan Mostaert. Closer in spirit to the young Mostaert than to Geertgen is the rather fatuous elegance of the languid, almost caricatured figures. Geertgen's figures are differently conceived, being solidly based and having a geometric structure, as in the *Adoration of the Magi* and *The Holy Kinship* (pp. 20–21). These are stylistic features in the van Eyck tradition, and in fact we know that a "Geertgen de Hollandere" was in Bruges from 1475 to 1476 as an apprentice in the Guild of Miniature Painters. In Bruges Geertgen must also have studied the work of Petrus Christus, who was closely concerned with the problems of volume and perspective. In the abstract feeling of the figures and in the relationship between them and the surrounding landscape, the work of Petrus Christus established a clear precedent for Geertgen.

GEERTGEN TOT SINT JANS. *Adoration of the Magi.*   *p. 20*

Geertgen's appearance on the scene had great significance for 15th-century painting in the Netherlands. Although he was preceded by the still mysterious figure of Albert van Ouwater, Geertgen may be considered the first great painter of the Haarlem School, which was to produce a number of important artists in the 16th and 17th centuries. In the limpid quality of his vision, Geertgen is a direct descendant of Jan van Eyck. The Dutch painter, however, does not have the incisive analytical feeling of van Eyck, nor does Geertgen's art have an epic and worldly tone. There is rather a contemplative and intimate character about his work. Geertgen has properly been seen as having some association with the spiritual movement known as the *Devotio Moderna,* which had great currency in the northern Netherlands during his time. Foreign to any sort of sentimental hysteria, this religious current emphasized a wholesome quietism. In the few paintings by the Haarlem artist that have come down to us — all of the highest quality — we are also struck by the prominence and the naturalistic straightforwardness given to the landscape. Geertgen's landscape backgrounds, as in this work, are always executed with great delicacy and are intimately connected with the main figures through an exquisite sense of space and atmosphere.

GEERTGEN TOT SINT JANS. *The Holy Kinship.*   *p. 21*

In a Gothic church, St. Anne with the Madonna and the Child are seated on the left; on the right is St. Elizabeth with the infant St. John the Baptist reaching out to Jesus. Behind St. Anne stand St. Joseph (with the lily in his hand) and St. Joachim; behind St. Elizabeth are Mary, the wife of Cleophas,

GEERTGEN TOT SINT JANS (?)
Leyden circa 1460 — Haarlem circa 1490
Perhaps this artist was the *Geertgen de Hollander* who was an apprentice in 1475–76 in the Guild of St. John and St. Luke at Bruges (booksellers and miniature painters). Subsequently, a pupil of Albert van Owater in Haarlem. He was called Geertgen tot Sint Jans, which means "Little Gerard of St. John's" because he lived with the Knights Hospitalers at Haarlem.
The Tree of Jesse
Oil on panel; 35″ × 23 1/4″.
Also attributed to the youthful Jan Mostaert. The kneeling nun on the left was revealed by cleaning in 1932. Acquired in 1956 with a contribution from the *Vereeniging Rembrandt.*

18

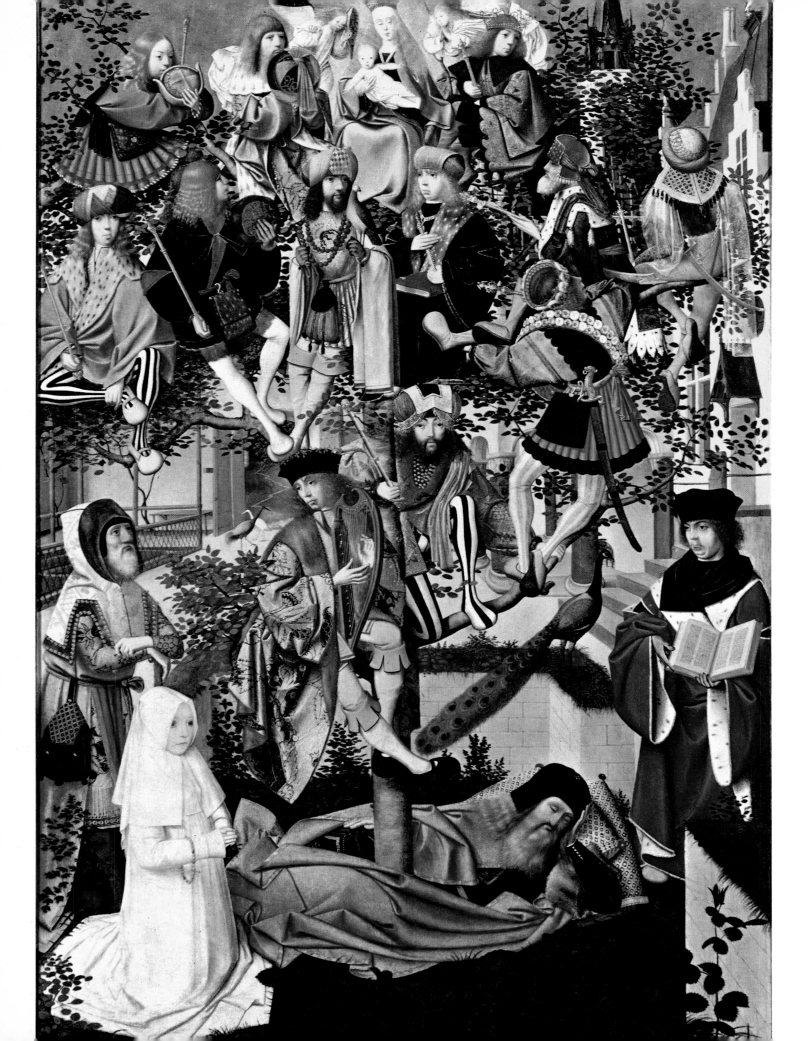

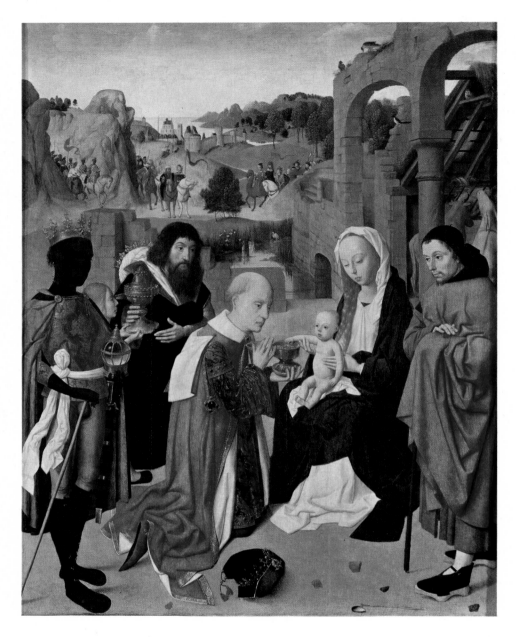

GEERTGEN TOT SINT JANS
Adoration of the Magi
Oil on panel; 35 1/2″ × 27 1/2″.
Acquired in Amsterdam in 1904.

and Mary Salome, watching her three children at play. Five male figures are seen about the altar, where a boy snuffs the candles. On the altar there is a sculpture representing the sacrifice of Abraham.

The painting is generally ascribed to the early working years of the artist, who died very young. But Geertgen shows that he has already posed and resolved the complicated problems of light, perspective and setting. The artist's independence and originality is apparent also in the symbolism, which is far from conventional. The figures in fact have a folksy, indeed somewhat wooden, aspect. Adolf Goldschmidt speaks of Geertgen's art as "secular, radical and veined with humor." Geertgen certainly eschewed the psychological and dramatic effects of Rogier van der Weyden; what interested him was clarity of form and purity of light.

GEERTGEN TOT SINT JANS
The Holy Kinship
Oil on panel; 54 1/4″ × 41 1/4″.
Acquired in Rotterdam in 1808.

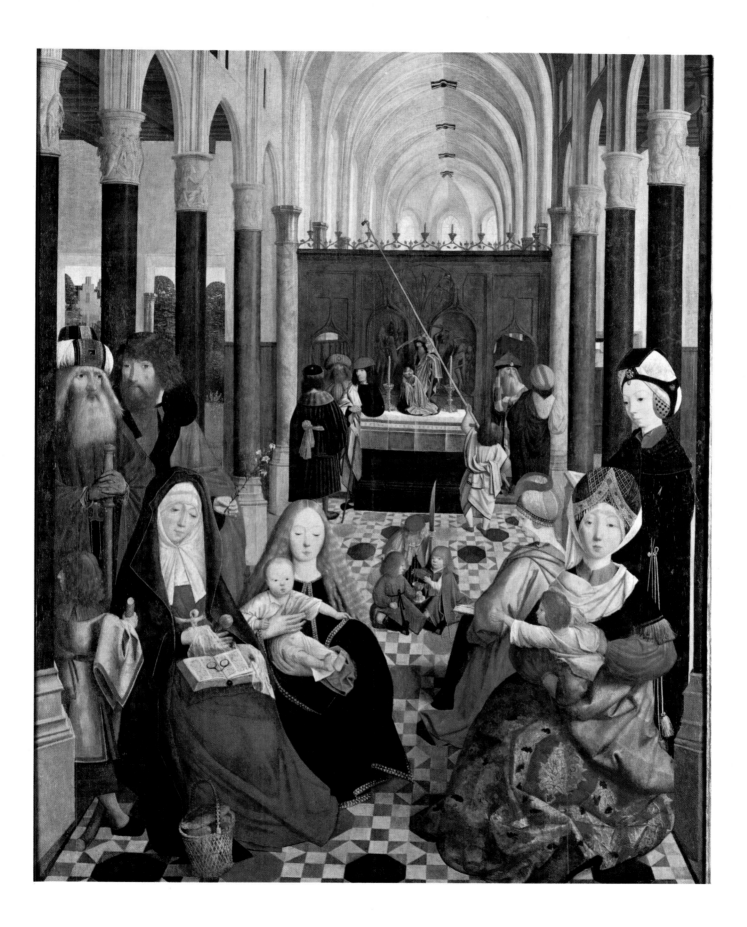

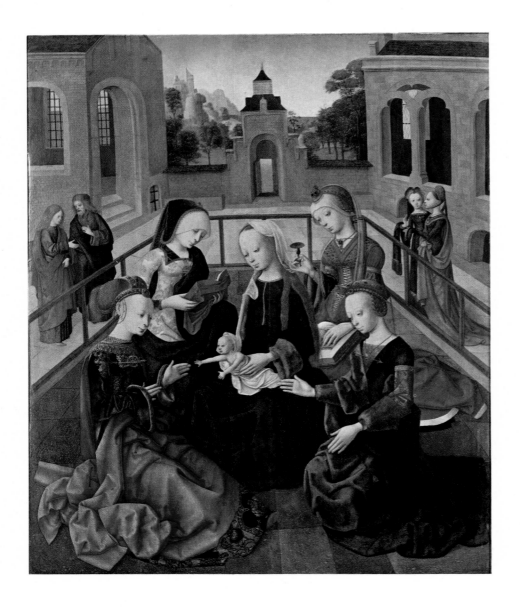

MASTER OF THE VIRGO INTER VIRGINES. *The Virgin among Virgins.*

The title of this painting, in Latin, has given a name to the sensitive, anonymous Dutch master who flourished around the last two decades of the 15th century, presumably at Delft. One art historian has described him thus: "An original artist in his choice of colors and their gradation, the master has left us intensely felt and sometimes violently expressive scenes of the Passion." In contrast with the classical art of the great Geertgen, who avoided any suggestion of psychological or decorative effect, this anonymous painter took pleasure in exaggerating the physical features of his figures, which are often richly dressed and eccentrically posed. He was, in fact, a stylist, who prefigured the Gothic Mannerists who appeared on the Netherlands' scene between 1500 and 1510. The four female saints accompanying the Virgin are Catherine, Ursula, Cecilia and Barbara. Each is identifiable by the shape of the jewel symbolizing her martyrdom that she wears on her breast.

MASTER OF
THE VIRGO INTER VIRGINES
Dutch painter so-called from *The Virgin among Virgins* in the Rijksmuseum. Active from about 1480 to about 1500, presumably at Delft. Perhaps trained at Ghent in the circle of Joos van Wassenhove (Justus of Ghent).
The Virgin among Virgins
Oil on panel; 48 1/2" ×40 1/4".
From the National Museum of The Hague to the Rijksmuseum in 1808.

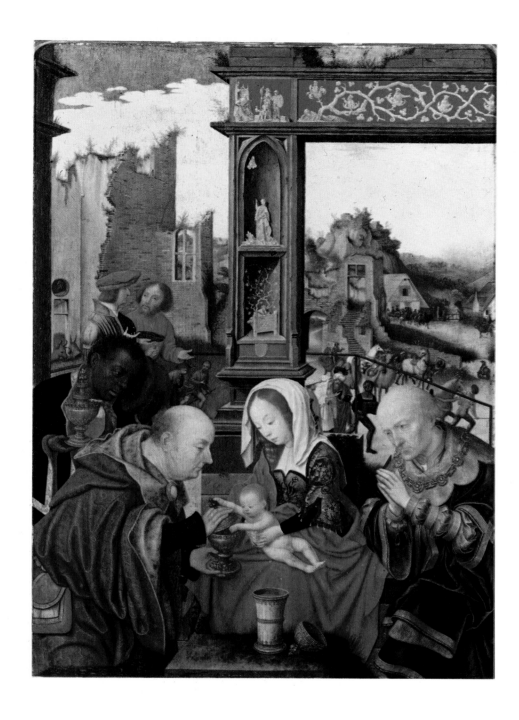

JAN MOSTAERT
Haarlem circa 1475 — Haarlem circa 1555
A pupil of Jacob Jansz at Haarlem, he was
trained under the influence of Geertgen. For
eighteen years he was court painter to Mar-
garet of Austria, Governor of the Netherlands (1507–1530), and perhaps was active
at Mechelen. The first works by Jan Mostaert were identified by G. Glück (1896)
and C. Benoit (1899).
Adoration of the Magi
Oil on panel; 19 1/4″ × 13 3/4″.
Acquired in Amsterdam in 1879.

JAN MOSTAERT. *Adoration of the Magi.*

The early works of Jan Mostaert, a Haarlem painter, show the obvious influence of his great compatriot, Geertgen tot Sint Jans. We know, however,
that Mostaert was too young to have been in touch with this master, who
died prematurely around 1490. According to Friedländer, *The Tree of
Jesse* is Mostaert's most important youthful work, and was inspired by
Geertgen. Jan Mostaert, who was long active in Brabant, painted curiously
squat and somnolent figures that appear to be made out of wax or porcelain.
Portraiture and landscape also have a special importance in his work.

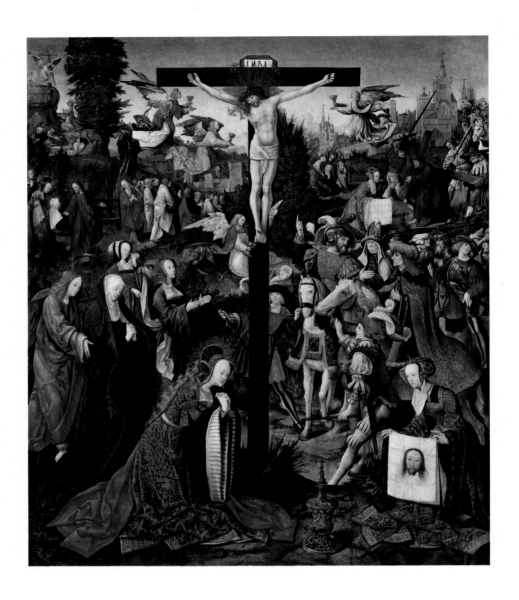

JACOB CORNELISZ VAN OOSTSANEN. *Crucifixion.*

Active in Amsterdam from the late 1400s to 1533, Jacob Cornelisz was the first important painter in that city, which had not yet become the metropolis of Holland. He was a very productive artist and was also the author of a notable series of woodcuts. In technique he was a solid craftsman, skillfully building up his paintings section by section. His compositional elements are densely interwoven with no great concern for spatial effects, but rather with a love of rich paint qualities. This is apparent in the numerous figures and teeming vitality of the present painting, in which the painter includes, besides the main subject, scenes of Christ's farewell to His Mother, the Agony in the Garden and the Way to Calvary. In its complex development, the art of Jacob Cornelisz belongs to the mainstream of Late Gothic Mannerism, which had its most refined exponents in Antwerp (Jan de Beer and Jan de Cock) and was represented at Leyden by Cornelis Engelbrechtsz.

24

JACOB CORNELISZ VAN OOSTSANEN
Oostzaan (near Amsterdam)
circa 1470 — Amsterdam 1533
Besides painting, he worked in woodcuts and designed stained glass and tapestries. Trained probably at Haarlem in the circle of Geertgen. Active in Amsterdam, where he is mentioned from 1500. He was the brother of Cornelis Buys (the Master of Alkmaar?), the father of Dirck Jacobsz and one of Jan van Scorel's masters.
Crucifixion
Oil on panel; 41″ × 34 3/4″.
Formerly in the Castle of Heeswijk.
Acquired in 1902 with the assistance of the *Vereeniging Rembrandt.*

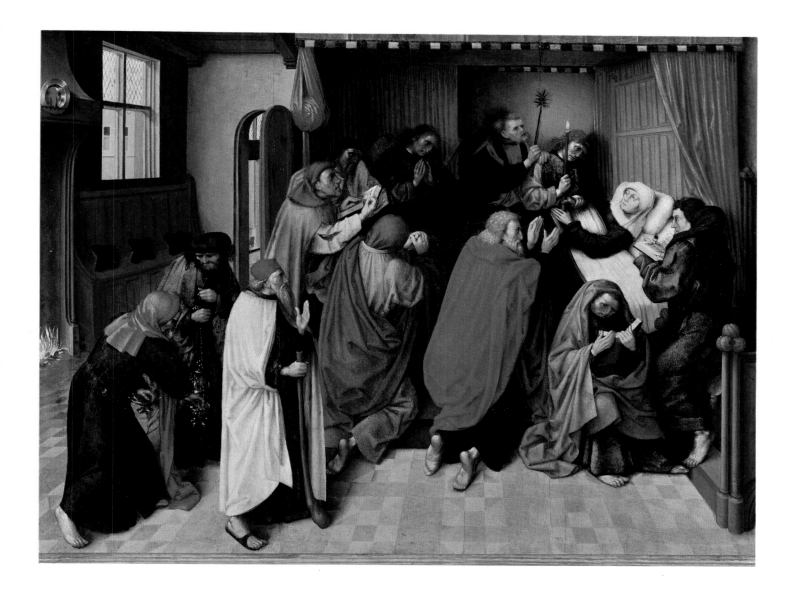

MASTER OF THE AMSTERDAM DEATH OF THE VIRGIN.

Death of the Virgin.

MASTER OF THE AMSTERDAM
DEATH OF THE VIRGIN
Northern Netherlandish painter, active
around 1480–1500, perhaps at Utrecht.
Named after the painting in the Rijksmu-
seum.
Death of the Virgin
Oil on panel; 22 3/4″ × 30 3/4″.
Formerly in the Hofje der Zeven Keurvor-
sten, Amsterdam; acquired in 1944.

Little is known about the painting of the School of Amsterdam before the
appearance of Jacob Cornelisz van Oostsanen. This interesting *Death of the
Virgin* has been taken to be an example of Amsterdam painting at the end of
the 15th century, and Friedländer has ascribed other pictures, including
some portraits, to the same hand. In any case, it should be observed that the
Amsterdam panel has a clearly archaic aspect both in the painting of the setting (recalling the Master of Flémalle and Rogier van der Weyden) and of
the figures (close to Petrus Christus). The relationship with Hugo van der
Goes (*Death of the Virgin* in Bruges) also shows that the Rijksmuseum's
picture is based on Flemish models. If it were to turn out that the work was
in fact executed in Amsterdam, it would be logical to suppose that the author was a Fleming who had settled there.

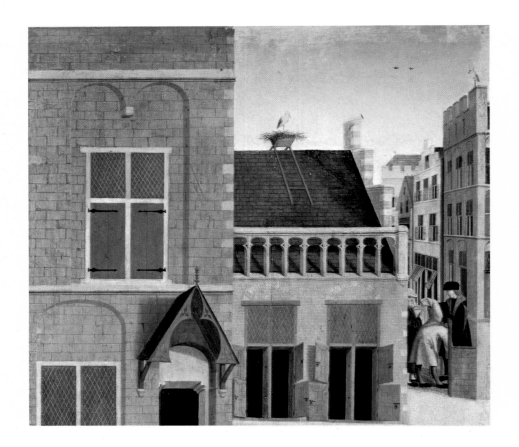 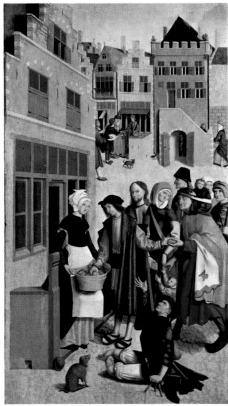

MASTER OF ALKMAAR. *The Seven Acts of Charity.*

In contrast to the *Death of the Virgin* discussed above, this impressive series of paintings is a rare example of early Dutch painting. The seven panels in a single frame (which bears the date 1504) represent the charitable acts of: feeding the hungry; refreshing the thirsty; clothing the naked; burying the dead; sheltering pilgrims; visiting the sick; comforting prisoners. On the frame below each composition are two verses in Dutch referring to the subject represented. Of the works of charity shown in the painting, six are mentioned by Jesus in Matthew 25:31–46, while the seventh (burying the dead) is taken from the Book of Tobit 1:21. In a spontaneous and straightforward way, the painter represents his scenes of human charity. In each he includes the figure of Christ — an unobtrusive background figure in six; a celestial apparition in *Burying the Dead*. The clarity and translucence of the various compositions is striking, and there is an evident inspiration from the great example of Geertgen. A novelty in this work is the delicate description of a town in the background and of scenes of daily life. *The Seven Acts of Charity,* which luckily escaped destruction by the iconoclasts in 1566, comes from a church in Alkmaar, and possibly it was painted by an artist from that city. We know from documents that the painter Cornelis Buys, who was the brother of Jacob Cornelisz van Oostsanen, worked in Alkmaar. It is difficult not to think that Cornelis Buys and the Master of Alkmaar were one and the same person.

MASTER OF ALKMAAR
So named after *The Seven Acts of Charity* in the Rijksmuseum, dated 1504, which came from Alkmaar (St. Laurenskerk). Probably he is to be identified with Cornelis Buys, the brother of Jacob Cornelisz van Oostsanen. Buys was active in Alkmaar, and there Jan van Scorel studied with him.
The Seven Acts of Charity
Oil on seven panels in a single frame; each panel measures 39 3/4" × 21 3/4", except the first and last which are 21 1/4" wide. Page 26: left, detail of *Clothing the Naked;* right, *Feeding the Hungry*. Page 27, from top to bottom and from left to right:
Refreshing the Thirsty
Clothing the Naked
Burying the Dead
Sheltering Pilgrims
Visiting the Sick
Comforting Prisoners
The work was acquired in 1918 with the aid of the *Vereeniging Rembrandt*.

26

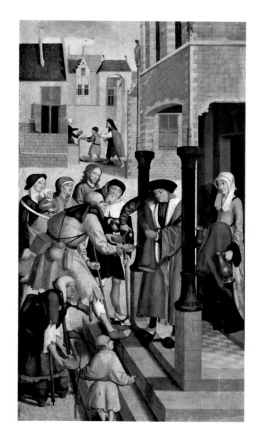
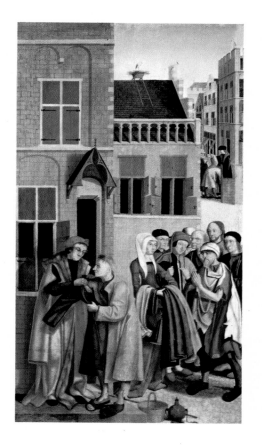
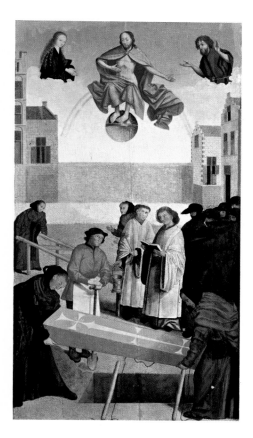
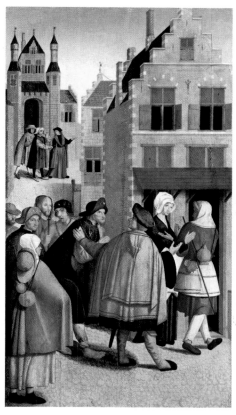
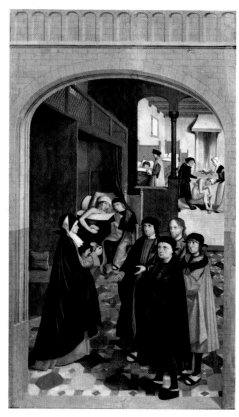
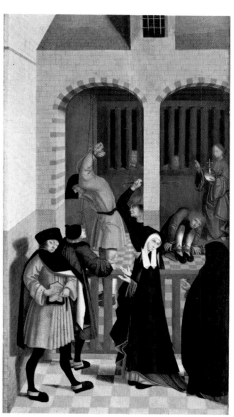

LUCAS VAN LEYDEN. *Adoration of the Golden Calf.*

Unquestionably Lucas van Leyden was one of the geniuses of 16th-century European art. His talent was precocious, for he executed his first dated engraving in 1508 when he was only sixteen years old. Beautiful engravings and woodcuts, which played an important role in the development of European painting (the influence on Bruegel was strong), represent the heart of Lucas van Leyden's activity, but he also left us some magnificent paintings. As with Dürer, the engraver's sensitivity is revealed in the paintings, where the linear design is emphatic.

Lucas was an attentive observer, and it may be said that in him the study of reality took the place of instruction by masters. Although he knew what had been done previously and what was being done around him, his work seems to have been born spontaneously out of brilliant creativity. At the same time, Lucas van Leyden's art shows a deep concern with problems of artistic creation. It is known that he closely studied Albrecht Dürer's writings, and he met the Nürnberg master himself in Antwerp, in 1521. Like few others, Lucas understood the crux of the problem of the "Italian Manner," and for him the crisis of the Italian Renaissance was a living experience. In his late engravings and paintings there is an evident approach to Marcantonio Raimondi and other Italian engravers. In these works, which are very different from the felicitous early creations with their domestic and realistic flavor, the artist adopted the heroic ideal of the human figure and the intellectually determined coordination of the forms.

The *Adoration of the Golden Calf* triptych is also a late work, datable around 1530. The three-dimensional figures moving easily in space show that the artist assimilated Italian ideals with happy effect. The linear tension and the active movement are so skillful as to place this work among the masterpieces of the first generation of European Mannerists. In the middle ground of the central panel of the triptych we see the Israelites dancing around the Golden Calf; in the foreground men, women and children are eating and drinking. Moses appears twice: on the left above, kneeling on Mount Sinai; below, in the act of smashing the Tablets of the Law, with Joshua beside him. The triptych was discovered only recently and was acquired by the Rijksmuseum in 1952.

LUCAS VAN LEYDEN. *The Sermon.* p. 30

A number of excellent painters were working in Leyden in the first half of the 16th century, but some of their personalities remain shadowy. The works of Engelbrechtsz' three sons — Pieter Cornelisz, Cornelis Cornelisz and Lucas Cornelisz — have never been clearly distinguished. The present, singular painting belongs in fact to this mysterious ambience. It has been generally attributed to Lucas van Leyden, although it does not have his rigorous spatial development nor his sensitive linear framework. Perhaps it should be ascribed to Pieter Cornelisz, who is known through a handful of fine drawings. It is certain, in any case, that the author of *The Sermon* was also responsible for four little pictures that are now at Hampton Court. The six male figures standing on the right were probably the donors, and the second from left of these, which is completely frontal, suggests a self-portrait.

28

LUCAS VAN LEYDEN
Leyden 1494 — Leyden 1533
Painter, engraver, woodcut maker and glass painter, he studied with his father, Hugo Jacobsz, and Cornelisz Engelbrechtsz at Leyden. In 1521 he was in Antwerp, where he met Dürer; in 1527, in Zeeland, Flanders and Brabant.
Adoration of the Golden Calf (central panel of a triptych)
Oil on panel; 36 1/2″ × 26 1/4″.
The triptych was acquired in 1952.

On page 30:
LUCAS VAN LEYDEN (?)
The Sermon
Oil on panel; 52 1/4″ × 38 1/4″.
Below right, the false monogram of Lucas van Leyden ("L"). The painting has also been attributed to Pieter Cornelisz and to Aertgen van Leyden. Acquired in London in 1897 with the aid of the *Vereeniging Rembrandt*.

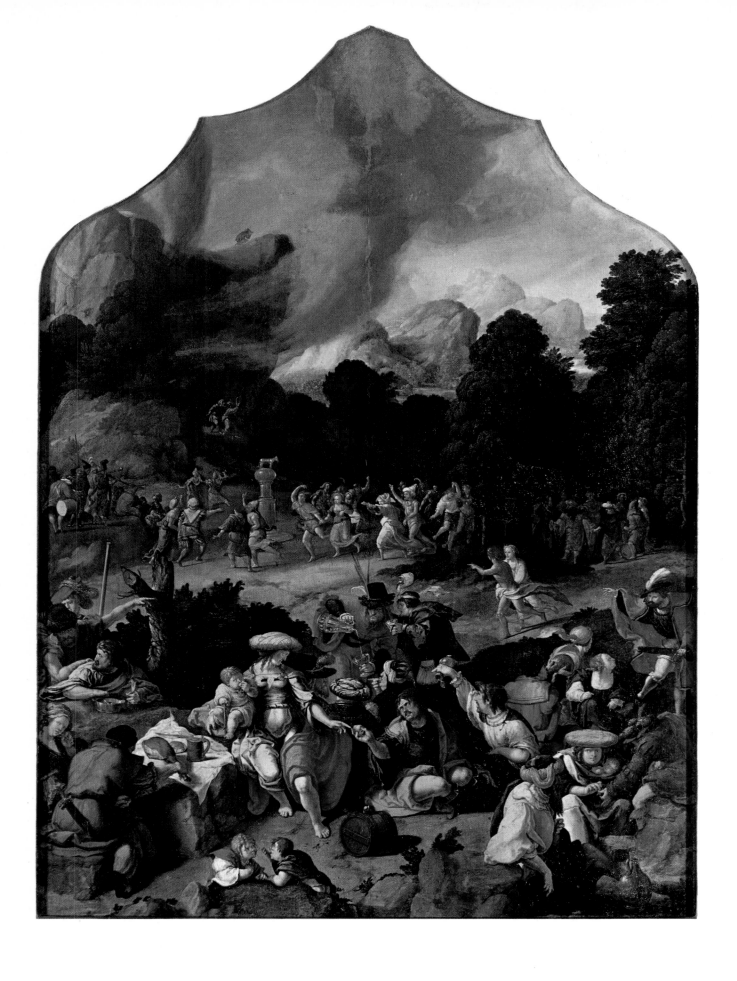

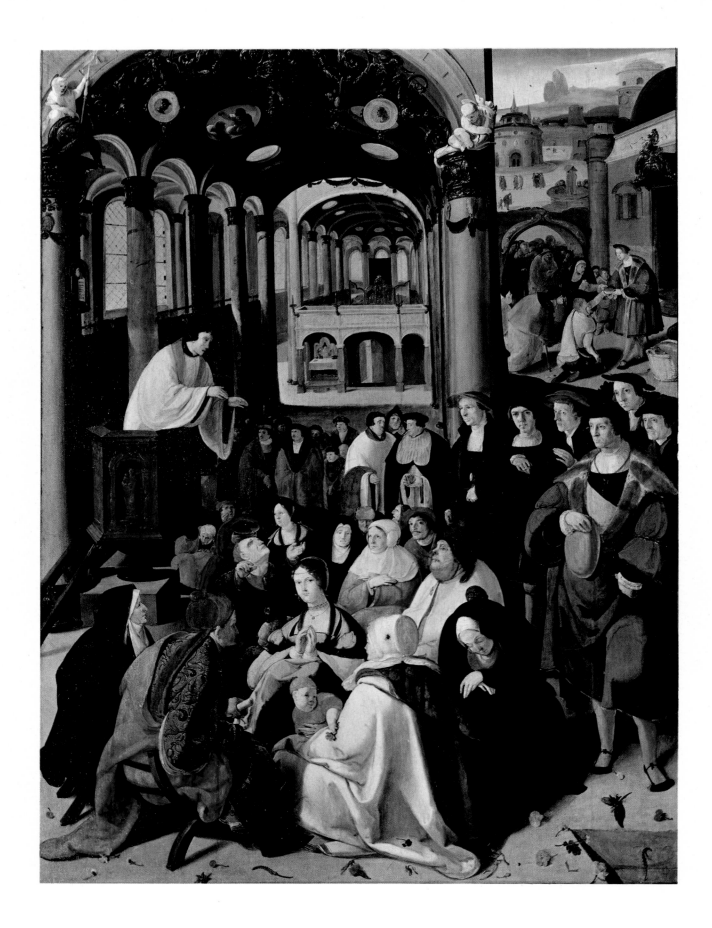

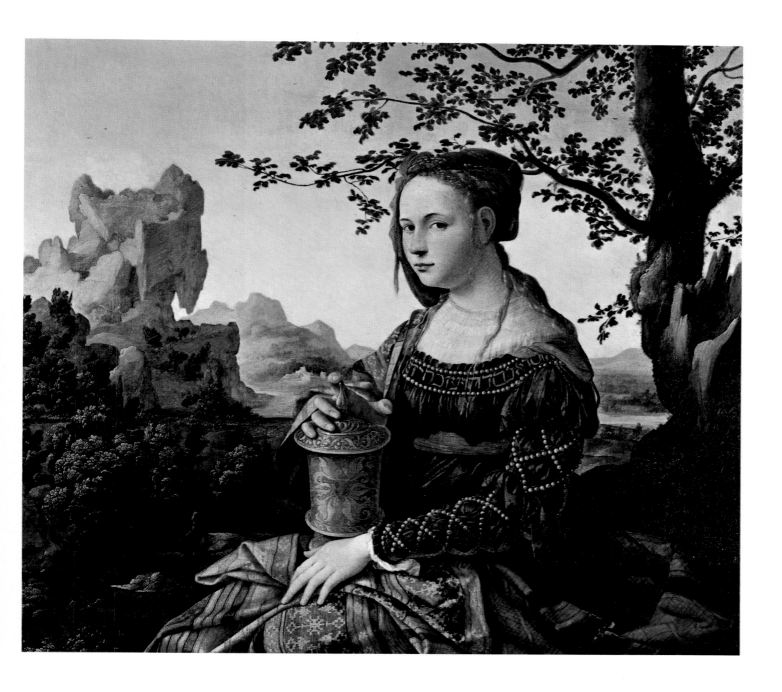

JAN VAN SCOREL
Schoorl (near Alkmaar) 1495 — Utrecht
1562
Pupil of Cornelis Buys at Alkmaar, of
Cornelis Willemsz at Haarlem and of Jacob
Cornelisz van Oostsanen at Amsterdam.
Between 1519 and 1524, he traveled to Ger-
many, Carinthia, Venice, Palestine and
Rome. From 1524 he was active at Utrecht,
except for a stay at Haarlem in 1527.
Mary Magdalene
Oil on panel; 26 1/4" × 30".
A band of painting above the head of the
figure is not original. In 1808 it was in the
National Museum of The Hague, from
which it later passed to the Rijksmuseum.

JAN VAN SCOREL.   *Mary Magdalene.*
Jan van Scorel, who described himself as a "lover of the art of painting,"
was also an architect, engineer, poet and musician. During his fruitful trav-
els as a youth — from 1519 to 1524 — which took him as far as Palestine,
he acquired a rounded education in painting by direct knowledge of the art
of the masters, from Gossaert to Dürer, and from Mantegna and Giorgione
to Raphael and Michelangelo. He returned home an Italianized artist, with
the aura of a great innovator. In this enchanting *Mary Magdalene,* executed
around 1528, the rich elaboration of the figure's dress is reminiscent of Raphael's *Madonna of the Chair;* the background rocks recall Patinir.

31

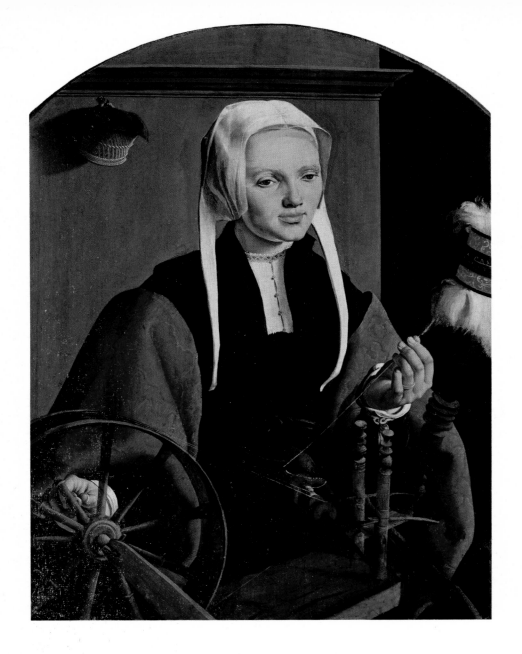

MAERTEN VAN HEEMSKERCK. *Portrait of Anna Codde.*
This work forms a pair with the *Portrait of Pieter Bicker Gerritsz* which is
also in the Rijksmuseum. Both paintings still have their original frames, and
on the lower part of these are inscribed the date of 1529 and the age of the
sitter — 26 for Anna Codde and 34 for Pieter Bicker Gerritsz, who was her
husband. The attribution of this delightful pair of portraits has been a problem for the critics. Long given to Jan van Scorel, they are now universally
recognized as the work of his brilliant pupil, Heemskerck, because of their
free and rapid execution, feeling of spatial illusion and spontaneous composition. The two portraits belong to Heemskerck's most creative period,
which began with his work in Scorel's studio (1527) and ended with his
departure for Rome (1532). In those five years Heemskerck painted a number of fine portraits and some compositions that were so completely like his
master's as to confuse his contemporaries and arouse Scorel's jealousy. The
sojourn in Italy alienated the artist from the sculptural and classical art of
Scorel and turned him into one of the most exalted Mannerists of his time.

MAERTEN VAN HEEMSKERCK
Heemskerk (near Haarlem) 1498 — Haar-
lem 1574
Pupil of Cornelis Willemsz at Haarlem and
of Jan Lucas at Delft. In 1527 he was ac-
tive in Jan van Scorel's studio in Haarlem.
From 1532 to 1535 he was in Italy (Rome),
and subsequently worked in Haarlem.
Portrait of Anna Codde (1529)
Oil on panel; 33 1/4″ × 25 1/2″.
With its companion piece, representing
Anna Codde's husband, Pieter Bicker Ger-
ritsz, it was given to the Rijksmuseum by
Messrs. D. and N. Katz in 1948.

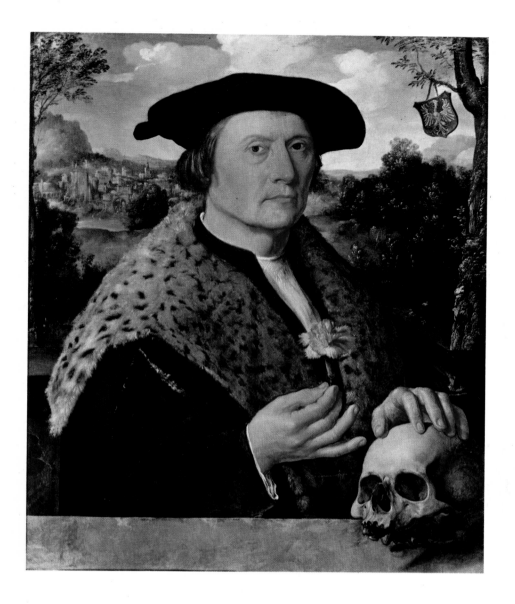

DIRCK JACOBSZ. *Portrait of Pompejus Occo.*

Thanks to the coat of arms hanging from the tree branch in the upper right corner of the picture, the subject has been positively identified. Pompejus Occo (1483–1537) was a banker, merchant and humanist. He bore the title of Count Palatine and was also agent of King Christian II of Denmark.

The artist Dirck Jacobsz was the son of Jacob Cornelisz van Oostsanen (see page 24), and also worked in Amsterdam. A number of portraits by him have come down to us, but few figure compositions. He was a provincial artist, yet his work displays a vigorous talent. His art is a reflection of the God-fearing society of Amsterdam, which was faithful to the papacy and to Spain, and — unlike Antwerp — not very receptive to Protestantism and national aspirations. The *Portrait of Pompejus Occo,* with the sitter shown behind the traditional parapet, is loaded with obvious allusions. The subject rests his left hand on a skull, while he holds in his right hand a carnation — a symbol of constancy in love often appearing in North European portraits.

DIRCK JACOBSZ
Amsterdam (?) circa 1497 — Amsterdam 1567
He studied with his father, Jacob Cornelisz van Oostsanen, in Amsterdam, and was then active in the same city. He was mainly a portraitist.
Portrait of Pompejus Occo
Oil on panel; 26″ × 21 1/4″.
Acquired in New York in 1957 with funds from the bequest of Jonkheer Dr. J. Loudon.

33

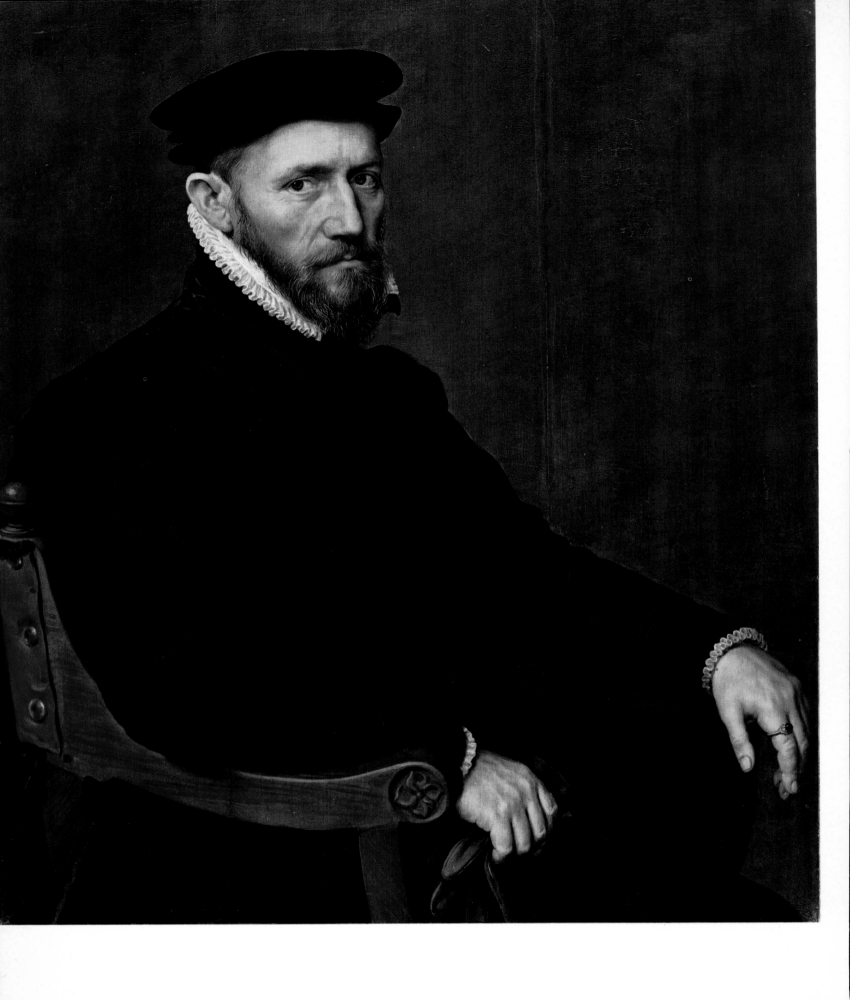

ANTHONIS MOR. *Portrait of Sir Thomas Gresham.*

The Rijksmuseum also possesses the artist's portrait of Lady Gresham, and she too is shown seated in an armchair, as it were opposite her husband. Sir Thomas Gresham, the financial agent of the English Crown in the Netherlands, was the founder of the London Stock Exchange and of Gresham College. This portrait was executed during the last decade of the life of Anthonis Mor, who died at Antwerp in 1576. Also known as Sir Anthony More and Antonio Moro, the English and Spanish versions of his name, the painter was born in Utrecht and studied with Scorel. He was famous as a portraitist throughout Europe.

A key figure in European portraiture, Mor assimilated elements from Titian and the Italians, but he had his own unmistakable personality and exerted a deep and lasting influence on the various schools of painting. Typical of Mor are his detached observation of the model, the exactness with which he rendered the features and the dress, and the sobriety of the setting and the details. His pictures usually appear cool and distant, thus very different from the palpitatingly vital portraits by Frans Floris and Titian. Around 1560, however, the painter's brushwork became freer and his subjects seem more relaxed. In the *Portrait of Sir Thomas Gresham,* the distinguished gentleman, comfortably posed, looks out at us almost casually, and the sobriety of his garb emphasizes the sound "bourgeois" character of the work.

PIETER AERTSEN. *Adoration of the Shepherds.*

Aertsen was born in Amsterdam, but may be considered an artist of the Brabant, as most of his working life (1535–60) was spent in Antwerp. Like van Amstel, who was also born in Amsterdam but worked in the Brabant, he was a precursor of Pieter Bruegel in being among the first Netherlandish artists to portray peasant life. Without troubling about inconsistencies, Aertsen sought monumentality of form and tackled the problem of movement. From the Mannerists he took whatever he needed, yet his pictures do not appear cerebral and have the warmth of life. What saves Aertsen from the coldness of many Italianate Mannerists is the richness of his dense, luminous color. The painting reproduced here gives a good idea of his gifts. It is a fragment of a large *Nativity,* probably the one painted by the artist for the Nieuwe Kerk in Amsterdam, which was destroyed by the iconoclasts in 1566.

CORNELIS CORNELISZ VAN HAARLEM. *Bathsheba.*   *p. 36*

Holland made an outstanding contribution to European Mannerism. Indeed, between the appearance of Scorel (the first real Dutch Mannerist) and the end of the century, Holland produced almost none but Italianizing artists. During the same period, Netherlandish painting of a realistic tendency was practiced predominantly in Antwerp — and it is there and not in Holland that the center of great 17th-century realistic Dutch painting is to be found. The personality of Cornelis Cornelisz takes us to the Haarlem art world, which was particularly lively from the end of the 15th century on-

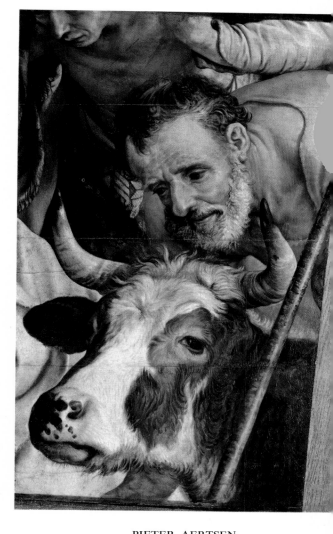

PIETER AERTSEN
Amsterdam 1508 — Amsterdam 1575
Master at Antwerp in 1535, and worked there until about 1560. Subsequently he returned to Amsterdam.
Adoration of the Shepherds (fragment)
Oil on panel; 35 1/2" × 23 1/2".
Formerly in the old Amsterdam Town Hall. On loan from the City of Amsterdam (1885).

ANTHONIS MOR
(SIR ANTHONY MORE or ANTONIO MORO)
Utrecht circa 1520 — Antwerp 1576
Pupil of Jan van Scorel in Utrecht. Master at Antwerp in 1547. In Rome from 1550 to 1551. Active at the courts of Portugal (1552), England (1554) and Spain (1559). He often returned to his native Utrecht and spent his final years in Antwerp.
Portrait of Sir Thomas Gresham
Oil on panel; 35 1/2" × 29 3/4".
With its companion piece, representing Anne Ferneley, Lady Gresham (wife of Sir Thomas), it was acquired in 1931, with the aid of the *Vereeniging Rembrandt.*

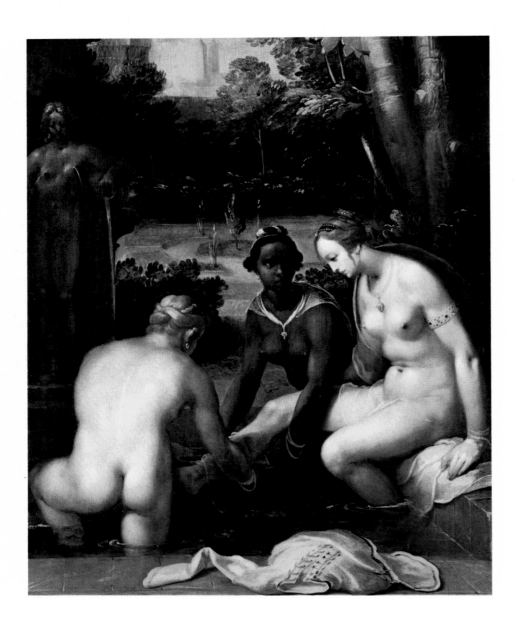

wards. In Haarlem around 1585, Cornelis sparked one of the last, brief up-
surges of northern Mannerism. His style stemmed from Spranger's art,
which was propagated in Haarlem by the painter and humanist, Carel van
Mander, and industriously engraved by Hendrick Goltzius. Stimulated by
this environment, Cornelis Cornelisz created large compositions full of
muscular nudes with proud expressions, seen in bold foreshortening. Thus,
the last phase of Mannerism in the Netherlands was born, and it was Cornelisz who provided the point of departure for such other excellent painters
as Bloemaert and Wtewael. The Rijksmuseum's *Bathsheba* (1594) does not
represent Cornelisz's painting at its moment of greatest tension. In fact,
after Goltzius's return from Italy in 1592 with a program of neo-Renais-
sance ideas, Cornelisz's Mannerism grew calmer and he then concentrated
on developing his gifts as a colorist.

36

CORNELIS CORNELISZ VAN
HAARLEM
Haarlem 1562 — Haarlem 1638
Pupil of Pieter Pietersz at Haarlem, and of
Gillis Congnet at Antwerp. In 1538, he re-
turned to Haarlem, where all his subse-
quent work was done. With Carel van Man-
der and Hendrick Goltzius, he founded an
academy of design.
Bathsheba (1594)
Oil on panel; 30 1/2″ × 25 1/4″.
Acquired in Paris in 1955.

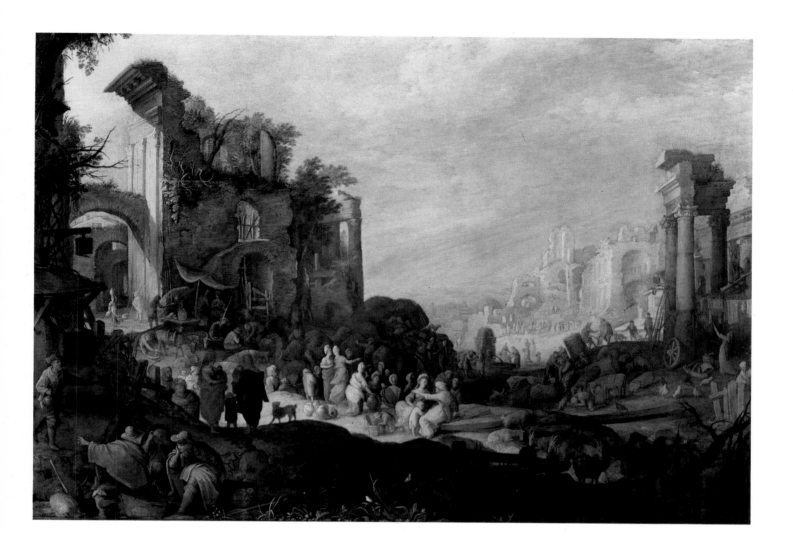

WILLEM VAN NIEUWLANDT. *Landscape with Ruins and Rebecca at the Well.*

WILLEM VAN NIEUWLANDT
Antwerp 1584 — Amsterdam 1635
Student of Jacob Savery at Amsterdam in 1599. At Paul Bril's studio in Rome in 1603, then at Antwerp. His final years were spent in Amsterdam.
Landscape with Ruins and Rebecca at the Well
Oil on copper; 16 1/4" × 22 1/2".
It bears the apocryphal signature of *P. Bril*. Identified in 1965 as a work of van Nieuwlandt by G. T. Faggin. In 1809, it was in the Kabinet van Heteren at The Hague from whence it came to the Rijksmuseum.

Carel van Mander, the great biographer of the Netherlandish painters, wrote in 1604: "Pauwels Bril for one year had a pupil from Antwerp, Willem van Nieuwlandt, who now is twenty-two years old, lives in Antwerp and has completely mastered his teacher's manner." This painting, which is generally credited to Paul Bril, in our view should be attributed to his pupil, Willem van Nieuwlandt, the author of similar works that are closely related to the art of his master. Van Nieuwlandt frequented Bril's studio in Rome at a time when that artist (who had been living in the Eternal City for twenty years) was particularly interested in drawing and painting ruins. The present landscape is built up in a series of receding "wings," following Bril's practice. The contrasts in light and shade are more contrived, however, than in Bril. We are reminded that van Nieuwlandt was an important poet as well as a painter by the gracefully gesticulating little figures, which are taken from the Biblical account.

37

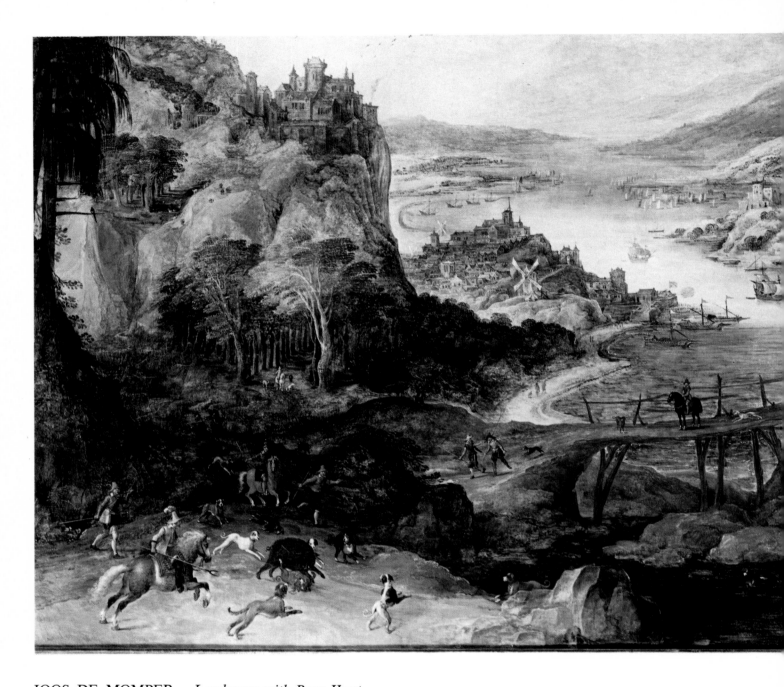

JOOS DE MOMPER. *Landscape with Boar Hunt.*

This is one of the most significant paintings of that productive landscapist Joos de Momper, who was active in Antwerp from 1581 to 1635. Although de Momper's works are almost never dated, and it is thus difficult to arrange them in a convincing chronological order, it seems certain that this landscape was painted before 1600, during the artist's youth. The main influence on de Momper comes from Pieter Bruegel, especially from his grandiose engravings of large landscapes. Joos de Momper, however, did not have Bruegel's organic feeling for nature. His landscapes are cerebrally constructed and belong to the mild climate of late Mannerism. But the summary, dashing technique — almost impressionistic — is notable.

JOOS DE MOMPER
Antwerp 1564 — Antwerp 1635
In 1581 Master at Antwerp, where he then stayed. He may have traveled in Italy.
Landscape with Boar Hunt
Oil on panel; 3'11 1/2" × 6'5 1/4".
The main figures are perhaps by Sebastiaen Vrancx. Acquired in Brussels in 1959 with the aid of the *Jubileumsfonds 1958.*

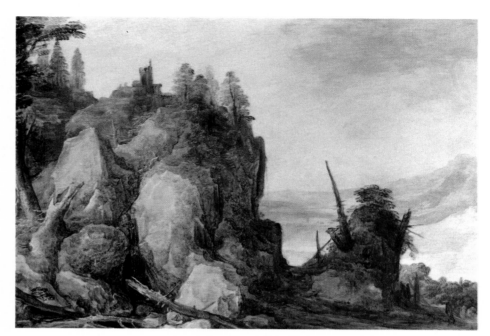

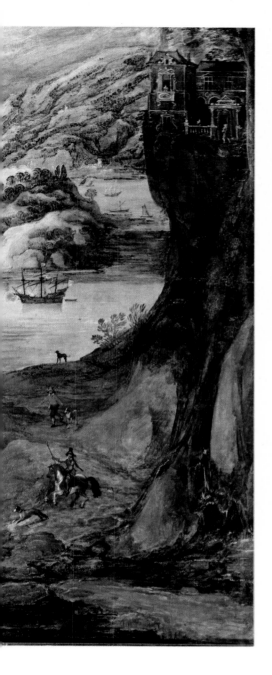

JOOS DE MOMPER. *Mountain Landscape.*

Joos de Momper's landscapes often have a conventional character, in color as well as in composition. The painter, in fact, usually laid out three distinct color areas: brown for the foreground, yellow green for the middle ground and blue for the distant planes. Also somewhat stereotyped are the mountain landscapes like this, in which the painter specialized. The romantic notes prevalent in de Momper's landscapes were to be carried further, with much greater lyric intensity, by the great visionary artist, Hercules Seghers.

ABRAHAM BLOEMAERT. *The Preaching of St. John the Baptist.*

p. 40

As mentioned already (p. 35) in connection with Cornelis Cornelisz's *Bathsheba,* the Dutch painters of the last quarter of the 16th century made an important contribution to international Mannerism. Cornelis Cornelisz van Haarlem was the innovator, the forerunner. Still, Abraham Bloemaert's art is no less intense and personal, for it also stemmed from the common source of the movement, the great personality of Bartholomeus Spranger. Compared to Cornelis' robust and monumental painting, Bloemaert's works are all grace. His closely studied, elegant drawings, often reproduced in prints, became a model for academic teaching. In color, too, there is a clear distinction between Bloemaert and Cornelis. But whereas the latter was a born colorist, who was fortunate enough to receive his training in Antwerp, where the Venetian influence was pervasive, Bloemaert had a rather abstract conception of color. He juxtaposed basic colors, without going on to blend them. *The Preaching of St. John the Baptist* is a typical example of the Mannerists' fondness for distorting Biblical themes. Here the subject is a pretext

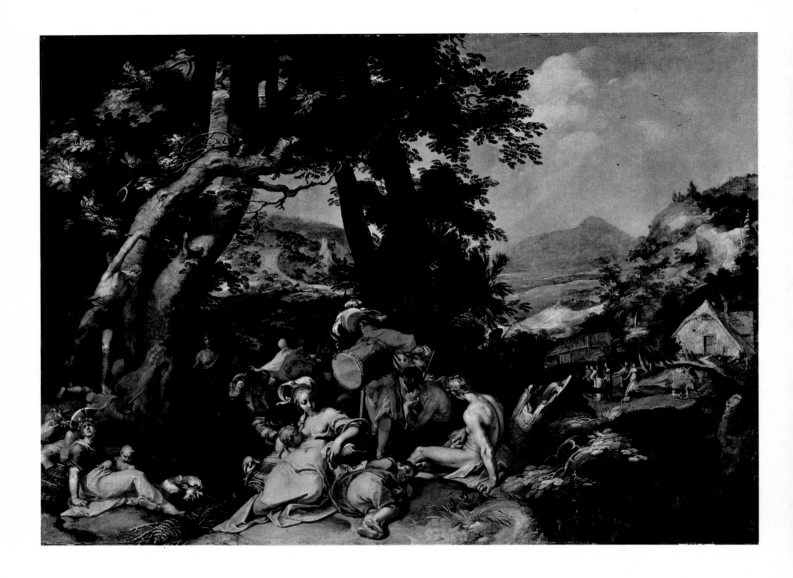

for painting beautiful, carefully posed figures in the midst of a leafy and varied landscape. The figure of the Baptist, having no importance for the painter, was relegated to an inconspicuous position; it was the theatrical scene in the foreground and landscape that interested Bloemaert.

JAN BRUEGEL. *Flower-Piece*.

Son of Pieter Bruegel the Elder, Jan was a highly gifted painter who has left us a great number of delicate landscapes, allegorical compositions and still lifes. He was essentially a master of precious, refined, miniaturistic effects. Some of his works, especially his flower-pieces, are astonishingly rich in details. Bruegel worked carefully from life, but then composed his gigantic bouquets with a taste for artifice and multiplicity that recalls the feeling of late Mannerism.

ABRAHAM BLOEMAERT
Gorinchen 1564 — Utrecht 1651
Studied with his father Cornelis (sculptor) and Joos de Beer at Utrecht. In Paris before 1583. From 1591 to 1592 in Amsterdam, then at Utrecht.
The Preaching of St. John the Baptist
Oil on canvas; 4′6 3/4″ × 6′2″.
Signed: *A. Blommaert*.
Acquired in London, 1950.

JAN BRUEGEL
Brussels 1568 — Antwerp 1625
Son of Pieter Bruegel the Elder (died in 1569). Pupil of Pieter Goetkint in Antwerp. From 1590 to 1596 in Italy (Naples, Rome, Milan), then in Antwerp. He is also known as "Velvet Bruegel."
Flower-Piece
Oil on panel; 44 1/2″ × 33 3/4″.
Gift of Mr. and Mrs. Kessler-Hülsmann, 1940.

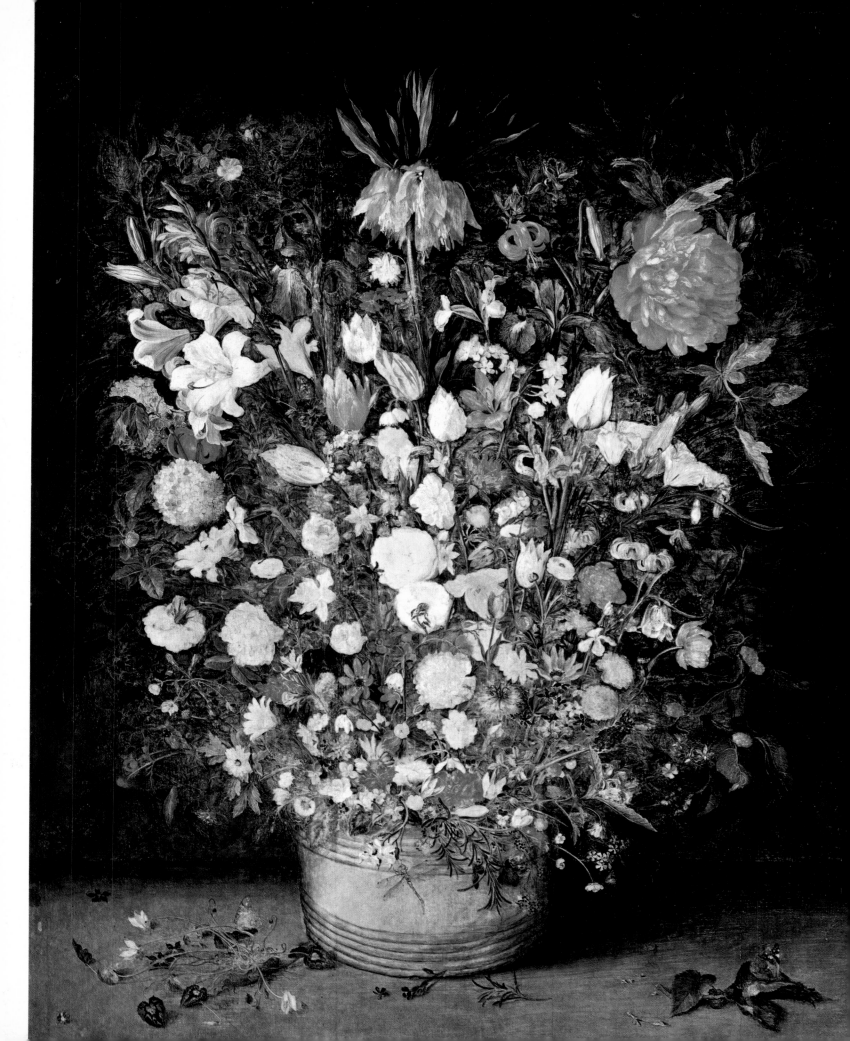

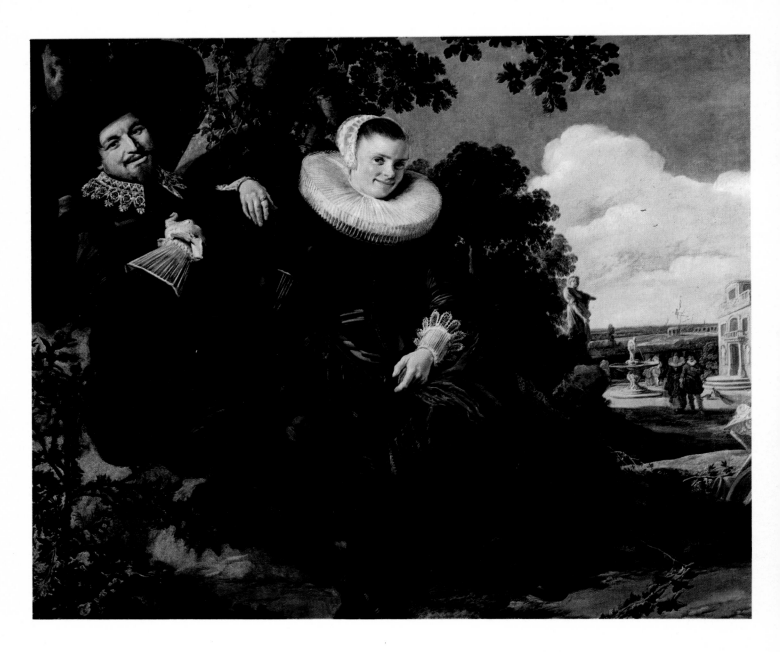

FRANS HALS. *Portrait of a Married Couple.*

Hals began his independent activity as an artist late in life, and this painting, executed around 1621, is accordingly a relatively early work. It seems certain that the two figures portrayed are Frans Massa (whom Hals also painted in 1626) and his wife, Beatrice van der Laen. The outdoor effect reflects Frans Hals's interest in the style of Terbrugghen and Honthorst, just as the architecture, the garden and the figures in the background show the influence of the Haarlem Mannerists. In this felicitous composition, Hals already demonstrated the assurance of his mature style.

FRANS HALS. *The Merry Toper.*

It seems that all of Frans Hals's genre pictures belong to the first half of his career, up to about 1635. These representations of drinkers, actors and mu-

FRANS HALS
Antwerp 1580 — Haarlem 1666
Portrait of a Married Couple
Oil on canvas; 55 1/4″ × 65 1/2″.
In the sales in Amsterdam of Jan Six, 1702, and Six van Hillegom, 1851.
Purchased by the Rijksmuseum in 1852.

FRANS HALS
The Merry Toper
Oil on canvas; 31 1/4″ × 26 1/4″.
Signed with the artist's monogram.
Acquired in 1816 at the sale of the van Leyden collection at Warmond.

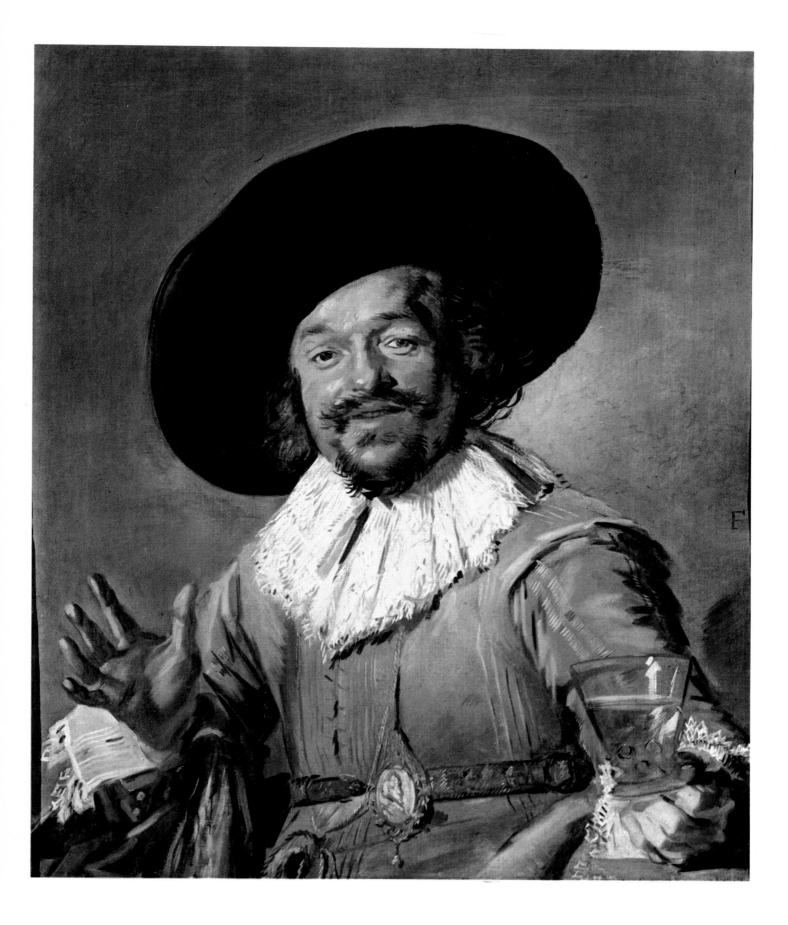

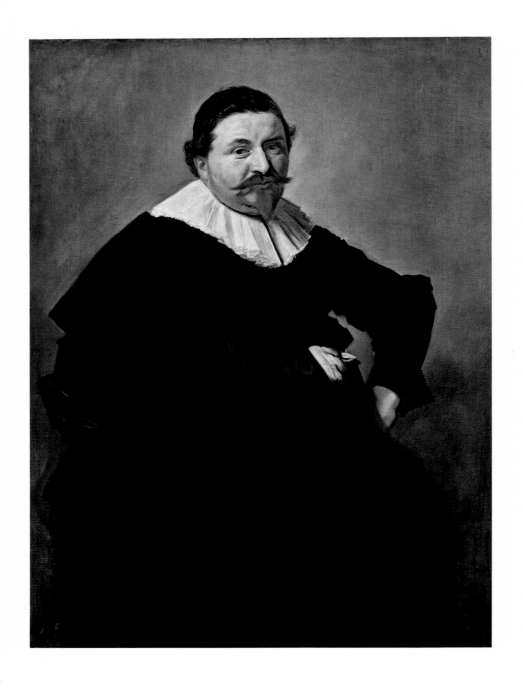

sicians shown life size, laughing and winking, were certainly inspired by the so-called "Utrecht Mannerists." Hals's most famous work of this kind is *The Gypsy* in the Louvre. The subjects, however, seem to be made for his style, and in his hands they are recreated with a vitality that is not to be found in Terbrugghen or Honthorst, although their works are also very fine. Note the painter's preference for light tones and the use of a large, highly colored passage for unexpected contrast. The dense, ragged brush strokes, summary in application, give the figures and objects they define an appearance of constant movement.

44

FRANS HALS
Portrait of Lucas De Clercq and
Portrait of Feyntje Van Steenkiste
Oil on canvas. The first portrait measures 49 3/4″ × 36 1/2″; the second, 48 1/2″ × 36 1/2″.
A Latin inscription on the back of the wife's portrait gives her age as 31. As she was born in 1604, the two paintings were executed in 1635. Given to the City of Amsterdam by the De Clercq family in 1891. On loan to the Rijksmuseum since that year.

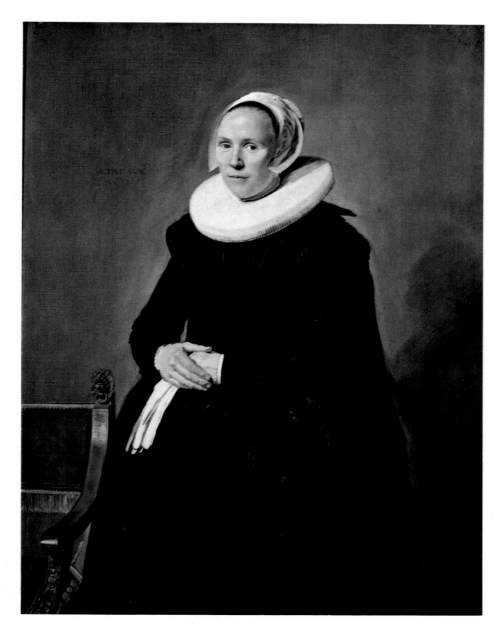

FRANS HALS. *Portrait of Lucas De Clercq* and *Portrait of Feyntje Van
                Steenkiste.*

It is well known that Frans Hals was primarily a great portraitist. It would
be an over-simplification, however, to attribute this specialization to the
pressure of commissions. The years between 1630 and 1640 are usually considered the most splendid period in the artist's style, and it is at this time
that he developed a type of portrait that remained a constant of his art. Intense monochrome effects replaced the clear, high-colored palette that emphasized the mobility of the subjects' expressions. The clothes are generally
dark (though this was of course called for by the fashion prevailing in Holland at the time). The figures are more contained in pose, yet still full of
the vitality that is typical of Hals. These companion portraits of a man and
his wife are among the finest of the period.

On pages 46-47:
FRANS HALS
*The Company of Captain Reynier Reael and
Lieutenant Cornelis Michielsz Blaeuw*
Dated: "A. 1637."
Oil on canvas; 42 3/4″ × 53 3/4″.
It was executed for the Guild Hall of the
Crossbow Archers in Amsterdam. Subse-
quently the painting was transferred to the
old Town Hall. On loan from the City of
Amsterdam since 1885.

45

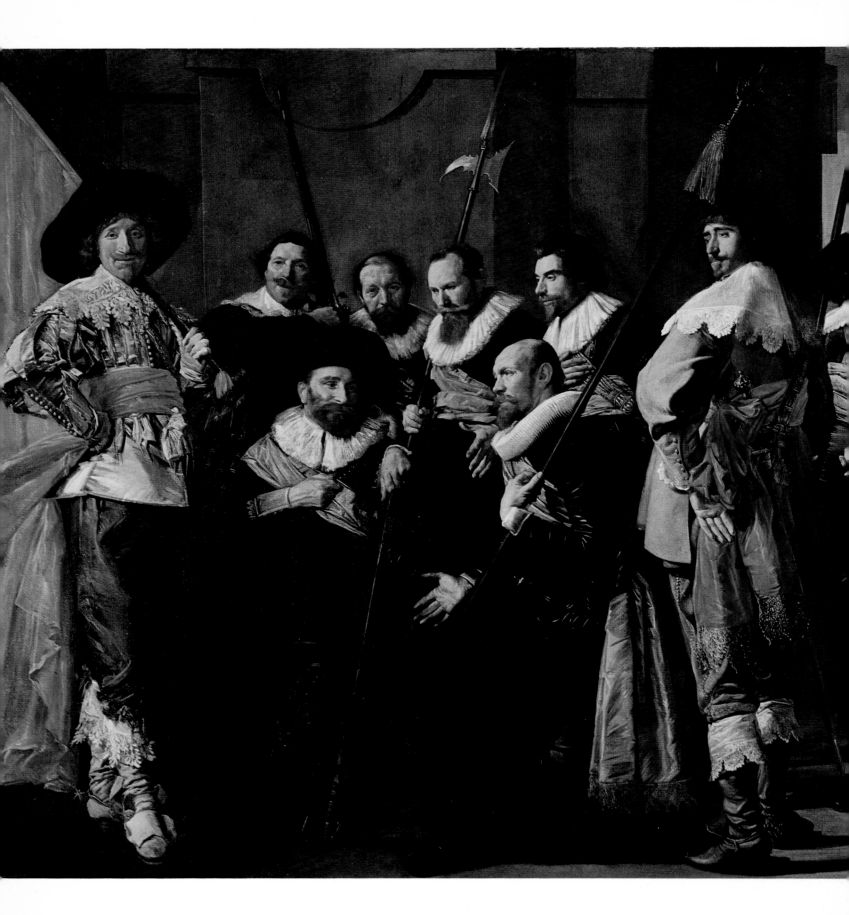

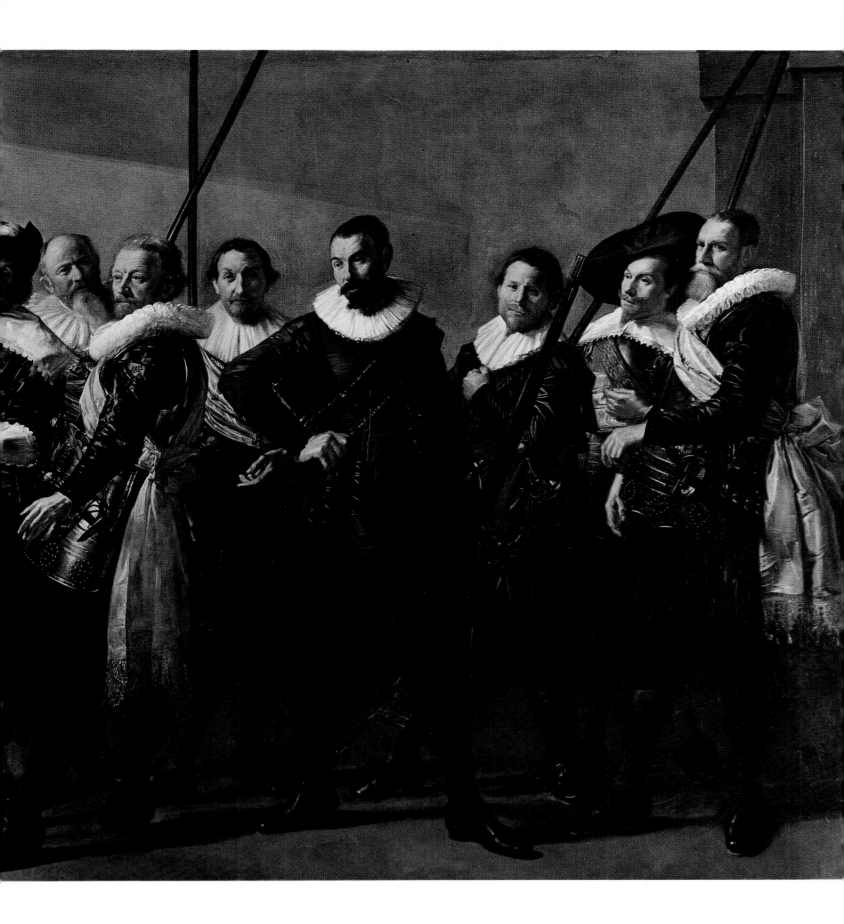

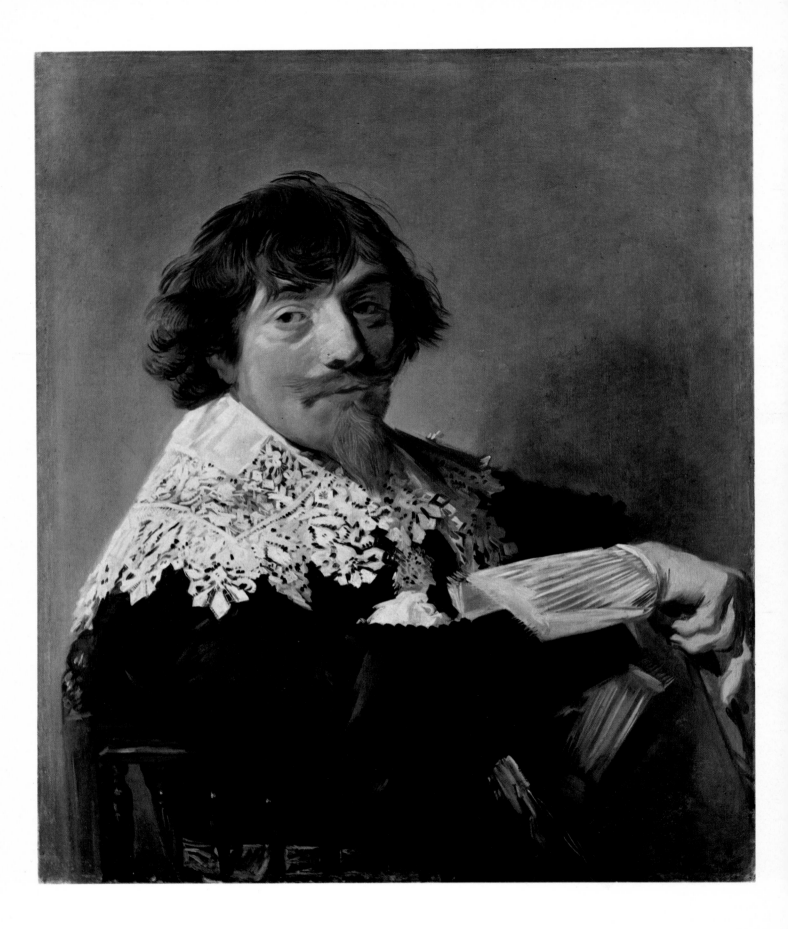

FRANS HALS. *The Company of Captain Reynier Reael and Lieutenant Cornelis Michielsz Blaeuw.* *pp. 46–47*

Commissioned in 1633, this painting still had not been finished three years later. It was given to Pieter Codde for completion, and he worked on some of the figures on the right. One of the "official portraits" typical of 17th-century Dutch painting, it is — along with the *Banquet of the Officers of the Civic Guard* — the most famous of the genre painted by Hals.

By comparing this masterpiece of a traditional kind of painting — though still among the greatest of its century — with Rembrandt's *Night Watch* (pp. 70–71), one can grasp the revolutionary impact of the latter work. In Rembrandt's painting all the figures have been caught in stop-action positions, with the suggestion that all the relationships in the composition will be changing. Here, on the contrary, the succession of figures acquires equilibrium from the repetition of some gestures and poses, and this is reinforced by the firm relationship between the foreground figures with their hands on their hips, elbows extended forward, and the figures to the rear that define the depth of the space. It is a typical "group picture," which belongs to a tradition of ceremonial portrayal that has lasted as a popular convention up to our time. Only here, the painter's genius has given dramatic definition to each figure. In Rembrandt's work the individual becomes a character in action, but here each is a portrait on its own, fully characterized but set apart in an official pose. The over-all spirit of the composition and its inner style is felt in the slightly ironic awareness of this official character. The figures acquire their identity largely through the splendor of their costumes, and it is to this magnificence and display that they adjust their poses and their expressions. Each appears to recognize himself in this other, official personality, and in turn must assume an attitude appropriate to the importance of his position. Yet the official character and the 17th-century pomp is turned into the liveliest human characterization.

It should not be forgotten, furthermore, that the "wide-screen" size of the canvas and the life-size figures meant that the artist's intention was illusionistic, and that this was certainly heightened and completed by the position in which the picture was placed. In this way the pomp became ritualistic, and the subjects human presences in the setting in which they had been portrayed, rather than civil or military officials.

FRANS HALS. *Portrait of Nicolaes Hasselaer.*

The subject, the mayor of Amsterdam, died at the age of 43 in 1635, and this portrait was probably painted between 1630 and 1635. Typical of those years, as we have seen, was Hals's tendency toward poised and monochromatic effects, as compared with the opulent portraiture of his youthful style. Here a vigorous element is the wide movement of the arm and the connection it makes, through the big lace collar, to the strong head shown in three-quarter view. The face is one of the most intense characterizations in all of Hals's portraits. The expression is somewhat official and suggests an awareness of the subject's position. It is more posed than those in the various group portraits of the Companies. Official dignity, however, is relieved by the unexpectedly human feature of the deep shadowing of the eyes.

FRANS HALS
Portrait of Nicolaes Hasselaer
Oil on canvas; 31 1/4" × 26 1/4".
Gift of Jonkheer J. S. R. van de Poll of Arnhem in 1885.

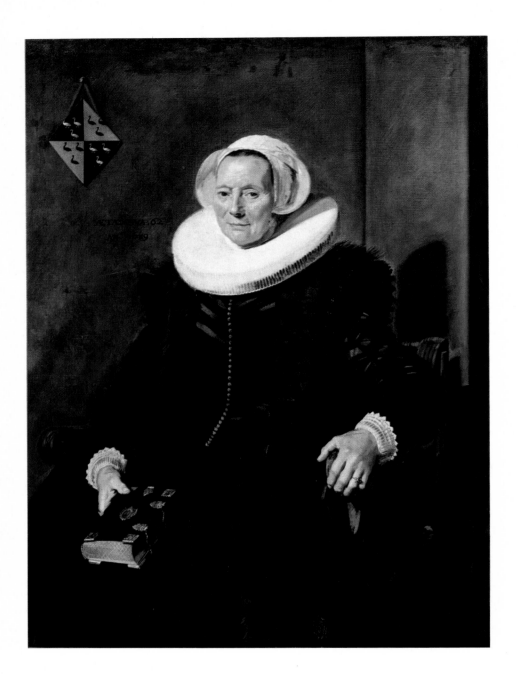

FRANS HALS. *Portrait of Maritge Voogt Claesdr.*

By 1639, the date of this painting, Hals had begun accenting the contrast of the brightness of the face with the monochrome harmonies of background and dress in his portraits. The poise of the old woman is exemplary. Firmly esconced in her armchair, she is enclosed in her stiff robe, exposing only her face and hands to the light. Her left hand grips the arm of the chair purposefully, while her right hand holds a Bible as if to declare her faith. In earlier portraits, each descriptive detail had the same emotional charge, but here, out of harmony with all the other elements of the composition, the head emerges in isolation from the white ruff and the geometrical headdress. The eyes gaze off into space and the mouth, though half smiling, is firmly set.

FRANS HALS
Portrait of Maritge Voogt Claesdr
Oil on canvas; 50 1/2″ × 37 1/4″.
In the upper left, in the family crest, a Latin inscription gives the subject's age — 62 — and the date of the painting: 1639. The sitter was the wife of Pieter Jacobsz Olycan, the subject of a companion portrait that is now in the Ringling Museum, Sarasota, Fla. Another portrait of Maritge by Hals is in an English private collection. The present work was for sale in Amsterdam in 1834. It subsequently belonged to the A. van der Hoop collection and was bequeathed to the City of Amsterdam in 1854. On loan to the Rijksmuseum since 1885.

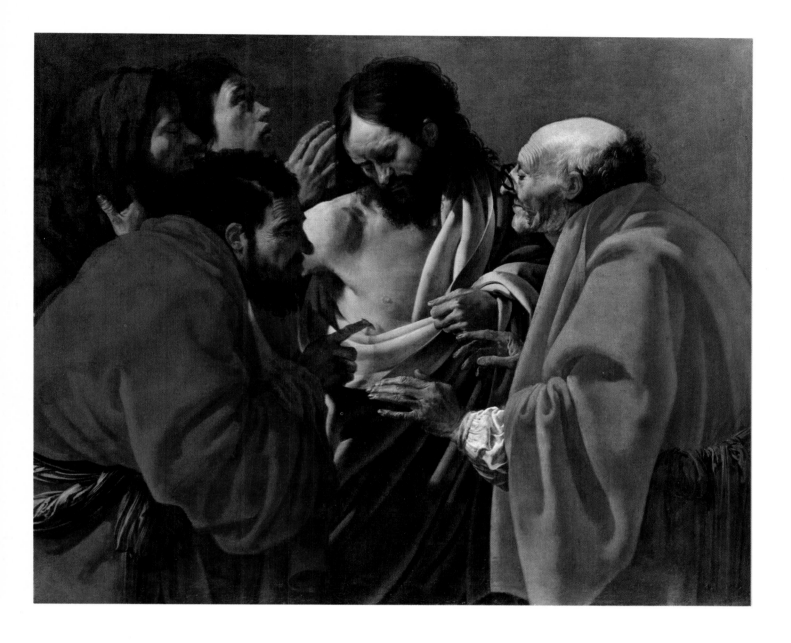

HENDRICK TERBRUGGHEN
Deventer 1588 — Utrecht 1629
The Incredulity of St. Thomas
Oil on canvas; 42 3/4″ × 53 3/4″.
It belonged to the S. Jackson collection, London, and was moved to Canada with the entire collection in 1880. Purchased from the dealers P. & D. Colnaghi, London, in 1956. Gift of the Commission for the Sale of Photographs.

HENDRICK TERBRUGGHEN. *The Incredulity of St. Thomas.*

It is well known that this composition is based on a similar work executed by Caravaggio for the Giustiani family, a painting that the Dutch artist had known and attentively studied during his visit to Rome. Perhaps more than his fellow artists of the Utrecht School, Terbrugghen intensified Caravaggio's lighting and used it to point up narrative elements. The light in his paintings usually has a single source and gives an exact account of the character and expression of the faces, while showing the gestures as tentative and human. The classical, unalterable cadence of Caravaggio is thus substantially reinterpreted, and the artist took those stylistic elements of the Italian master that could most easily be incorporated into the Dutch pictorial tradition.

51

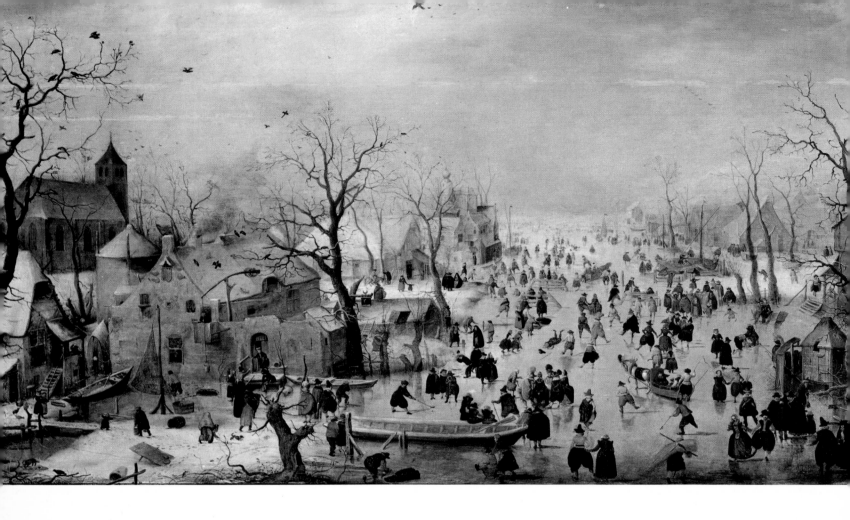

HENDRICK AVERCAMP. *Winter Scene.*

As a landscapist, Avercamp shows close familiarity with Flemish painting and with the work of Jan Bruegel. This typical work, which is certainly one of his greatest, illustrates these influences very clearly. The high viewpoint allows the maximum depth of field up to the clear-cut horizon line, which shows up light under the variegated browns and grays of a lowering sky. In this strongly receding space, the gay activity of the figures is shown with a cheerful, wholesome humor that is one of the original elements in the master's style. The composition records the happy pastimes of a winter's day, perhaps a Sunday. From the snow-covered houses behind the trees, by the banks of a frozen stream, the little figures emerge to join in ice sports. A sense of common enjoyment is conveyed, without splintering the composition into episodes. A perfect balance has been achieved between figures and background. The human intimacy of the scene is intensified by the contrast between the animated pleasure seekers and the closed, leaden oppression of the winter sky. Winter cold makes the village houses seem more snug and inviting, and the church in the left background sums up the picture of close-knit community life.

HENDRICK AVERCAMP
Amsterdam 1585 — Kampen 1634
Winter Scene
Oil on panel; 9 3/4″ × 14 3/4″.
Signed with the initials: "H. A."
Given to the Rijksmuseum by
Sir Henry Deterding in 1936.

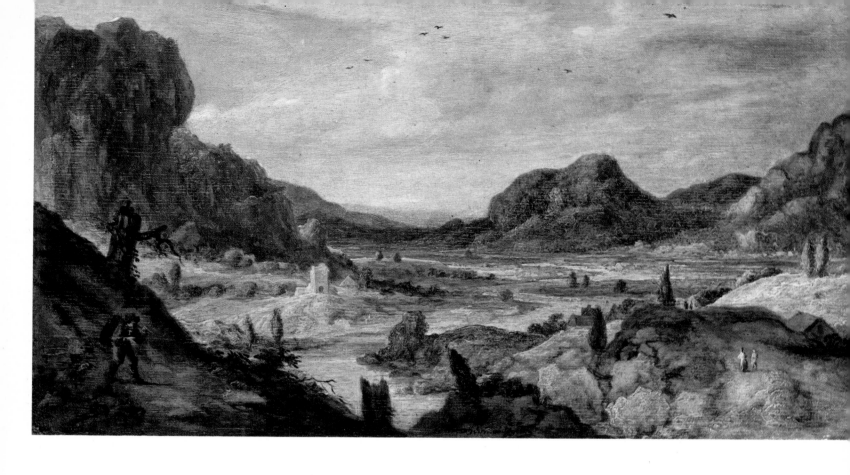

HERCULES SEGHERS. *River in a Valley.*

Mainly known for his engravings, Seghers did few paintings, and until the beginning of this century these were inadequately studied. Like the other great Dutch landscape painters of the 17th century, he was much influenced by the works of the German master, Elsheimer. In a general way, though, Seghers continued Momper's and Savery's tradition of the fantastic mountain landscape. Rembrandt, in turn, looked to him in developing his own style. In fact, Rembrandt was the owner of eight paintings by Seghers and reworked one of his etchings. Like his prints, Seghers's paintings are full of fantasy even though they are based on views in nature. The light corresponds to a specific moment of the day, but the landscape takes on a legendary aspect which is not dissimilar in feeling from Leonardo's work in this direction.

HERCULES SEGHERS
Haarlem (?) 1589 or 1590 — The Hague or
Amsterdam circa 1638
River in a Valley
Oil on panel; 11 3/4″ × 21″.
Signed in lower center: "Hercules Seghers."
In the collections of Hugo Graf Enzenberg
of Musbruck and of C. Hofstede de Groot.
The latter bequeathed it to the City of Groningen. Acquired by exchange in 1931.

53

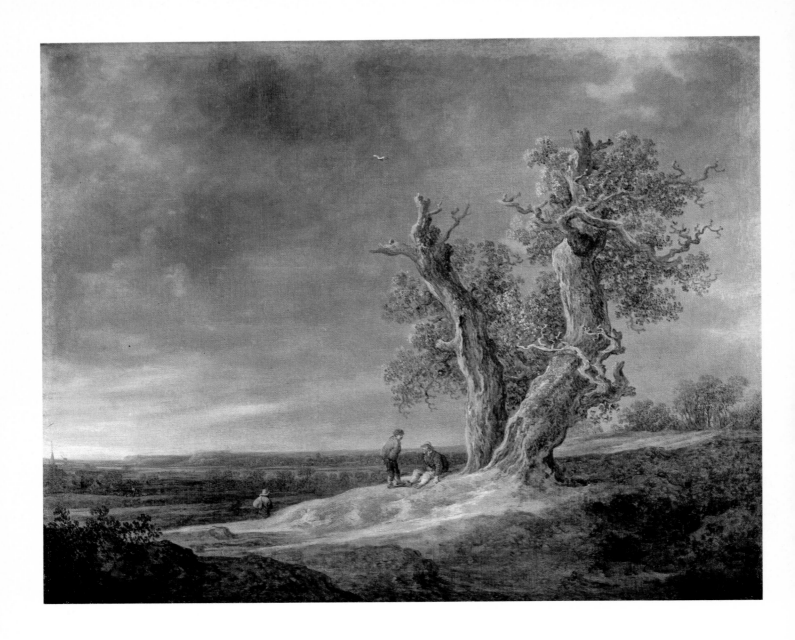

JAN VAN GOYEN. *Landscape with Two Oaks.*

The scene is set at the edge of the dunes, perhaps somewhere between The Hague and Leyden — though van Goyen painted invented as well as observed landscapes. This one has the most dramatic contrasts of any of his pictures. The composition is highly simplified: along the low horizon on the left stretch the dunes; on the right the ground rises and is covered with trees. The sky looms above, occupying the canonical two-thirds of the picture surface. Here there is a virtuoso play of nuances in light and atmosphere. The principal point in the "narrative" is provided by the minutely described wind-blasted oaks, which establish a connection between the sky and the ground. The weight of the oaks is balanced by the broad light passage at their feet. Two little figures in conversation beneath the trees, and a third further down the slope, create a domestic note that sets off the immensity of the horizon.

JAN VAN GOYEN
Leyden 1596 — The Hague 1656
Landscape with Two Oaks
Oil on canvas; 34 3/4″ × 43 1/2″.
Initialed and dated: "V G 1641."
In the Lacoste sale, Dordrecht, 1832; it belonged to the Cabinet J. Rombouts in the same city. Bequest of L. Dupper Wz. of Dordrecht in 1870.

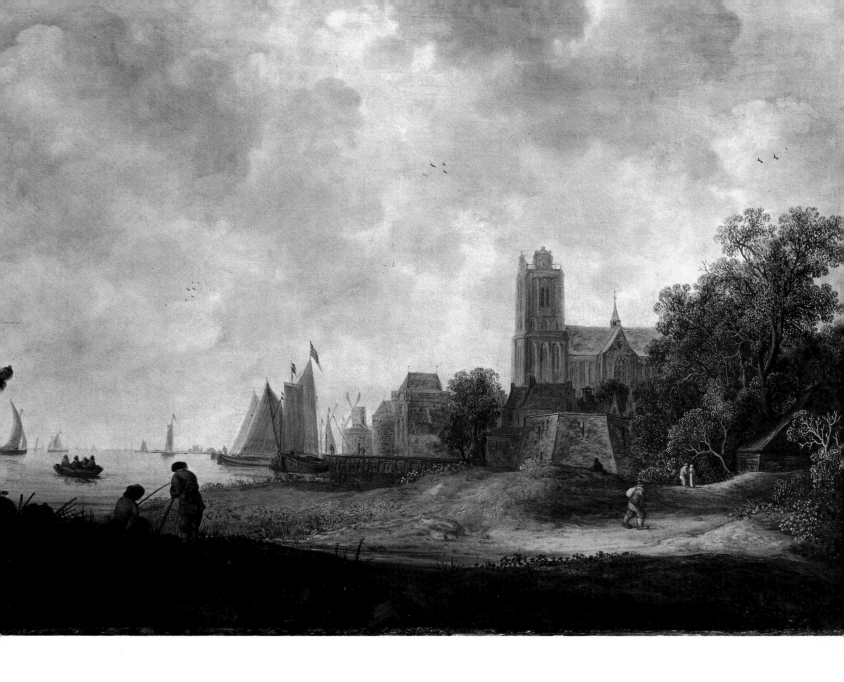

JAN VAN GOYEN
View of the Dordtse Kil Before Dordrecht
Oil on panel; 21 3/4″ × 28 1/4″.
In the sales of J. van der Mark, 1773, and
J. J. de Bruyn, 1709, in Amsterdam; A. van
der Werff van Zuidland, 1811, and Adr.
Lacoste, 1832, Dordrecht. In the Cabinet J.
Rombouts, Dordrecht, 1850. Bequest of L.
Dupper Wz., Dordrecht, in 1870.

JAN VAN GOYEN.   *View of the Dordtse Kil Before Dordrecht.*
Van Goyen liked to paint the great waterways of Holland, showing the rivers and canals busy with people going about their daily tasks. Yet, he did not allow this mundane activity to diminish the broad atmospheric effects he wished to create. An example of van Goyen's mature style, this painting shows an unusually high horizon line, occupying a third of the canvas and rising to the right where the most interesting elements of the composition are grouped. On the left the water reflects the sky and there is a view of boats and fishermen going about their business. The old landmark, with its tower, on the right, creates a new diagonal movement, as seen in the *Landscape with Two Oaks*. This is one of the best-known compositional devices in Dutch landscape painting.

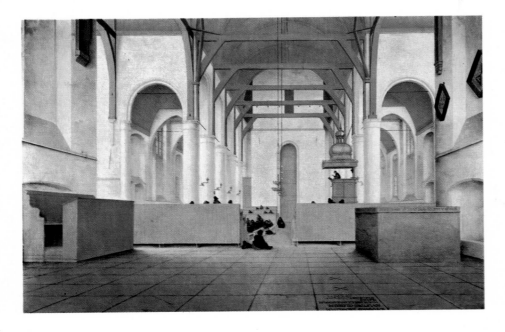

PIETER JANSZ SAENREDAM. *Interior of the St. Odolphuskerk at Assendelft.*

Set in the pavement in the foreground is the tombstone of the artist's father. To the right is the tomb of the van Assendelft family. The composition is signed and dated on a pew on the left. Typical of interiors in Dutch 17th-century painting, the composition is laid out symmetrically in one-point perspective. In many works by the artist the symmetry is perfect. Here a slight displacement to the right emphasizes the rhythm of the spacing and the recession of the columns.

In contrast to painters who created a geometrical play of light and dark elements, Saenredam painted broader and more diffused light effects. Another characteristic of the artist is the freeing of the perspective "stage" of any narrative elements that might disturb its metrical development. The figures, which were perhaps executed by Adriaen van Ostade, are placed in the background, in the second space of the composition. Foreground and background spaces are united by a single perspective scheme, but have the relationship of the real space of a stage to its painted backdrop.

PIETER JANSZ SAENREDAM. *The Old Town Hall of Amsterdam.*

A few figures appear on the porch of the Town Hall and its surroundings, but the main subject of the picture is the building itself. There are few anecdotal elements: besides the figures, only the whale's rib hanging on the façade — a souvenir of Dutch whaling expeditions — is of incidental interest. The inscription in Dutch on the canopy of the house on the right states that "Pieter Saenredam first drew this after life in all its colors in the year 1641 and painted it in the year 1657." Another inscription on the step of the porch adds that: "This is the old Town Hall of the city of Amsterdam, which was burned down in the year 1651 on the 7th July, in no longer than 3 hours' time." Thus the artist, after the destruction of the landmark, did a finished painting of the building based on his earlier watercolor.

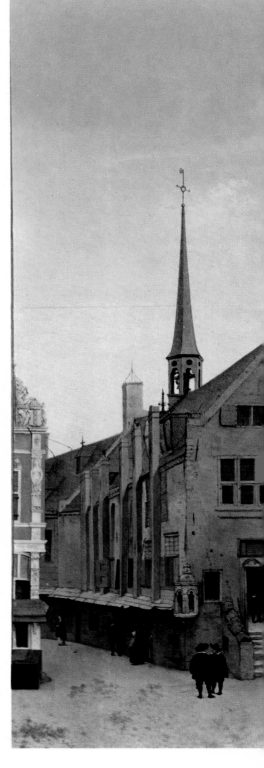

PIETER JANSZ SAENREDAM
Assendelft 1597 — Haarlem 1665
*Interior of the St. Odolphuskerk
at Assendelft*
Oil on panel; 19 3/4″ × 30″.
The Dutch inscription on a pew on the left

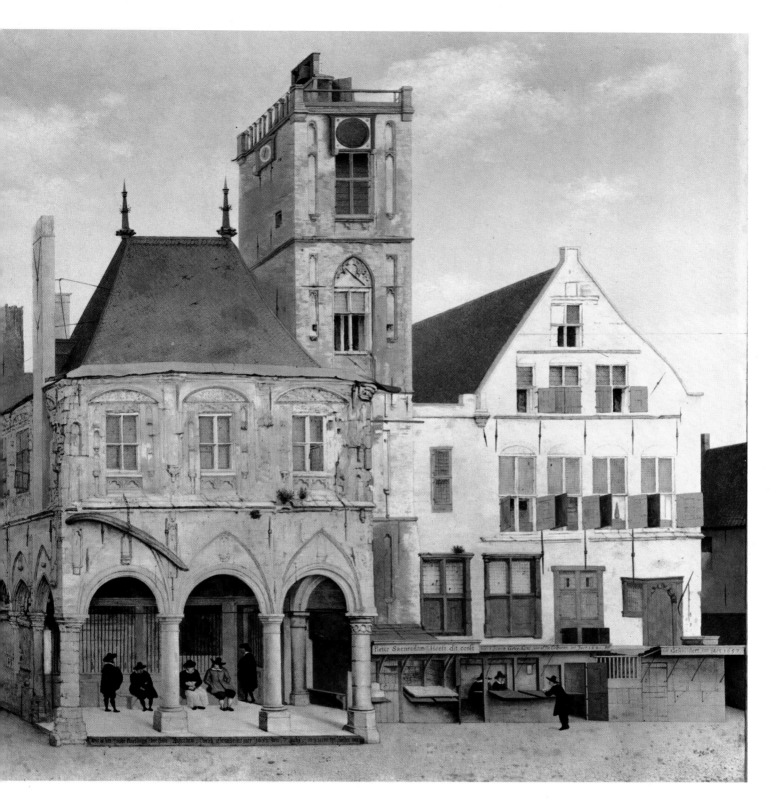

gives the name of the artist and the date: "This is the church at Assendelft a village in Holland, by Pieter Saenredam, this was painted in the year 1549 on the 2nd October."

PIETER JANSZ SAENREDAM
The Old Town Hall of Amsterdam
Oil on panel; 25 1/2″ × 32 3/4″.
The name of the artist and the date of exe-

cution of the work are given in the inscription on the canopy of the house represented at the right.

57

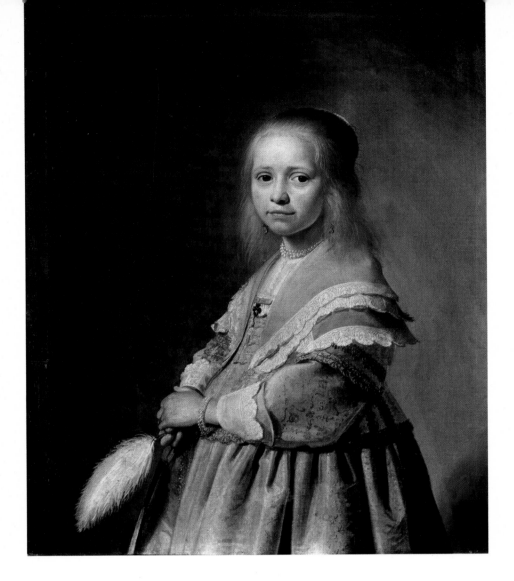

JOHANNES CORNELISZ
VERSPRONCK
Haarlem 1597 — Haarlem 1662
Portrait of a Girl
Oil on canvas; 32 1/4″ × 26 1/4″.
Signed and dated: "J Verspronck an 1641."
From 1805 it was in the Augusteum of
Oldenburg. On loan from M. P. Voûte.
Amsterdam, 1922. Purchased from his es-
tate by the *Vereeniging Rembrandt* and
donated to the Rijksmuseum in 1928.

JOHANNES CORNELISZ VERSPRONCK. *Portrait of a Girl.*
A pupil of Frans Hals, Verspronck was undoubtedly the most original
among the numerous portraitists of Amsterdam who kept alive the tradition
established by the great master. An able but uneven artist, he produced
some highly finished works that look as if they were done by formula; but
in others — such as this one — he achieved a completely independent expression that sets him apart even from the style of Hals. The subject has been
placed in the conventional three-quarter pose, and is three-quarter length.
The girl is dressed in pale blue, holds a white feather fan and stands against
a muted background. Coming from a single source on the left, the light
strikes the whole figure, creating a broad division into light and dark that
is somehow disquieting. Besides creating the diagonal structure of the composition, the light brings out the details of the dress and the features of the
girl's face. Her innocently wise childish expression is the most fascinating
element in the picture.

THOMAS DE KEYSER. *Portrait of Pieter Schout on Horseback.*
Equestrian portraits were not very common in egalitarian 17th-century Holland. Here the painter, who is better known for his "mythological," family

THOMAS DE KEYSER
Amsterdam 1596 — Amsterdam 1667
Portrait of Pieter Schout on Horseback
Oil on copper; 33 3/4″ × 27 1/4″.
Monogrammed and dated 1660.
Bequest of
Jonkheer J. S. H. van de Poll,
Amsterdam, 1880.

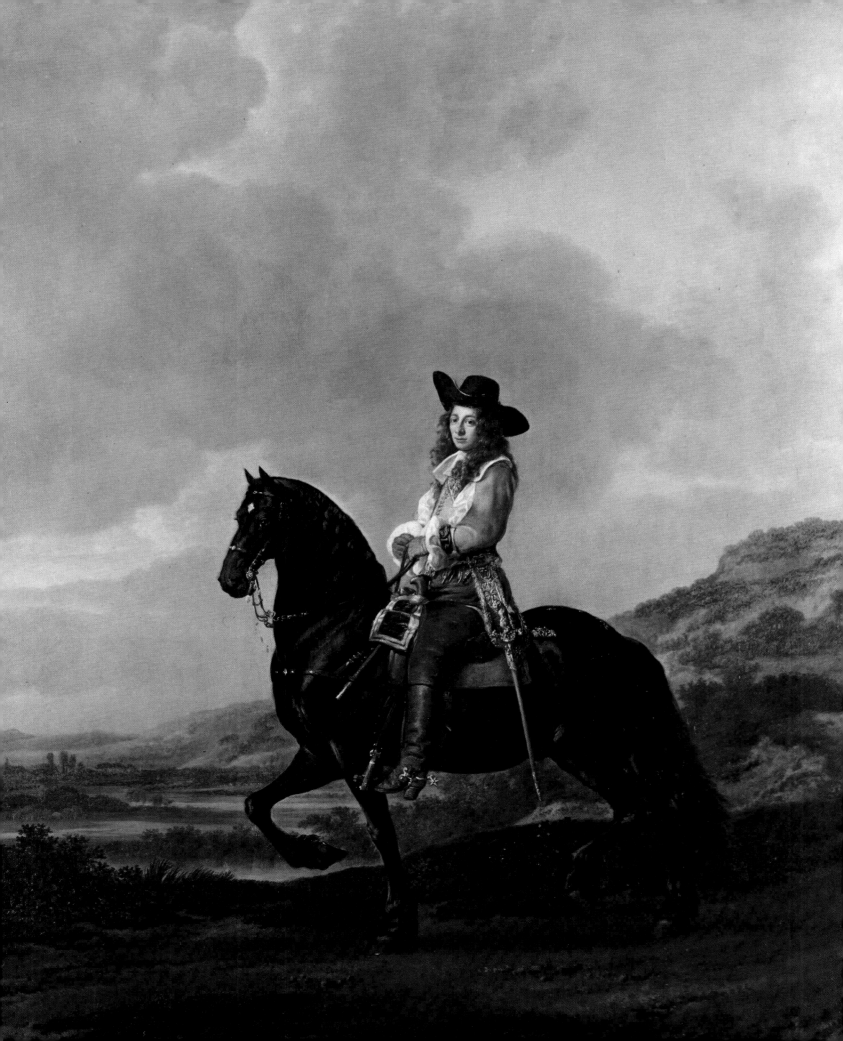

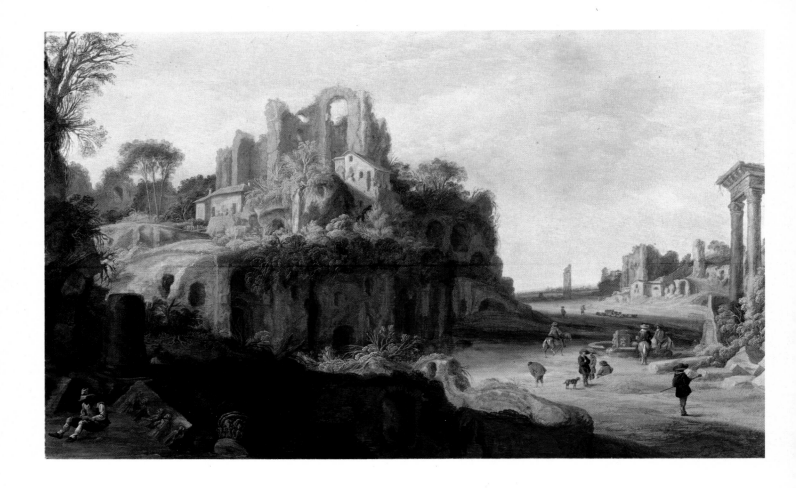

BARTHOLOMEUS BREENBERGH
Deventer 1599 or 1600 — Amsterdam 1657
Roman Landscape
Oil on canvas; 22" × 35 1/2".
From the Dienst R. V. K., 1948.

and official group portraits, has given the theme a particular interpretation. He has placed the horseman in the midst of a canonically composed landscape that could stand by itself as an example of the genre. Adriaen van de Velde may have been the author of the landscape background, and this separate authorship would explain in part its unusual importance. In any case, the aspect of horse and rider is also changed by this factor, as they lose any heraldic impressiveness. Pieter Schout, despite his martial turnout, merely seems to be enjoying a jaunt in his native countryside.

BARTHOLOMEUS BREENBERGH. *Roman Landscape.*
From 1620 to 1627, Breenbergh studied and worked in Rome, where he was the pupil of Paul Bril and was much influenced by Adam Elsheimer. He is one of the most notable of the Amsterdam Romanists. His art reflects an interest in a wide range of painters, from Claude Lorrain to the Carracci, but in most of his little panels the subtly imaginative transformation of the scene, the calibration of light and shade and the atmospheric harmony comprise a distinctive vocabulary. Thus the artist's Romanism, in which the rules of Dutch landscape painting remain unaltered, is all his own.

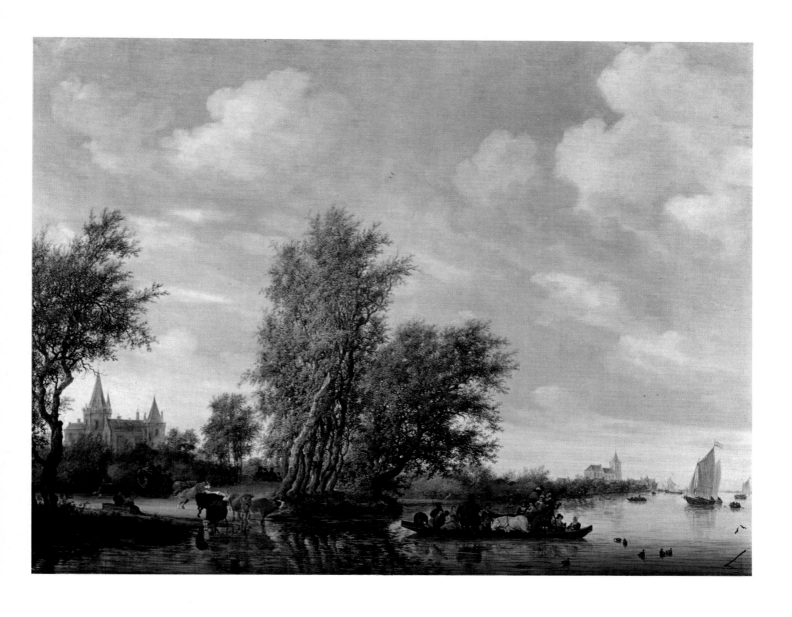

SALOMON VAN RUYSDAEL. *River Scene with Ferry.*

Salomon first worked in the circle of Pieter van de Velde. Along with Pieter Molijn and Jan van Goyen, he was subsequently the major representative of the so-called "New Haarlem Style," in which the favorite subject for landscapes was the local dunes and the human figure was subordinate to the panorama. After 1630, Ruysdael's style became clearly distinct from that of his colleagues. His scenes acquired greater depth in the recessions of the firm shapes of trees and bushes. In composition they were built up on the diagonal, and two subjects became typical: the halt at the inn and the river crossing. In this last genre, there are marked affinities with Jan van Goyen during the same years, but van Goyen's descriptive vivacity is very different from Ruysdael's elaborate, measured color harmonies. Here, as in the atmospheric rendering of the trees, the color may be light and free, but the picture as a whole shows strong intellectual control.

SALOMON VAN RUYSDAEL
Naarden circa 1600 — Haarlem 1670
River Scene with Ferry
Oil on canvas; 39 1/4" × 52 1/2".
Signed and dated: "SVRuysdael 1649."
Sales of G. Wilbraham of Northwich
(Cheshire), London, 1930; and of
Messrs. J. Goudstikker, Amsterdam.
From the Dienst R. V. K., 1948.

61

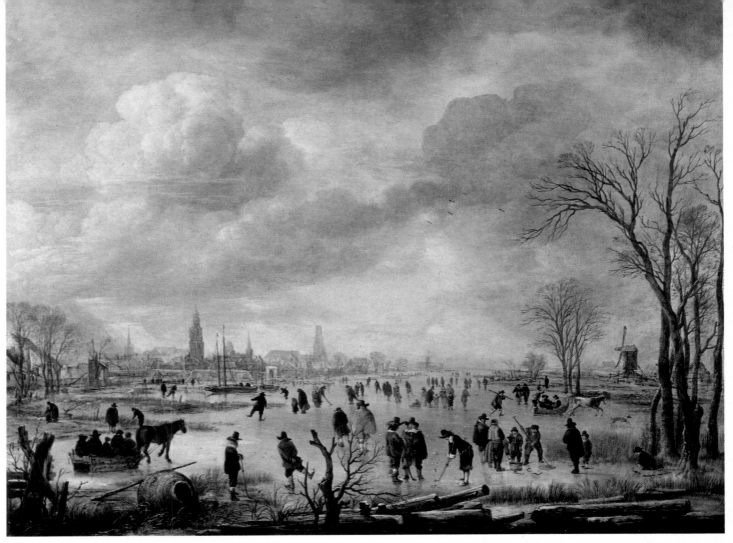

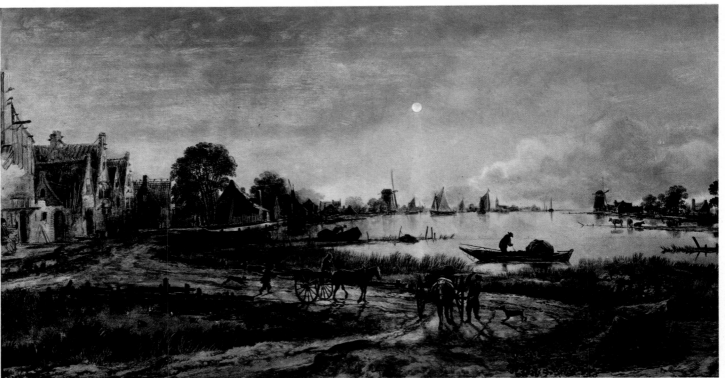

AERT VAN DER NEER. *River Scene in Winter.*

If, as some maintain, Dutch landscape painting in the 17th century was created to satisfy the desire of the middle class to see themselves portrayed in their familiar surroundings, then van der Neer is certainly one of the painters whose works reflect this proposition. The nature of this style, however, is much more complex in its methods of composition, its derivations and the personalities of its practitioners than this contention would allow. But it is also undeniable that a taste for this subject remained constant in succeeding centuries in Holland and by transmission in England and France. The theme of the frozen river peopled with little figures going through the typical motions of skating, sleighing and playing a kind of solo hockey (called *kolf*) keeps recurring from Avercamp on. The setting usually shows villages, mills, churches and trees, along the embankments and in the distance. In van der Neer's paintings the figures are larger and fewer, more documentary and less anecdotal. The style is broader, the tone and form heavier. Although still imaginative, his works convey a large degree of factual reality.

AERT VAN DER NEER
Amsterdam 1603 or 1604 — Amsterdam 1677
River Scene in Winter
Oil on canvas; 25 1/4″ × 31 1/4″.
Monogrammed.
In the collections of Edward Gray, Harringhay; A. Brondgeest, 1839; and A. van der Hoop, Amsterdam. Bequeathed to the City of Amsterdam, and on loan to the Rijksmuseum since 1885.

AERT VAN DER NEER
River Scene by Moonlight
Oil on canvas; 21 1/2″ × 40 1/2″.
Signed with the artist's initials at lower center. It was in the collection of Jonkheer J. Six, then was sold in 1928. Sir Henry Deterding gave it to the Rijksmuseum in 1936.

AERT VAN DER NEER. *River Scene by Moonlight.*

One of the first paintings by the artist, it shows a theme for which he later became famous. The recurrent Dutch subject of a view of one of the waterways is here enriched by rendering it at night. The eye of the moon, opening at the edge of the clouds, beams a firm light upon the landscape, sharply defining the elements of the composition in silvery surfaces and dark silhouetted effects. The reality of the wintry skating scenes, such as the preceding work, is here replaced by limpid revery. Life here has been overtaken by sleep, but the figure of a boatman bent over his oar brings human feeling into the dreamlike scene.

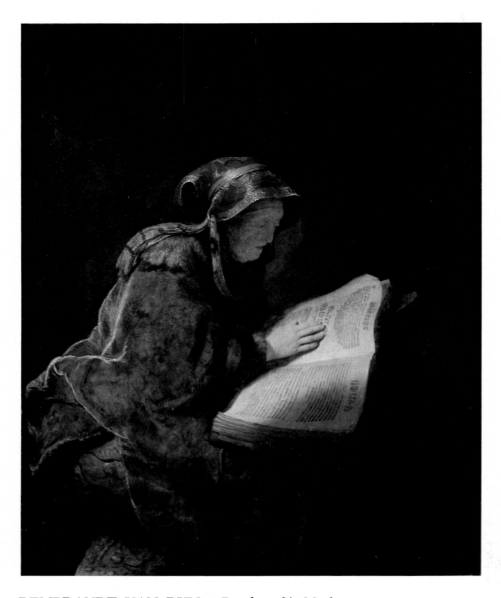

REMBRANDT VAN RIJN
Leyden 1606 — Amsterdam 1669
Rembrandt's Mother (1631)
Oil on panel; 23 1/2″ × 19″.
Monogrammed "RHL" and dated.
In 1719 the painting was in the Schönfeld collection in Pommersfelden. Acquired by the Augusteum of Oldenburg in 1867 at the Schönborn sale in Paris. On loan from M. P. Voûte in 1922. Bequest to the *Vereeniging Rembrandt* in 1928.

REMBRANDT VAN RIJN. *Rembrandt's Mother.*

Cornelia Willemsdochter van Zuytbroeck, the mother of the master, in keeping with her status as a simple well-to-do woman of the middle class, was firmly pious. This is one of the few portraits of her that have come down to us. Rembrandt painted it during the years of his success as a portraitist, a success that was to culminate in 1632 with the execution of the celebrated *The Anatomy Lesson of Dr. Tulp,* immediately after he moved from Leyden to Amsterdam. References to the style of Thomas de Keyser are obvious, but the elaborate dress of the figure adds a new dramatic atmosphere. During the 19th century it was thought that the subject was meant to represent the Prophetess Hannah, but this supposition is now considered doubtful.

REMBRANDT VAN RIJN. *Joseph Telling His Dreams.*

The tendency toward monochrome seen in Rembrandt's major works here takes the form of *grisaille,* which intensifies the highlights and shadows

REMBRANDT VAN RIJN
Joseph Telling His Dreams
Oil on paper; 20″ × 15 1/4″.
Signed and dated: "Rembrandt 163 . . . ."
In all likelihood it was executed in 1636–37, and was thus contemporary with the *Tobias* in Stuttgart and the *Parable of the Vinedressers* in the Hermitage, Leningrad. Sale of W. Six, Amsterdam, 1734; Prince de Carignan, Paris, 1742; Duc de Tallard, Paris, 1756; J. de Vos, Amsterdam, 1833; Jonkheer J. W. Six van Vromade, Amsterdam, 1920. From 1928 in the A. W. Volz collection, The Hague. In the Rijksmuseum since 1946.

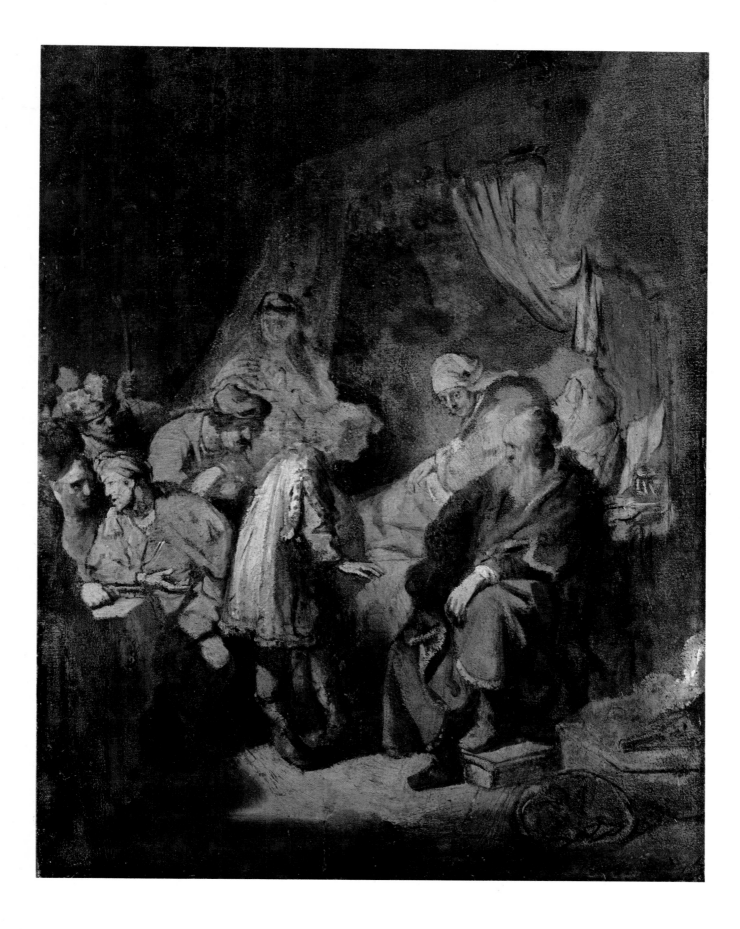

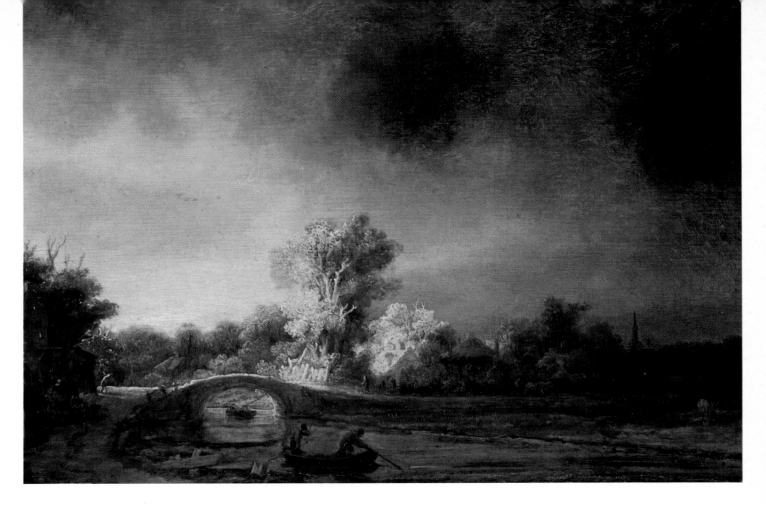

of the web of light in the composition. In a small space, the light picks out the faces and figures of the actors as the narrative unfolds. Standing beside his mother's bed, the youthful Joseph tells his dreams and explains them to members of his family.

REMBRANDT VAN RIJN. *The Stone Bridge.*
There are comparatively few landscapes in the catalogue of Rembrandt's works. Comparison with the major Dutch scene painters of the time, especially van de Velde, van Goyen and Jacob van Ruisdael, clarifies Rembrandt's development in this genre. But from the beginning he diverged from his sources of influence; instead of following the general, equilibrated atmosphere common to all these painters, Rembrandt defined his space in violent contrasts. Here, under a heavily clouded sky, dense trees are hit by sunlight. The sun also edges the stone bridge over the canal on which boats can be seen. In the shadow in front of the inn on the left stands a cart with a few figures in it. From the shadow on the right rises a church tower.

REMBRANDT VAN RIJN. *Jeremiah Lamenting the Destruction of Jerusalem.*
This is a detail of a painting that shows the old prophet in solitude, sitting on the moss-grown steps of the Temple, meditating on the misfortunes of the Holy City. The body of the figure is set between light and shade, where details like the embroidery on the robes are most minutely described. On the face and the broad brow, however, the light becomes more intense, as if to reveal the flash of prophecy.

REMBRANDT VAN RIJN
The Stone Bridge (circa 1638)
Oil on panel; 11 1/2″ × 16 3/4″.
Possibly a view of Ouderkerk, where a stone bridge, the Binnen Benningbrug, was situated. It was demolished in 1649. In the Lapeyrière sale, Paris, 1817. In the collections of James Gray, Versailles (1863) and of the Marquis of Lansdowne, Bowood, 1883. Acquired at the James Reiss sale in London, 1900, with the financial aid of the *Vereeniging Rembrandt* and of Dr. A. Bredius.

REMBRANDT VAN RIJN
Jeremiah Lamenting the Destruction of Jerusalem
Detail.
Oil on panel; 22 3/4″ × 18″.
Monogrammed and dated 1630.
About 1760 it was in the Cesar collection in Berlin, then in the Stroganoff collection, St. Petersburg, and Rasch, Stockholm. In 1939 it was donated to the Rijksmuseum by the *Vereeniging Rembrandt,* with the aid of private citizens.

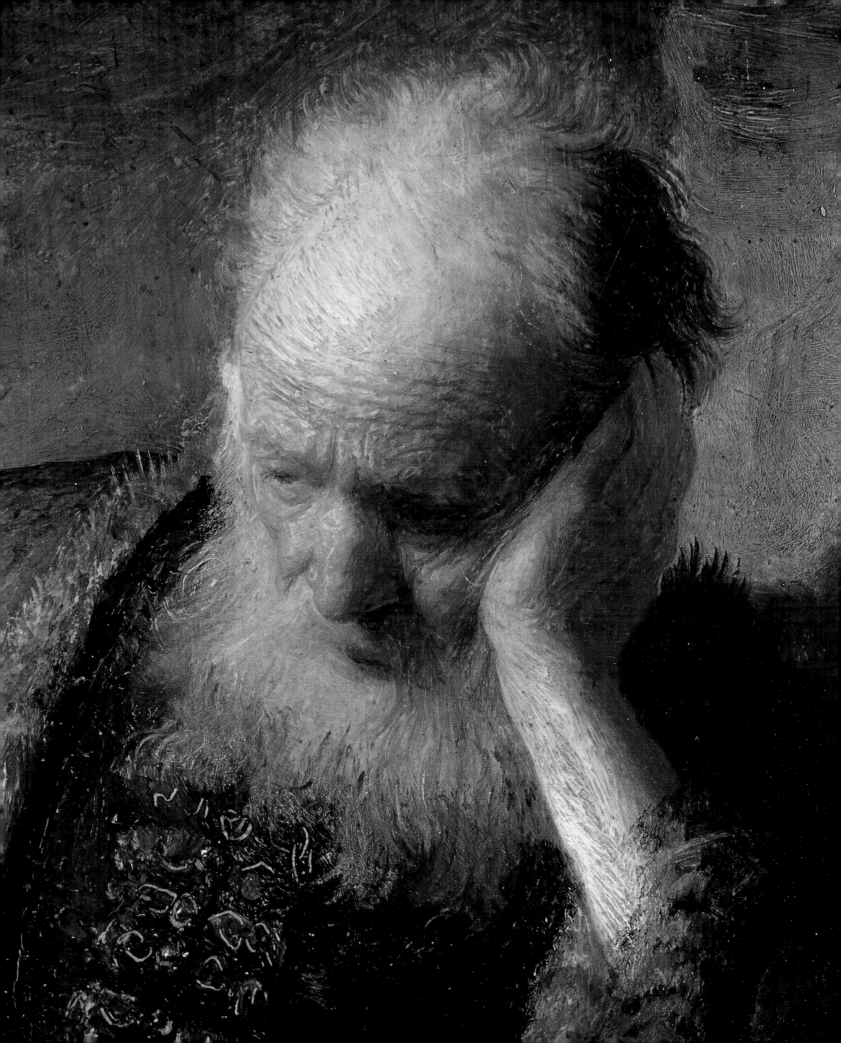

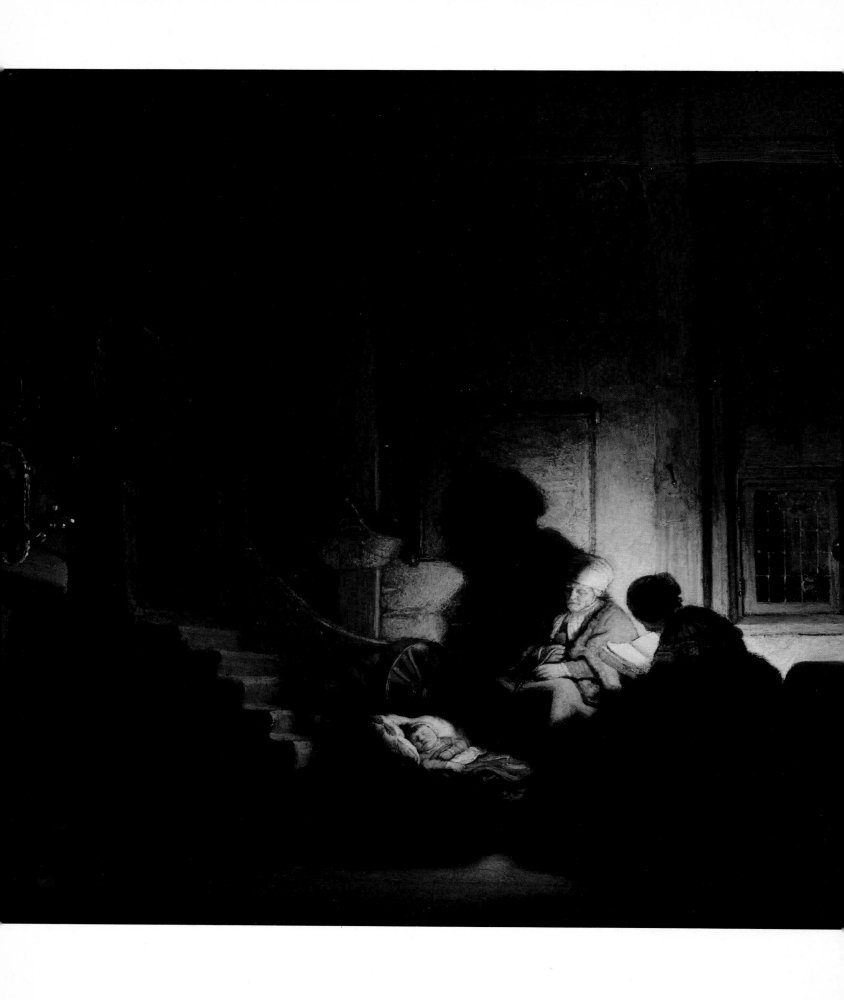

REMBRANDT VAN RIJN. *Holy Family by Night.*
Very probably this little panel was painted around 1645, since there are evident similarities to paintings of the same subject that were executed between 1645 and 1646. Here, in a lofty room, light emanates from things themselves and is the element that measures off the space and establishes the feeling of the interior. The figures are perfectly in harmony with this element, which gives them their stylistic and emotional definition in the narrative. It is in this sense that the master's choice of a "nocturn" should be understood: not as an excuse for pictorial effects, but as a means of expressing the intimacy of family life in domestic quietude.

REMBRANDT VAN RIJN
Holy Family by Night (1645?)
Oil on panel; 23 1/2″ × 30 1/4″.
Recently acquired by the Rijksmuseum.

REMBRANDT VAN RIJN. *The Night Watch.*   *pp. 70–71*
This impressive work was commissioned as one of three large group portraits for the Hall of the Civic Guard — perhaps to commemorate Marie de' Medici's visit to Amsterdam in 1638. Contemporary convention in this kind of painting called for a static succession of figures, in which the higher ranking subjects were generally given some prominence by their gestures or positions.

Rembrandt, however, revolutionized the tradition by conceiving the Company of Frans Banning Cocq in action, as it sets off on a march. The figures making up the group are strongly individualized, but not isolated. In fact, the interrelationships are multiplied and involve marginal, anecdotal elements like the somewhat caricatured children and the dog barking at the drum major. The vivid portrayal of the action is emphasized by the radiating directions in the composition. From the central group under the arch to the two officers in the foreground, each figure establishes a different movement in space toward the spectator. The entire company is arranged as if on a stage, with a fixed stage setting of central arch and architecture, in the classical tradition. But the barrier of the proscenium has been breached, and the space represented surges out and mingles with the space in which the spectator moves. The symmetrical balance of the setting is annulled by the pulsating light, which multiplies the spaces and creates many different centers of interest.

The pivotal figure of the entire composition, that of Frans Banning Cocq (center, in black) — designed as the single balancing point — lost its function when the canvas was cut down on the left. Mutilated, probably to fit into a smaller space when it was moved in the 18th century, the composition went askew, the two central figures became more prominent and the halberdier on the left became a sort of statuary wing. On the right, which was also cut down, the drummer became the other wing closing off the scene, whereas originally both this figure and the halberdier served as fulcrums for further action. Despite these major damages, Rembrandt's genius triumphs and the emotional intensity, the concentrated human feeling in every detail of this monumental canvas, still make *The Night Watch* one of the world's greatest masterpieces.

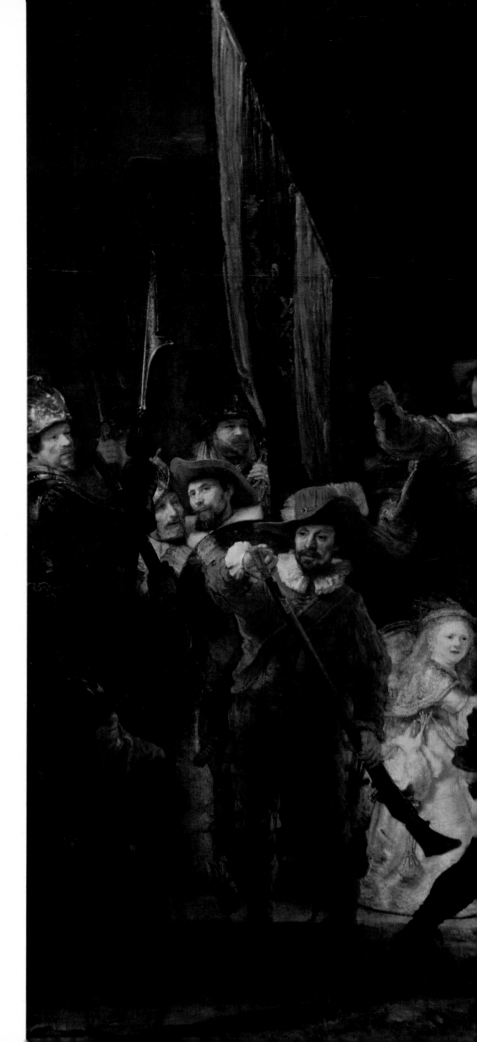

REMBRANDT VAN RIJN
The Night Watch
Oil on canvas; 11'9 1/4" × 14'4 1/4".
Signed and dated: "Rembrandt f. 1642."
The copy by Gerritt Lund in the National Gallery, London, shows that this painting must have been cut down when it was moved from its original place in the Guild Hall of the Arquebusiers (Civic Guard) to the old Town Hall of Amsterdam, where it was reduced to fit between two doors (1715). The most extensive mutilation was on the left, where a vertical strip more than a yard wide was removed. The halberdier who now appears at the edge of the picture was at the center of a group extending to the left. About a foot of canvas was removed on the right. The setting shown was a narrow shaded street rather than a night scene, but the progressive oxidation of the paint has helped create the nocturnal effect. In 1815 it was moved to the Trippenhuis.

70

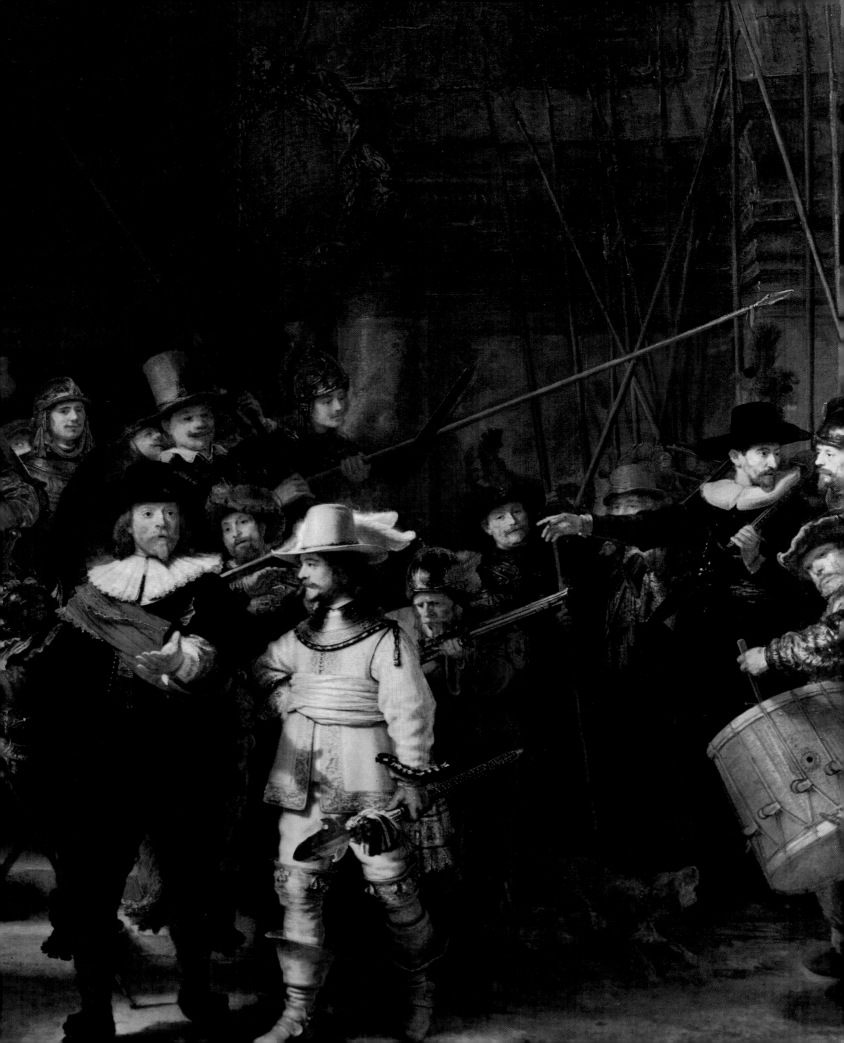

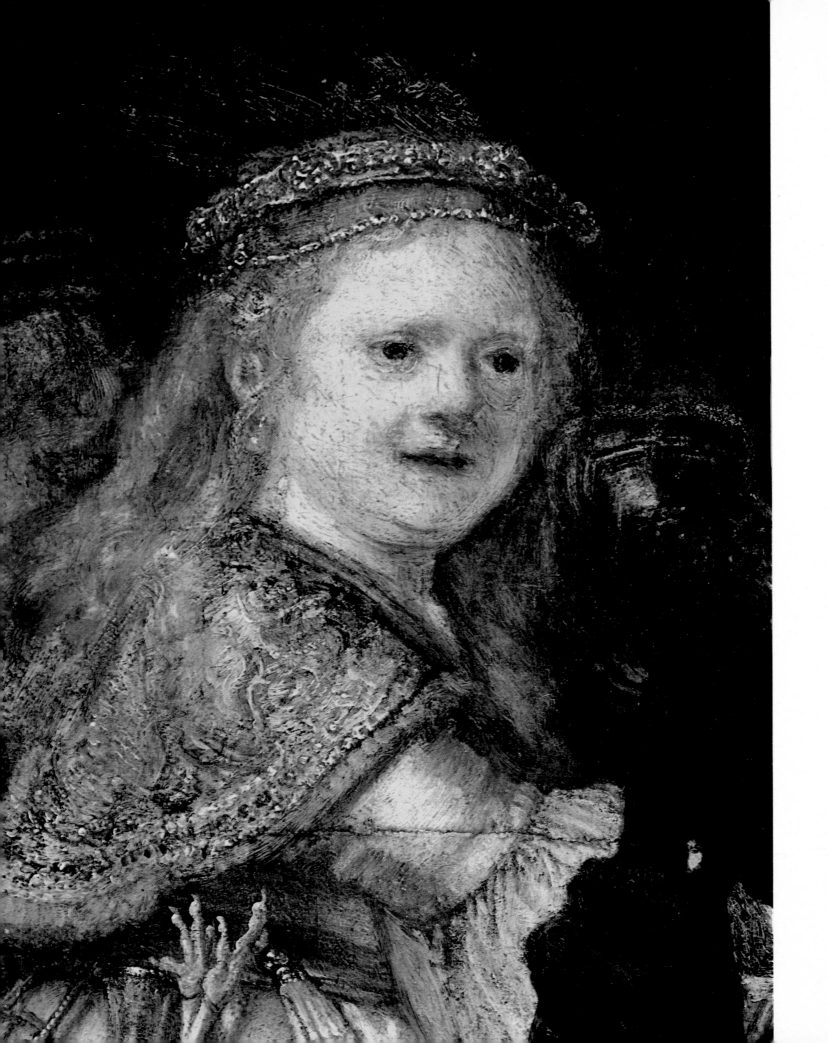

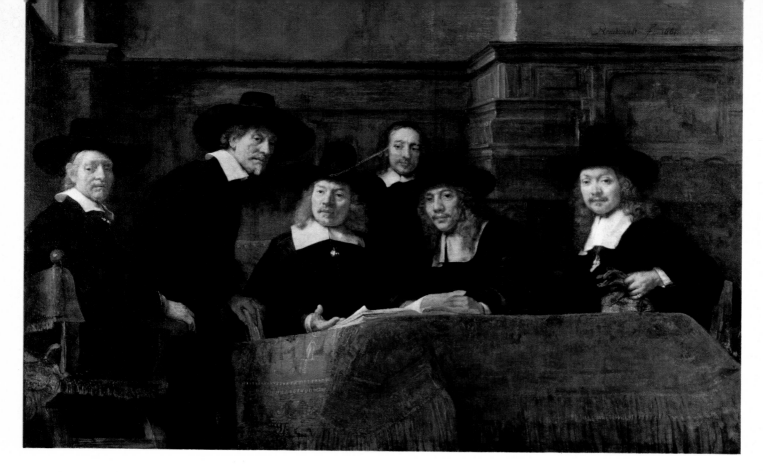

REMBRANDT VAN RIJN
The Syndics of the Cloth Guild
Oil on canvas; 6′3 1/4″ × 9′1 3/4″.
Signed and dated: "Rembrandt f. 1662."
The identity of the subjects has not been securely established. An X-ray examination has shown that Rembrandt started the composition with a different idea in mind, but changed it in the course of his work. It was painted for the Drapers' or Cloth Guild, and was installed in the Guild Hall, in Staalstraat, Amsterdam. In 1771 it was moved to the Town Hall, and in 1808 the City of Amsterdam lent it to the Rijksmuseum.

REMBRANDT VAN RIJN
The Night Watch
Detail.

REMBRANDT VAN RIJN. *The Syndics of the Cloth Guild.*

The last of Rembrandt's group portraits, this work was painted in 1662 to continue a series of similar pictures hanging in the Cloth Guild's headquarters at Amsterdam. The years from 1655 to around 1660 were the saddest in the artist's life. His reputation declined, he went bankrupt after commissions became scarce and his house and goods were sold at auction to pay his creditors. Around 1660 his financial situation improved, but the death of people he loved and further disappointments embittered Rembrandt's old age. Yet this great portrait breathes serenity, and the painter has rendered his subjects with affectionate sympathy. As the canvas was to be placed above a mantelpiece, the perspective is constructed from a low viewpoint. According to the Guild's tradition, five Syndics were portrayed. The sixth figure, bareheaded in the background, is the valet, who, unlike the others, was not required to pay for his portrait. The group looks out as if caught during a momentary interruption of business, but the composition of this apparently casual scene has been worked out with extreme care.

REMBRANDT VAN RIJN. *Dr. Deyman's Anatomy Lesson.*

pp. 74–75

A drawing, also in the Rijksmuseum, shows what Rembrandt's original composition looked like, before a fire in 1723 destroyed three-quarters of the work. It was symmetrical, with the corpse in the center and behind it the professor in the act of dissecting the brain. Around him stood the students under arches, in two groups. The assistant on the left is holding the top of

73

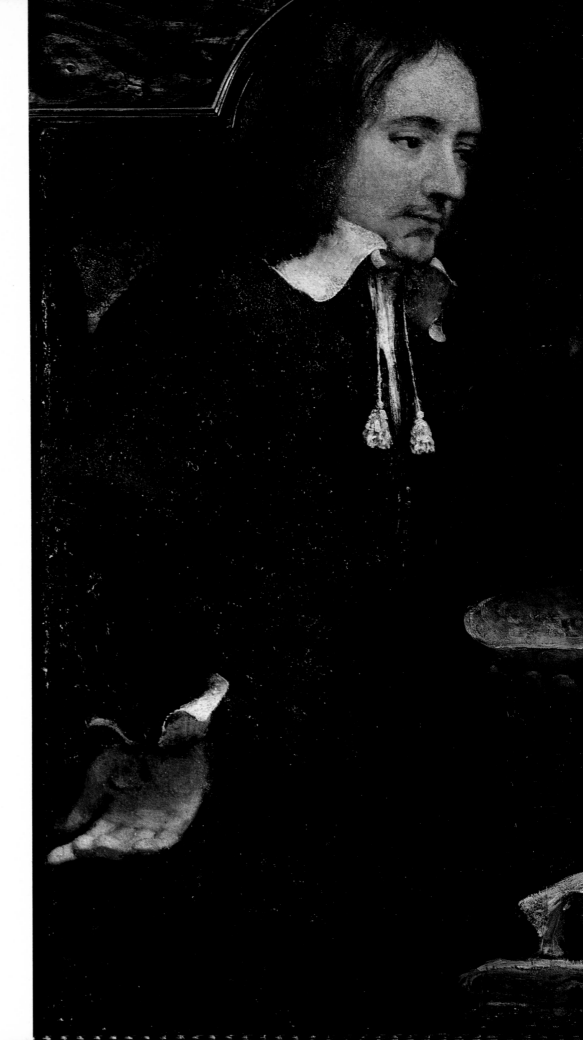

REMBRANDT VAN RIJN
Dr. Deyman's
Anatomy Lesson
(fragment)
Oil on canvas;
39 1/4″ × 52 3 /4″.
Signed and dated:
"Rembrandt f. 1656."
The cadaver shown in this fragmentary painting is that of one Joris Fonteyn, alias Zwarte Jan, who was sentenced to death for theft on January 27, 1656, and buried on February 2. The picture was executed for the dissection room of the Surgeons' Guild in the Sint Anthonieswaag, Amsterdam. Sold in 1841, it entered the collection of the Rev. E. Pryce Owen at Cheltenham. Bought by the City of Amsterdam in 1885.

74

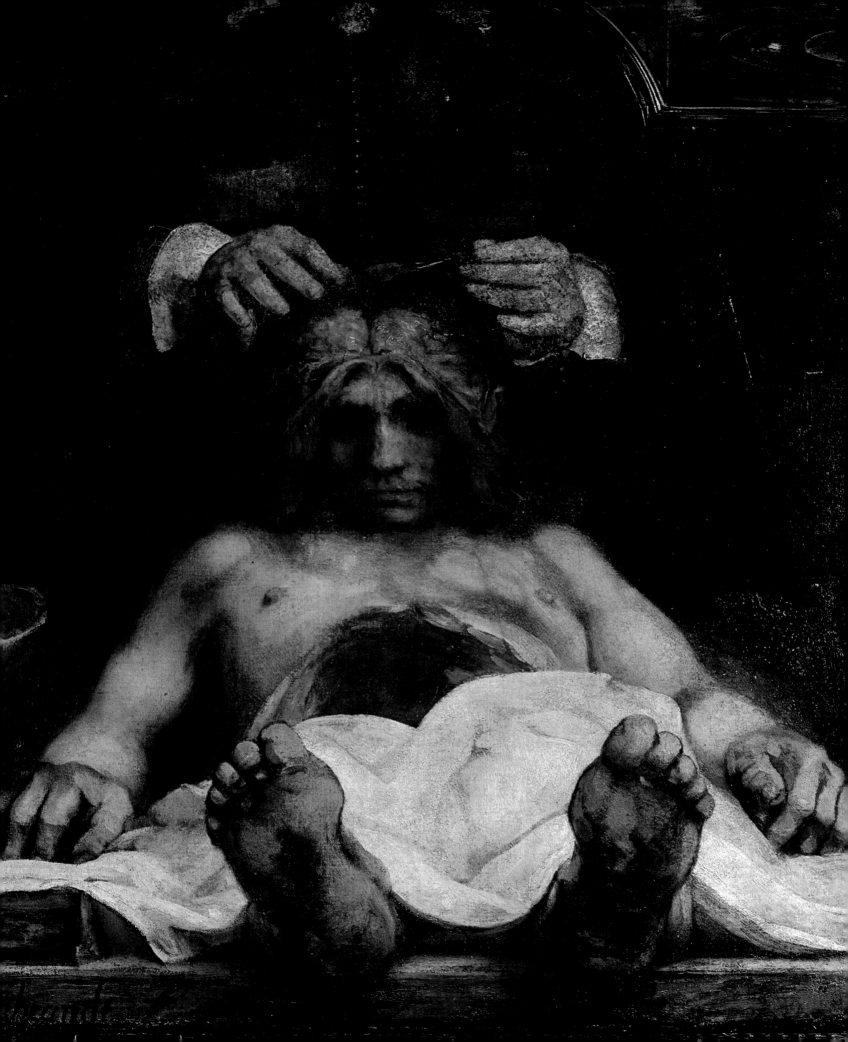

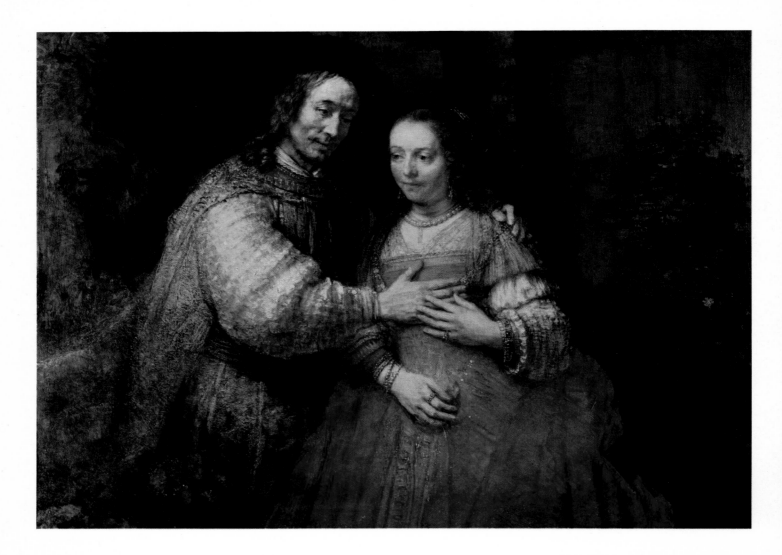

the skull, which has been removed from the cadaver. The most symmetrically constructed of all Rembrandt's works, it was very different from his other famous painting of a similar subject, *The Anatomy Lesson of Dr. Tulp*. In that picture, executed in 1632 and now in The Hague, the group of the instructor and students was dynamically disposed around the foreshortened cadaver, seen in three-quarter view. Here the mutilation of the canvas has accentuated the resemblance to Mantegna's *Dead Christ,* which was already very strong in the painting as Rembrandt conceived it. Thus, the tragic isolation of the dead figure has become more marked and is further emphasized by the detached professionalism of the figure on the left.

REMBRANDT VAN RIJN.   *The Jewish Bride.*

In this wedding portrait, representing the Jewish poet, Don Miguel de Barrios, and his wife, Abigael de Pina, the painter unquestionably intended to suggest a Biblical parallel. A drawing, very probably contemporary, in the Kramarsky collection, New York, which shows Isaac and Rebecca in the same pose, is considered to be a preliminary sketch for this painting. Iconographically, the husband's affectionate gesture, which is meant to signify the

REMBRANDT VAN RIJN
The Jewish Bride
Oil on canvas; 47 1/2″ × 65 1/2″.
Signed and dated: "Rembrandt f. 16 . . . ."
Painted probably after 1665. It belonged to the Vaillant and A. van der Hoop collections. In 1854 it was donated to the City of Amsterdam. On loan to the Rijksmuseum since 1885.

REMBRANDT VAN RIJN
Self-Portrait as St. Paul
Oil on canvas; 35 3/4″ × 30 1/4″.
Signed and dated on the left, above the shoulder:
"Rembrandt f. 1661."
In the collections of Tournier, Paris; Corsini, Rome, until 1807; Lord Kinnaird, Rossie Priory near Dundee. On loan from Mrs. J. G. de Bruyn-van der Leeuw, Muri.

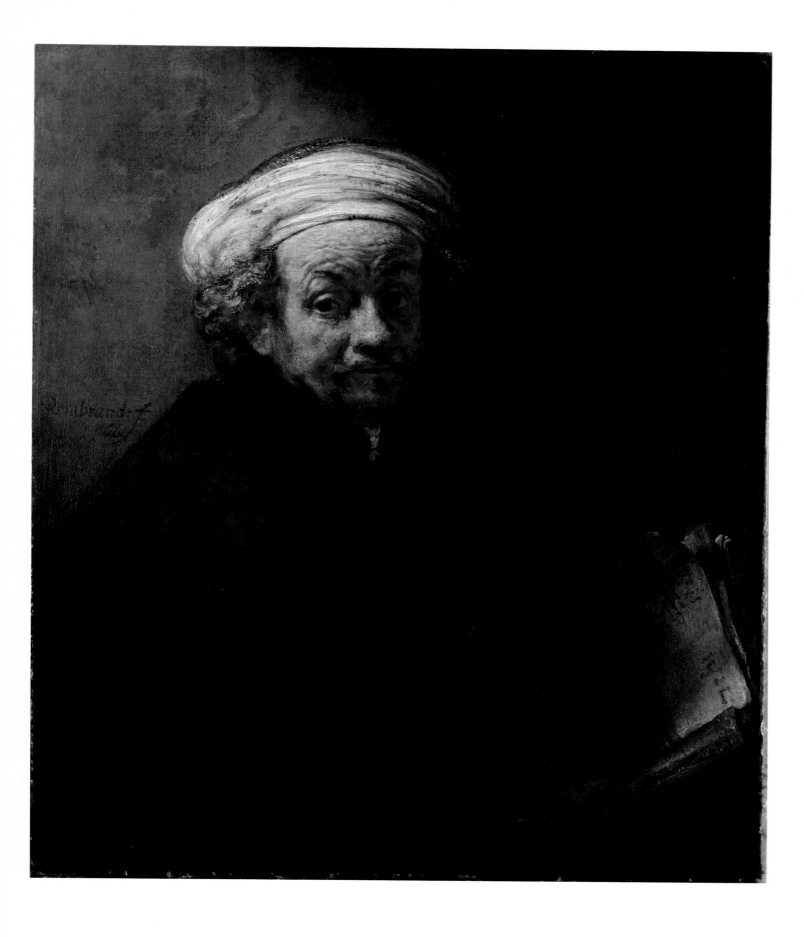

woman's fertility, belongs to the contemporary convention of representing the marriage of Jacob and Rachel. It has also been suggested that the two figures might be identified as Esther and Ahasuerus or Tobias and Sarah. In any event, the connection with some Biblical couple does not alter the symbolism. The work is one of the finest of Rembrandt's late period. The transformation and costuming that is typical of Rembrandt as a portraitist are imbued here with particular feeling and intensity. The light springs upon the intensely absorbed faces of the couple, and their serene awareness makes them as much universal as individual figures. The reds, browns and golds of the fabulous, almost ceremonial, costumes, are now smooth and now clotted, as they were rapidly applied by strokes of the palette-knife.

REMBRANDT VAN RIJN. *Self-Portrait as St. Paul.*   *p. 77*
Rembrandt was his own favorite model. About seventy self-portraits, or at least representations of his own face, have come down to us. From the youthful one in Kassel to the shaggy *Self-Portrait as Democritus* in Cologne, there is no moment of the artist's biography that he did not vividly represent. Such personal statements are a complete record of Rembrandt's view of the world, and of his relationship to it, expressed with great feeling and intensity.

In this example, one of his last self-portraits, Rembrandt adopts — as he often did — a disguise. He sees himself dressed in Oriental style, holding a Hebrew scroll. The hilt of a sword emerging from under his coat identifies him as St. Paul, the conventional symbol for the Apostle to the Gentiles. The work thus connects with a series of the Apostles, including the St. James in the Stephen Clark collection and the St. Matthew of the Louvre, in which Rembrandt's son Titus was the model for the angel. Compared to the aged suffering seen in the Uffizi self-portrait and the painful laughter of the *Democritus,* this image of Rembrandt's old age seems peaceful and meditative, with a veiled hint of irony.

REMBRANDT VAN RIJN. *Portrait of Titus.*
Rembrandt's beloved son Titus, who died still young, only a year before his father's death in 1669, was often portrayed by the master. The first and most famous of these portraits, now in the Boymans–Van Beuningen Museum, Rotterdam, was painted in 1655 and shows Titus as a thirteen-year-old boy with pen, ink and paper, pondering over what he is going to draw or write. The Rijksmuseum's painting is the last portrait of the young man. For us, who know his tragic future, his pallor and the melancholy of his eyes foreshadow his premature death.

78

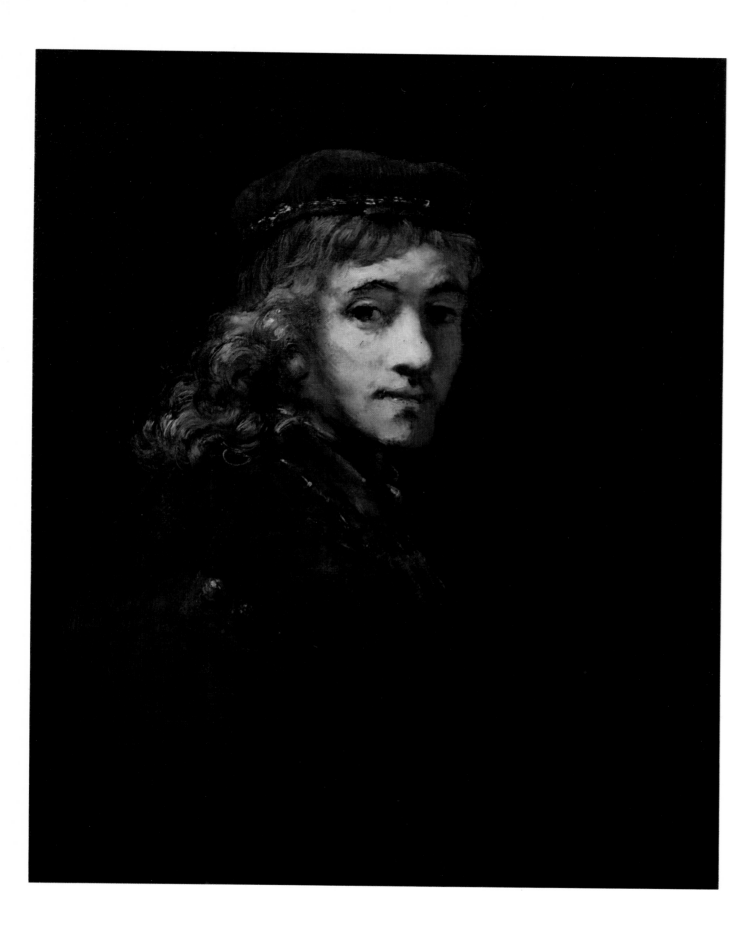

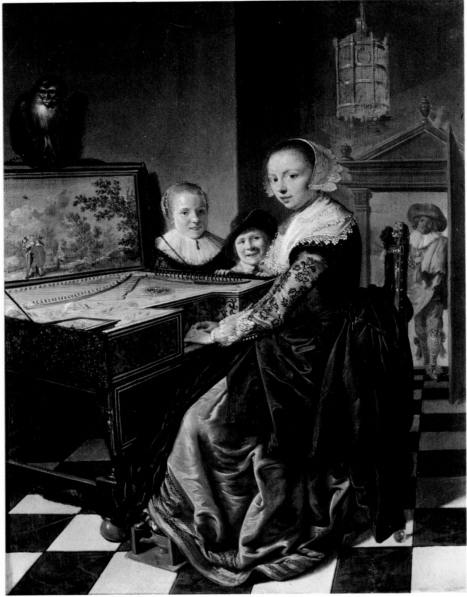

JAN MIENSE MOLENAER
Haarlem 1610(?) — Haarlem 1668
*A Lady with Two Children at
a Harpsichord.*
Oil on panel; 15 1/4″ × 11 1/2″.
Formerly attributed to Dirck Hals. Belonged to the A. van der Hoop collection, Amsterdam. Bequest to the City of Amsterdam, 1854. On loan to the Rijksmuseum since 1885.

JAN MIENSE MOLENAER.   *A Lady with Two Children at a
Harpsichord.*

According to tradition, the lady at the harpsichord is Judith Leyster, the
wife of the artist and a painter in her own right. But even if this identification is correct, the two children cannot be Molenaer's daughter and son as
they were born in 1660 and 1665, respectively, whereas the painting is unanimously held by scholars to have been executed in 1635. A pupil of Frans
Hals, Molenaer was one of the most able and interesting of those masters
who resolved the problem of group portraits by composing them as genre
scenes. In the small format of the cabinet picture, a scene from family life
is represented in careful perspective and is enlivened by a play of light that
brings out the salient features. In fact, the entire tone of the representation
is pleasantly anecdotal.

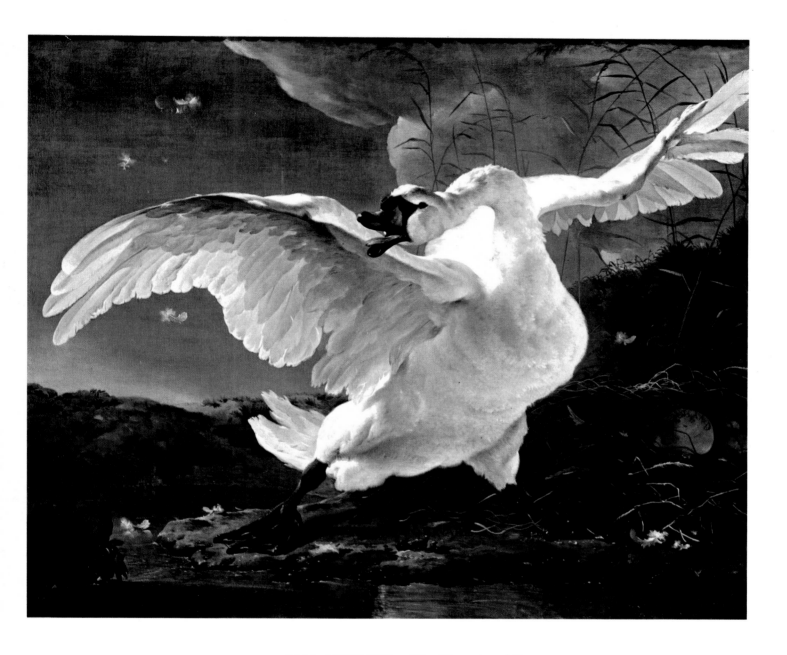

JAN ASSELYN
The Threatened Swan
Oil on canvas; 56 1/2″ × 67 3/4″.
Monogrammed.
In the sales of Jean Deutz, in
Amsterdam, 1784; and Gildemeester,
Amsterdam, 1800. It belonged to
the National Museum; at the
Rijksmuseum since 1808.

JAN ASSELYN.   *The Threatened Swan.*
Jan Asselyn, one of the best known of the Dutch Romanists, painted this
picture for Jan De Witt. In theme it is unusual but not rare. The execution
is firm and vigorous, while the bluish clarity of the color and the rugged
background are typical of the Italianizing movement in the northern Netherlands. Asselyn, in fact, worked for some time in Rome and was influenced
by Claude Lorrain. Sometime after Asselyn's death Jan De Witt was ap-
pointed Grand Pensionary of the Republic, and inscriptions in Dutch were
added to the painting by another hand. These give it the meaning of a political allegory; the words are: "The Grand Pensionary," beneath the swan;
"Holland," on one of the eggs; and "Enemy of the State," above the dog
(lower left). The intention of the allegory is clear, even though we do not
know who was the "Enemy of the State." 81

JUDITH LEYSTER.   *Serenade.*

A pupil of Frans Hals and the wife of Jan Molenaer, the artist possibly studied with Hendrick Terbrugghen at Utrecht in 1628. The hypothetical contact with Terbrugghen is used by some scholars to explain the Caravaggesque play of light over the figures seen in some of her works. In subject, this panel is typical of the Utrecht School, but such themes are also part of the iconography associated with the circle around Frans Hals. The direct inspiration for these elements thus remains an open question. The painter handled the composition of the young man playing a lute with ease and confidence, building up the structure in broad masses. The planes recede neatly, cleanly revealed by the light, which has a single source on the left, as in Terbrugghen.

ADRIAEN VAN OSTADE.   *The Fish Vendor.*   *p. 84*

This genre scene, of which there is a variant in the Budapest Museum, is not among the most typical works of the artist, who is best known for his interiors with peasants. Van Ostade lived in Haarlem all his life and was a pupil of Frans Hals. The major influences on his work were Adriaen Brouwer, who stayed in Haarlem in 1627, and Rembrandt.

As with many painters who were also engravers, van Ostade's paintings tend to be neglected in favor of his black and whites. Some artists and critics entertain a romantic notion that drawing and engraving are more immediate or "instinctive" than painting. Indeed, graphic work can permit a more spontaneous expression, but in his etchings van Ostade generally multiplied his compositional planes fantastically and accentuated the linear development of figures and objects. Here, on the contrary, he firmly established the spatial relationships, stating the distances from the tower in the background to the middle-ground pillar that delimits the episodes depicted and the movement of the principal figure. How much the artist learned from Frans Hals is evident in the lively color and luminous quality of the fish, as well as in the natural gesture of the fish vendor.

82

JUDITH LEYSTER
Haarlem 1609 — Heemstede 1660
Serenade
Oil on panel; 18″ × 13 3/4″.
Monogrammed and dated 1629.
In the Winter collection, ascribed to
Frans Hals. Six collection, Amsterdam.
Acquired by the Rijksmuseum in 1908.

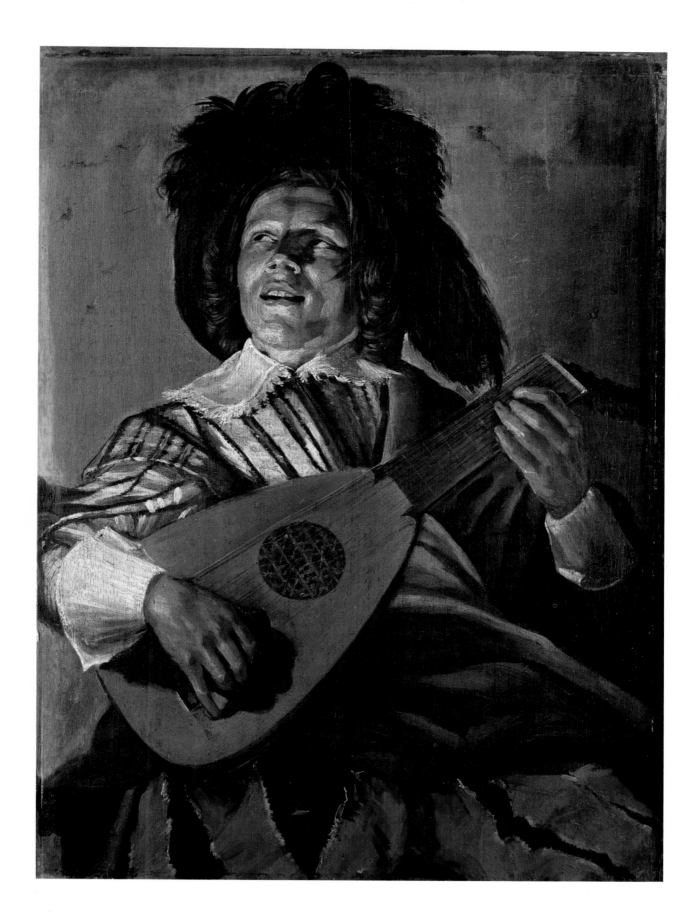

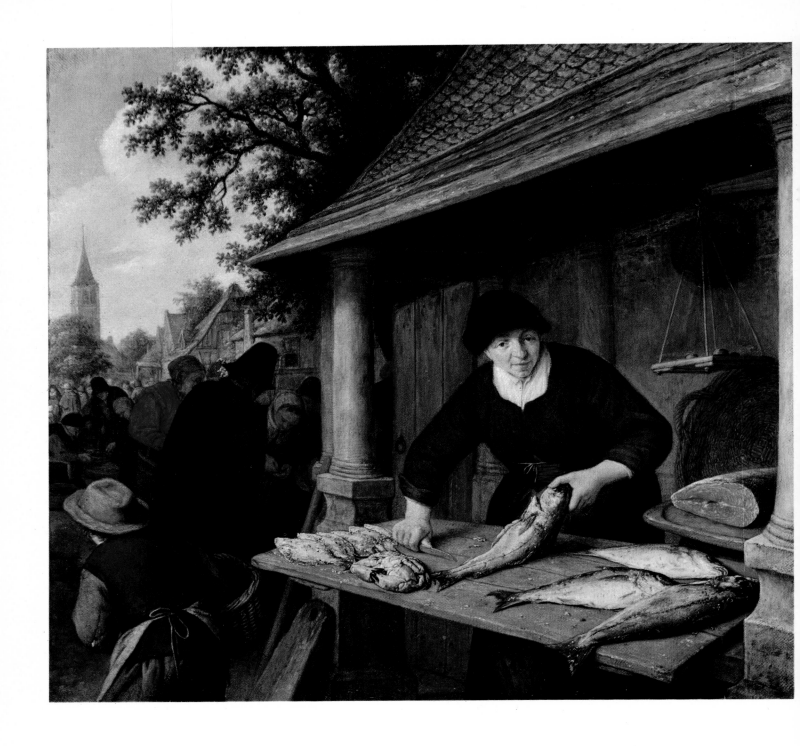

ADRIAEN VAN OSTADE. *Interior with Peasants.*
This is one of van Ostade's interiors in which the influence of Adriaen
Brouwer is most apparent. There is no doubt that van Ostade was in touch
with Brouwer when the Flemish artist stayed in Haarlem in 1627, working
in the circle of Frans Hals. In some cases their choice of subject is identical,

ADRIAEN VAN OSTADE
Haarlem 1610 — Haarlem 1685
The Fish Vendor
Oil on canvas; 14 1/4″ × 15 1/2″.
Signed and dated: "Av. Ostade 1672."
In the Gerard Braamcamp sale, Amsterdam,
1771. Belonged to the Six van Hillegom and
J. Six collections, Amsterdam. Gift of Sir
Henry Deterding, 1936.

ADRIAEN VAN OSTADE
Interior with Peasants
Oil on canvas; 17 1/4″ × 14″.
Signed and dated: "Av. Ostade 1650."
H. Sorgh sale, Amsterdam, 1720.
Belonged to the van Winter and Six van
Vromade collections. Acquired in 1908.

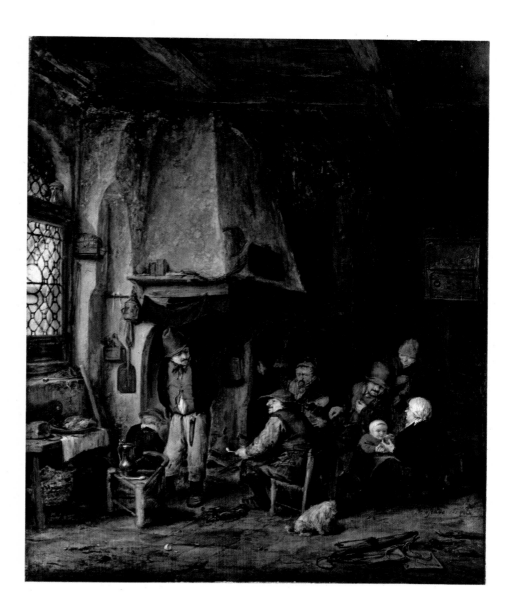

and the features of their figures have a family resemblance, though van Ostade's are less caricatural. The soft, diffused light also is often the same in both "little masters."

What is very different, however, is the relationship between the figures and the setting. Brouwer frequently made use of a monochrome ground, against which the figures stand out. In van Ostade there is an exact rendering of interior and exterior space and architectural framework, with objects and details carefully noted. Also in his etchings, every figure and object is a reference point in the recession of the scene into depth. This precision does not detract from the human feeling for the everyday activity that informs his vision.

85

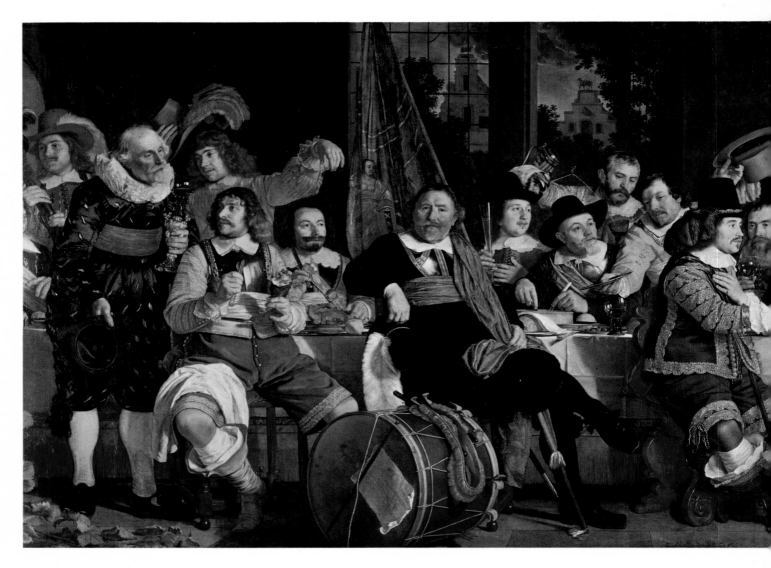

BARTHOLOMEUS VAN DER HELST. *The Banquet of the Civic Guard.*

The artist was one of the most successful of the "official" portraitists active in 17th-century Amsterdam. He was clearly exceptional in the lively and elegant rendering of the individual figure, as well as in executing large compositions. Here the subject is the traditional one of the banquet. Each figure at the table is placed so as to be as prominent as possible. The occasion being celebrated was the conclusion of the Peace of Westphalia on June 18, 1648. The banquet took place in the St. Jorisdoelen — the Hall of the Crossbow Archers' Guild of St. George — in Amsterdam. In the center sits the standard-bearer of the Guild. On the right, one of the two officers shaking hands holds the celebrated silver drinking-horn of the Guild. The sheet of paper on the drum bears a poem by Jan de Vos celebrating the Treaty.

FERDINAND BOL. *Four Governors of the Amsterdam Leper Asylum.*

Bol was one of four pupils of Rembrandt who were closest to the master in style and spirit. Yet when Rembrandt's fortunes were at an ebb, Bol, Flinck,

BARTHOLOMEUS VAN DER HELST
Haarlem 1613 — Amsterdam 1670
The Banquet of the Civil Guard
Oil on canvas; 6'7 1/4″ × 17'8 1/4″.
Signed and dated: "Bartholomeus van der Helst fecit A°. 1648." Executed for the St. Jorisdoelen, it was subsequently moved to the old Town Hall, Amsterdam. Lent by the City of Amsterdam, 1808. The names of the men portrayed are known.

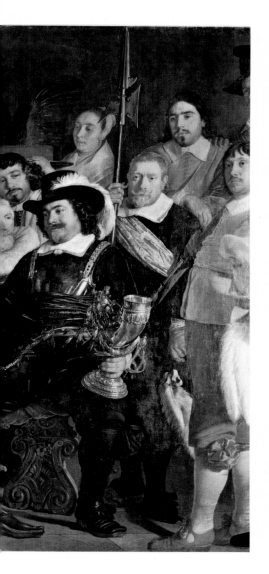

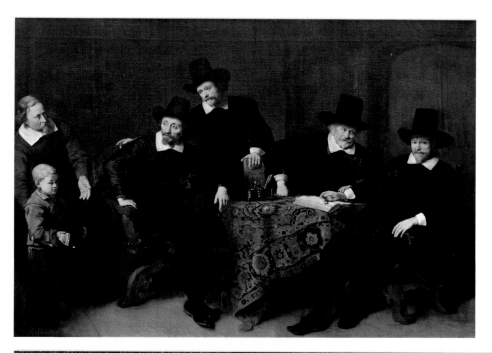

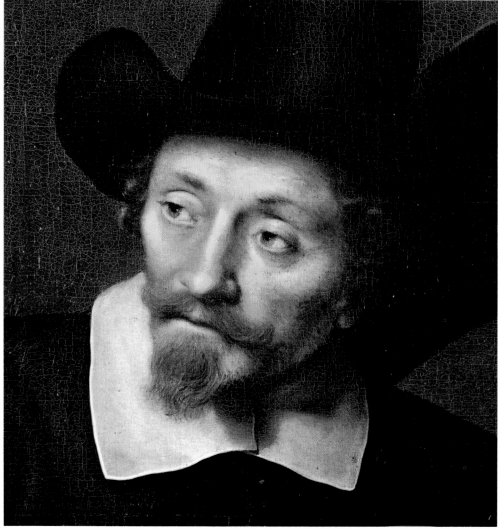

Backer and Jacob Adriaensz remained in high demand with private and official patrons in Amsterdam. In fact, during Rembrandt's old age these painters, and Bol in particular, maintained their prestige and were more famous than he. Bol even won an important official commission to decorate the Amsterdam Town Hall.

Rembrandt's influence in the rendering of the light and in the tensions and resolutions of the composition is obvious in the present work. But Bol did not go as far beyond the realities as his master did, a fact that may explain why he was preferred by the powers of Amsterdam. His heads are very fine, but they do not breathe with Rembrandt's disturbing originality. The detail on the left of the picture, of the master of the asylum bringing in a little boy whose head is covered with sores, balances the composition and provides a narrative interest. This episode illustrates Bol's detached observation and adherence to tradition.

GERARD DOU. *Night School.*

Two candles and a lantern provide the sources of light that define the shadowy space in the foreground of this painting, while the rapt expressions of the faces are intensified by the gloomy atmosphere. Dou was a pupil of the youthful Rembrandt at Leyden, but did not grasp or did not care to acquire the master's inner, intellectual powers. He was drawn more to the example of the Utrecht School, especially to Honthorst.

GERARD TER BORCH. *A Company in an Interior.*   *p. 90*

Among the greatest portraitists and painters of interiors of the century, Ter Borch, like Pieter de Hooch and Gabriel Metsu, is more famous for the latter genre. His portraits, however, are conceived, as are his interiors, in terms of an exact relationship between figure and space. In this canvas, which was formerly known as the *Paternal Admonition,* the composition is impeccably regulated by the positioning of the figures and objects. The placing of the woman seen from the back and the turn of her body call in turn for the positions assumed by the seated man and woman. It is a closely linked group and leaves the rest of the space, which is not strictly in perspective, in a secondary role.

Concentrating the composition on a strong central group is a fundamental element of Ter Borch's style. He established an exact focus in the center, at which the axes of the main compositional ground lines intersect like a St. Andrew's cross. A vertical axis bisecting the composition also passes through this point. This carefully worked out structure is the framework for the feeling of great intimacy, in a moment of private conversation.

88

GERARD DOU
Leyden 1613 — Leyden 1675
Night School
Oil on panel; 20 3/4″ × 15 3/4″.
Monogrammed: "GDOV."
In the Cabinet de Brye, 1665.
Belonged to the collections of
Allart de la Court, Leyden, until 1766;
and of G. van der Pot, until 1808.

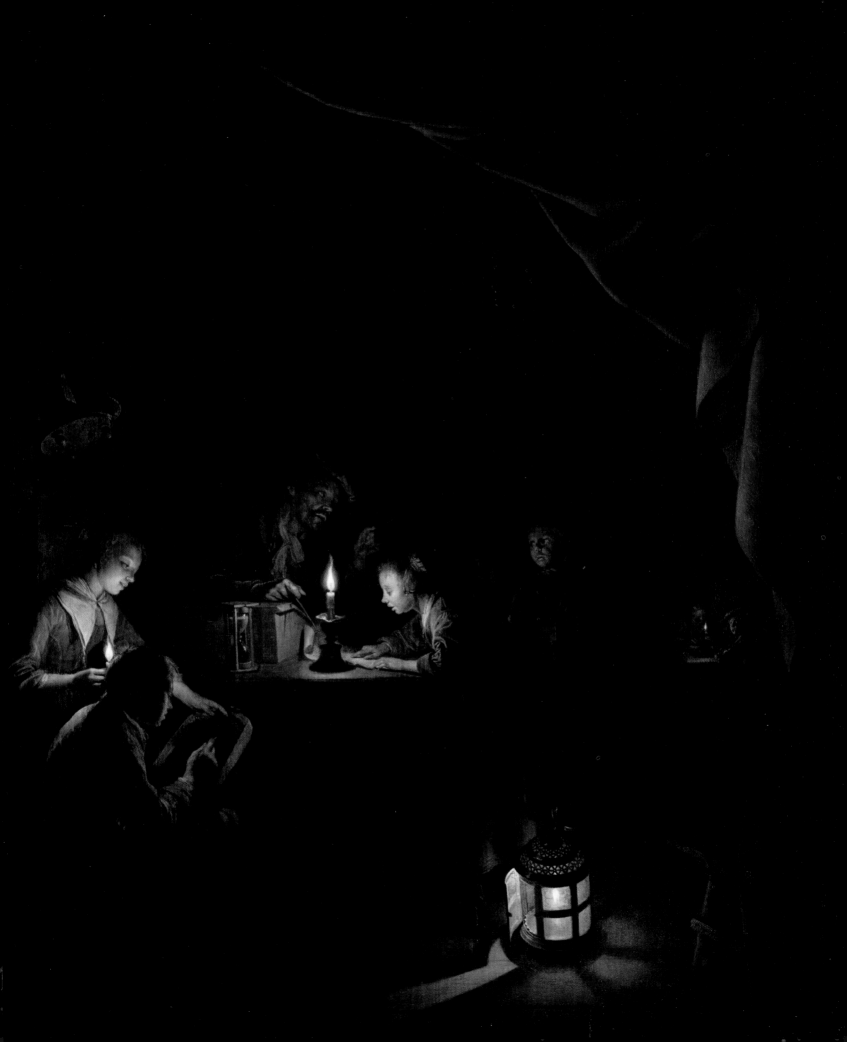

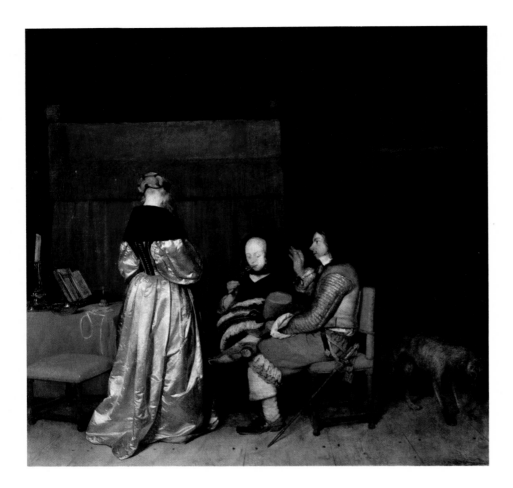

GERARD TER BORCH
Zwolle 1617 — Deventer 1681
A Company in an Interior
Oil on canvas; 28″ × 28 3/4″.
D. Ietswaart collection.
Sale of W. Lormier, The Hague, 1763.
Cabinet van Heteren. The Hague, 1809.

GERARD TER BORCH. *Portrait of Helena van der Schalke.*
The artist's typical composition has a triangular floor plan and a central vertical axis. In his portraits of men he had his subject advance the right foot, as in a dancer's position, and the foot was made the fulcrum to the balance of the entire composition. In this portrait of a child, he reinforced the triangular plan and vertical axis with the reflecting surface of the pavement, which throws a white light on the figure. The neutral ground creates an abstract space in which the subject stands out like a little idol. The broad folds of the dress and the big collar are unmoving, and the basket hangs weightless from her arm. In keeping with this playful and somewhat macabre rigidity, the child's face is long and pointed, with a long nose and a grownup's mouth. Her large eyes have a fixed, inward look.

GERARD TER BORCH
Portrait of Helena van der Schalke
Oil on panel; 13 1/4″ × 11 1/4″.
Acquired in 1898.
Portraits of all the members of the van der Schalke family are in the Rijksmuseum. With the artist's *Self-Portrait* at The Hague, they represent the highest point in Ter Borch's portraiture.

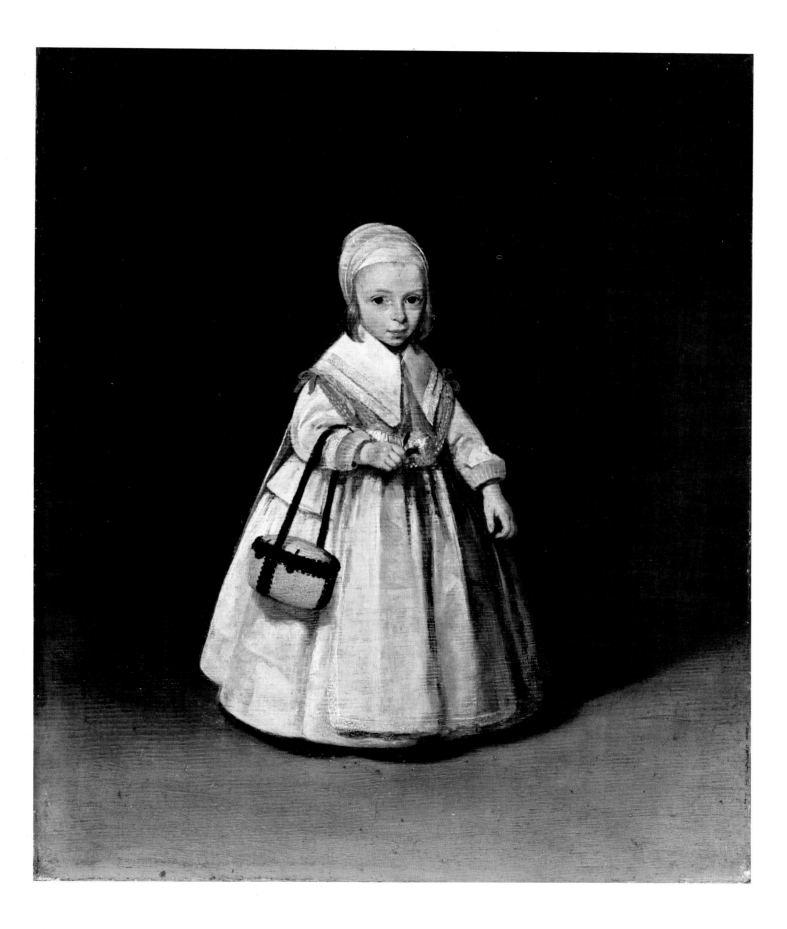

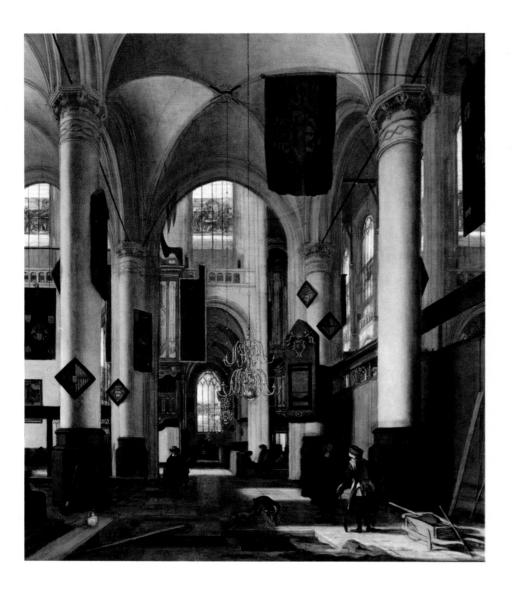

EMANUEL DE WITTE. *Interior of a Gothic Church.*
In this composite view, the south aisle seen from the choir contains motifs of the Nieuwe Kerk in Amsterdam, while the piers and stalls are those of the city's Oude Kerk. The figures in the foreground and middle ground include a sexton and a gentleman, who are in conversation beside an open grave. As in many of De Witte's interiors, the perspective is centered and the composition falls into two more or less equal areas. The light is rendered in contrasts, which provides a means of measuring the space. Although they brought him little success, church interiors were an ideal subject for De Witte. The complicated articulation of the space, the alternation of columns and great windows and the relationship between figures and architecture offered the artist many more compositional possibilities than domestic interiors could provide. For such artists as Vermeer, who preferred to represent large foreground spaces seen close up, the opposite was true.

92

EMANUEL DE WITTE
Alkmaar 1617 — Amsterdam 1692
Interior of a Gothic Church
Oil on canvas; 48″ × 41″.
In the A. van der Hoop collection, Amsterdam. Bequest to the City of Amsterdam, 1854. Lent to the Rijksmuseum in 1885.

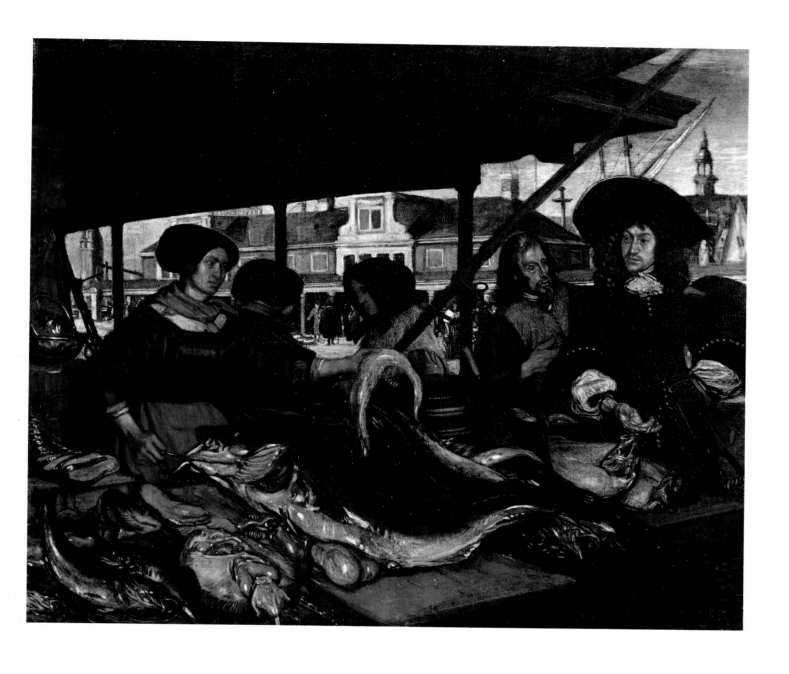

EMANUEL DE WITTE
The Fishmarket (circa 1672)
Oil on canvas; 20 1/2" × 24 1/4".
Sale, Fr. Muller & Co., Amsterdam, 1911.
A companion piece, *The Chicken Vendor,*
is in the National Museum of Stockholm.

EMANUEL DE WITTE. *The Fishmarket.*
The foreground fishmongers with their wares and customers are seen under
a shed, while an Amsterdam street scene forms the background of the picture. As in the artist's interiors, the structure of the composition is carefully
articulated. Here the architectonic elements are provided by the figures. The
complex system of perspective is keyed to the figure in the middle.

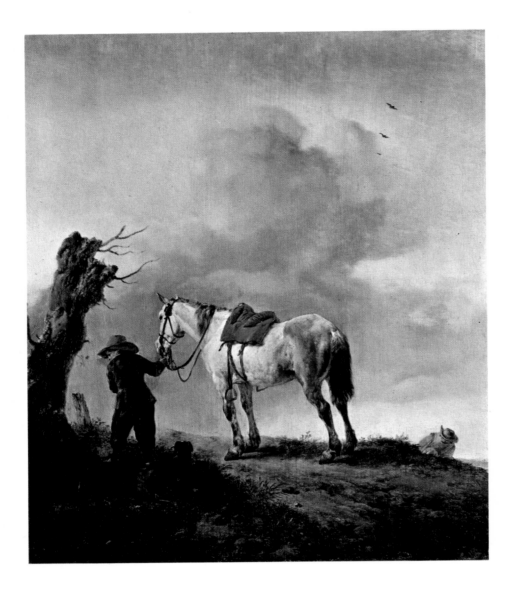

PHILIPS WOUWERMAN
Haarlem 1619 — Haarlem 1668
The White Horse
Oil on panel; 17″ × 15″.
Monogrammed.
Sale, Dirk Versteegh, Amsterdam, 1823.
Collection of W. F. van Lennep, Amsterdam. Sale, Messchert van Vollenhoven,
Amsterdam, 1892. Acquired in 1894 with
the aid of the *Vereeniging Rembrandt*.

PHILIPS WOUWERMAN. *The White Horse.*

Wouwerman is generally known as one of the major animal painters of 17th-century Holland. As a genre, this kind of painting also includes battle and hunt scenes, and many such works appear among the 1,200-odd pictures attributed to the artist. Imaginative and open to a wide range of influences, from Roman classicism to Rubens, Wouwerman was apt to dwell on his landscape settings, which often absorbed the nominal subject of the picture. Here the atmosphere, or climate, of the narrative is strongly characterized. Figures and objects are foreshortened and diminished against the immensity of the autumnal sky.

ABRAHAM VAN BEYEREN. *Still Life.*

Van Beyeren ranks with Jan Jansz van de Velde and Jan I. Davidsz de Heem among the major still-life painters of the latter part of the 17th cen-

ABRAHAM VAN BEYEREN
The Hague 1620(?) — Overschie 1690
Still Life
Oil on canvas; 49 1/2″ × 41 3/4″.
Monogrammed.
Collection of A. de Labrouche de Labordie,
Paris. Sale, Amsterdam, 1922. Collections of
Messrs. Katz, Dieren; Merrs. Eug. Slatter,
London. Purchased from Messrs, D. A.
Hoogendijk, Amsterdam, 1958, with the aid
of the "Jubileumfonds 1958."

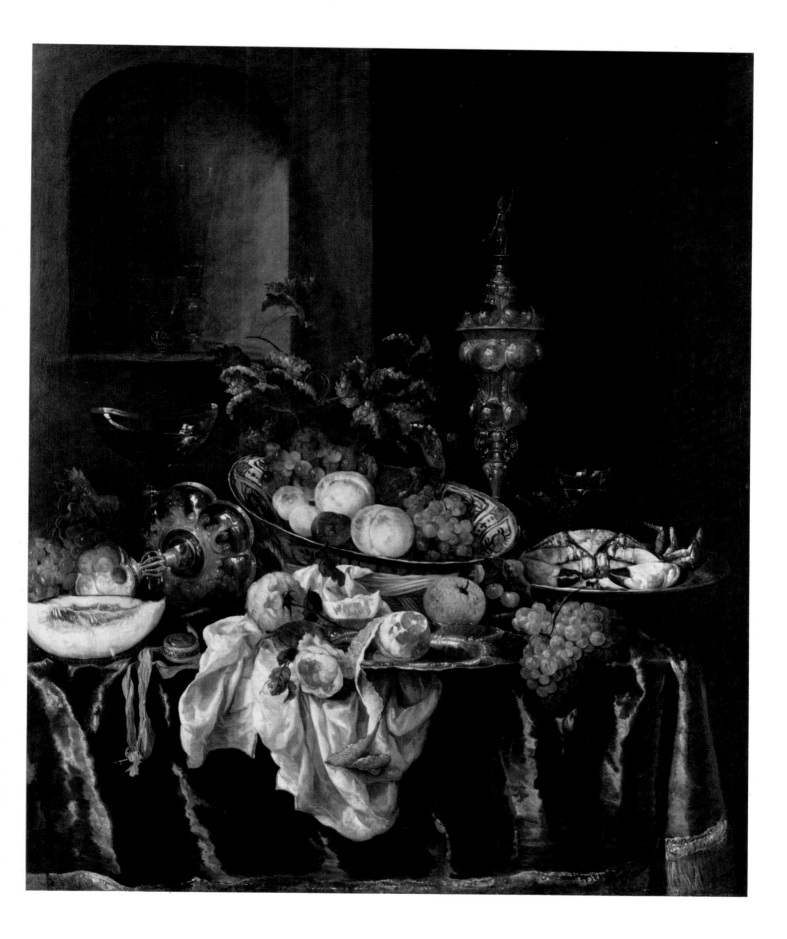

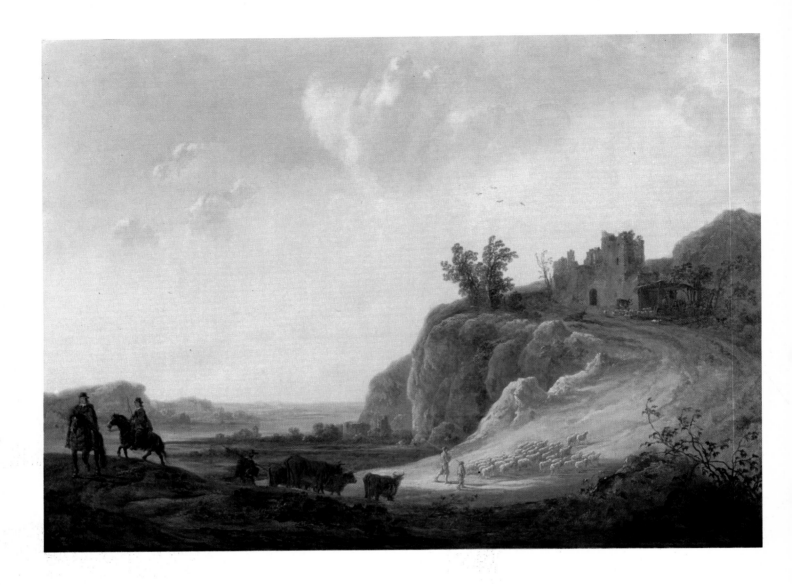

tury in Holland. During this century, as is well known, still-life subjects were exceptionally popular in Holland and Flanders. In the hands of the Dutch and Flemish artists, this genre (like the others of landscapes and interiors) was developed in terms of rhythmical disposition of the elements and carefully constructed compositions. Van Beyeren was often in financial straits and obliged to keep on the move to avoid his creditors, but his still lifes are sumptuous statements of serene opulence. Silverware, porcelain, glassware, wine, flowers and fruits were never painted together directly from life, but sketched and put together as an act of the artist's imagination.

AELBERT CUYP. *Mountain Landscape* and *Landscape with Figures.* The "grandiose landscape" was a separate genre, especially in 17th-century Dutch painting. Vast horizons lie beyond successions of valleys and receding plains; the skies are clear or swollen with clouds, but always full of reflected light. And the national theme of waterways, frozen or seen in spring or fall, is a constant motif. Aelbert Cuyp rendered the vastness with a par-

AELBERT CUYP
Dordrecht 1620 — Dordrecht 1691
Mountain Landscape
Oil on panel; 26 1/4″ × 31 3/4″.
Signed: "A. cuijp."
Collection of A. de Lelie, 1810.
Cabinet J. Rombouts, Dordrecht, 1850.
Bequest of L. Dupper Wz., Dordrecht, 1870.

96

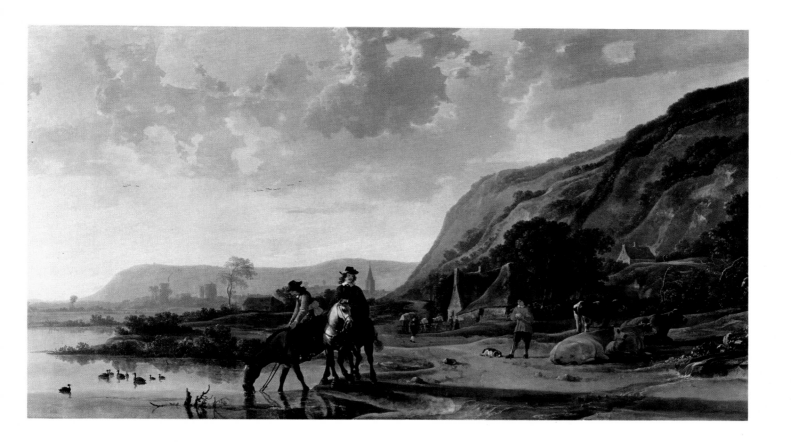

ticularly measured rhythm. Often, as in his two landscapes shown here, ground and sky each occupy half the picture and are laid out on a diagonal.

The narrative elements we have observed in winter and river scenes have been discarded. Figures have become incidents in the landscape, establishing spatial relationships, giving the measure of distances or creating movements. Seghers, as painter, transfigured natural events and made them imaginary. Ruisdael exalted them into something pantheistic and cosmic. Cuyp's contemplative imagination evoked the natural scene, stripped of any reference to events and of any immediate emotion. The effect is musical, as in a fugue. The two paintings here seem to be variations on one landscape theme, but the different distances create a marked change in the poetic quality of each view. In the first, the vast, bright, reflecting sky opens a broader view of the receding valley. In the second, the valley is closer and more domestic, giving the figures more important roles.

97

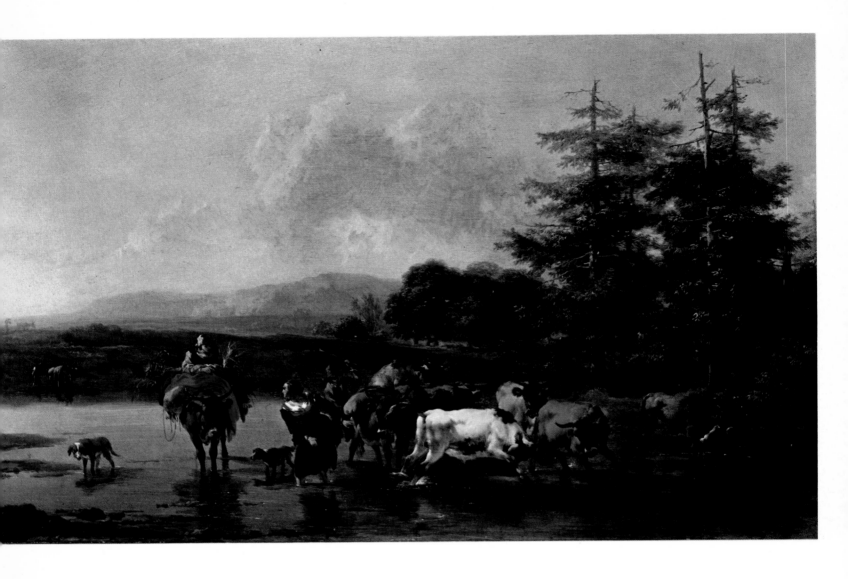

CLAES PIETERSZ BERCHEM. *Crossing the Ford.*

Berchem was one of the principal Dutch Italianizers of the 17th century. With his cousin, the painter Jan Baptist Weenix, he traveled to Italy in 1642, and lived in Rome for three years. Very probably he returned to Italy again between 1653 and 1656. The results of his Roman education, during which he got to know the works of Claude Lorrain, the Carracci and Elsheimer, are naturally most evident in his numerous Italian landscapes, with or without ruins. This picture, painted in Rome or immediately after the artist's return to Haarlem, shows a typical Italian landscape. But the bucolic theme adopted in homage to the classical tradition takes a narrative and realistic turn that is typical of Berchem.

ADAM PYNACKER. *The Shore of an Italian Lake.*

Of all the Dutch painters who went to Rome and were in touch with the so-called "classicists," Pynacker stands out, especially in this picture, for his vivid natural scenes that seem to anticipate 19th-century Romanticism. Un-

CLAES PIETERSZ BERCHEM
Haarlem 1620 — Amsterdam 1683
Crossing the Ford
Oil on panel; 15″ × 24 1/2″.
Signed and dated: "Berchem. f: 1656."
It belonged to the collections of van Heemskerk, The Hague (until 1770), and van Heteren, in the same city (until 1809).

ADAM PYNACKER
Pijnakker (Delft) 1622 — Amsterdam 1673
The Shore of an Italian Lake
Oil on panel; 38 1/4″ × 33 1/2″.
Signed: "APijnacker."
Neufville collection, Rotterdam.
Van der Pot sale, Rotterdam, 1809.

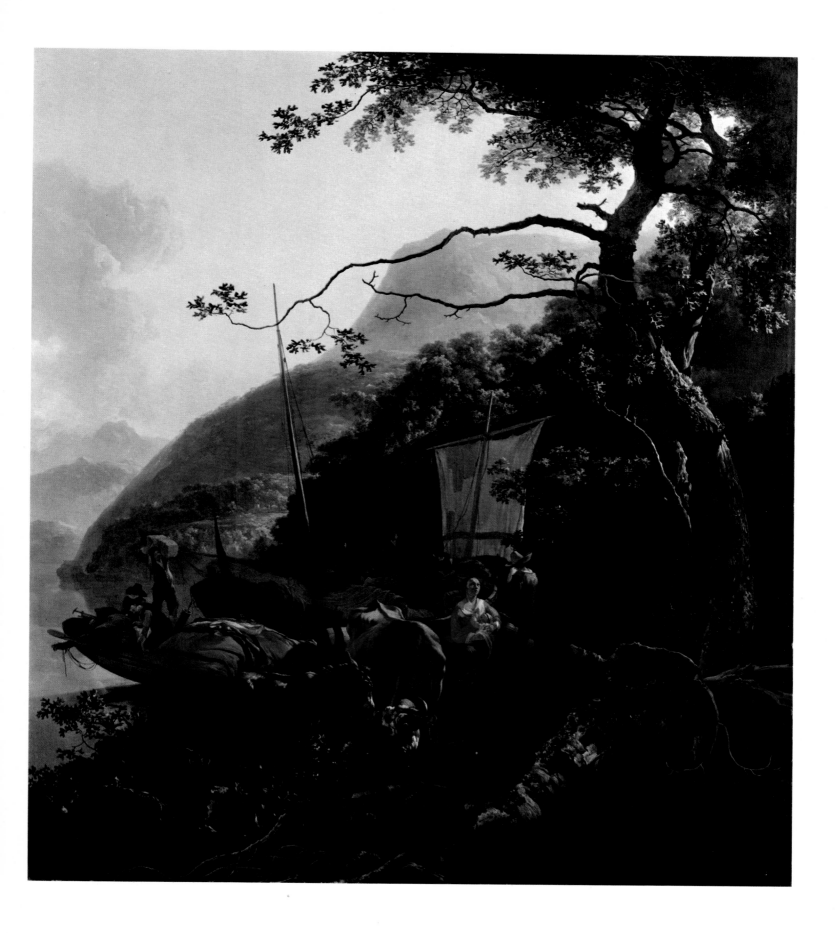

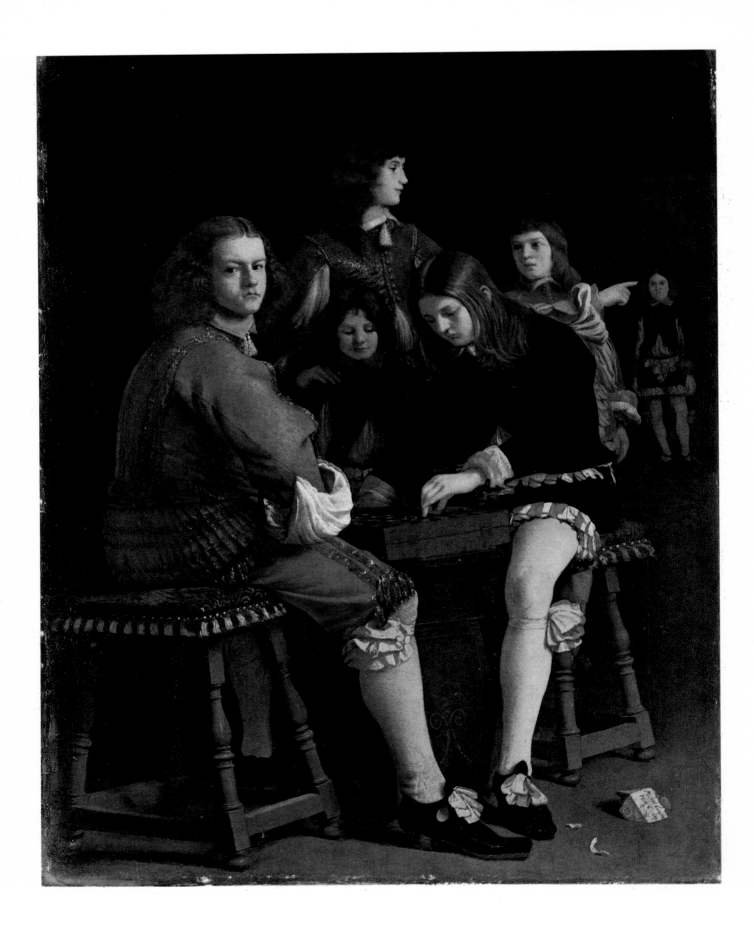

conventional in composition, the image has a high viewpoint which takes us immediately into the foreground. This is boldly described and enlivened by a light in which the figures are extraordinarily free and alive. The diagonal development permits a steep and dramatic rendering of the space, while figures and trees animate it with their tensions and movements.

MICHIEL SWEERTS. *A Game of Checkers.*

Sweerts went to Rome in 1646 and stayed there for six years. Neither a landscapist nor a classicist, he worked in the circle of Pieter van Laer, who was nicknamed Bamboccio (Italian for a fat, lively baby). Van Laer's paintings of low life — along with those of other 17th-century Dutch and Flemish artists living in Italy — are called Bambocciate. Their works are Caravaggesque, but they contain an emphasis on descriptive details that was foreign to Caravaggio. Their major themes are the events of daily life, transitory moments caught as they occur.

Sweerts was one of the principal painters of the Bambocciata and belonged to the bohemian movement that was in violent opposition to the official, classical culture of the papal court. In the 17th and 18th centuries these painters were held to have degraded themselves by their devotion to inferior subjects, but in the 19th century they were revaluated and honored as genre painters. Sweerts' early works are often confused with those of van Laer and the Roman painter Cerquozzi. In this painting he is close to van Laer in the dense brown monochrome that derives from Caravaggio, and in the way in which the light is used to emphasize narrative details. The composition is firmly anchored in the foreground by the legs of the two players. Successive planes, defined by the light, then carry back to the clearly profiled background figure. This system of tensions and balances unexpectedly reveals the artist's grasp of the "classical" approach.

MICHIEL SWEERTS. *A Painter's Studio.*   *p. 102*

This is perhaps the most ambitious and complex work of Michiel Sweerts. In a painter's studio, the master is working from a nude model, his pupils from a plaster cast. Casts and ancient fragments lie in a heap on the right. Two visitors converse on the left. A contrast in feeling is created by the vivid narration of the scene and the broken bits of excavated statuary. A glimpse of the town is seen through the rear door of the studio. This opening and a high window on the left provide light that gives a measure of the ample space. But the most dramatically telling elements in the picture take their light from an outside source on the left, which illuminates the attentive figure of the boy drawing in the foreground, the heap of studio props and, finally, the anatomical flayed figure.

MICHIEL SWEERTS
Brussels 1624 — Goa (India) 1664
A Game of Checkers
Oil on canvas; 18 3/4″ × 15″.
Signed and dated: "Michael Sweerts fecit an 1652 Roma." Gift of C. Hoogendijk, 1912.

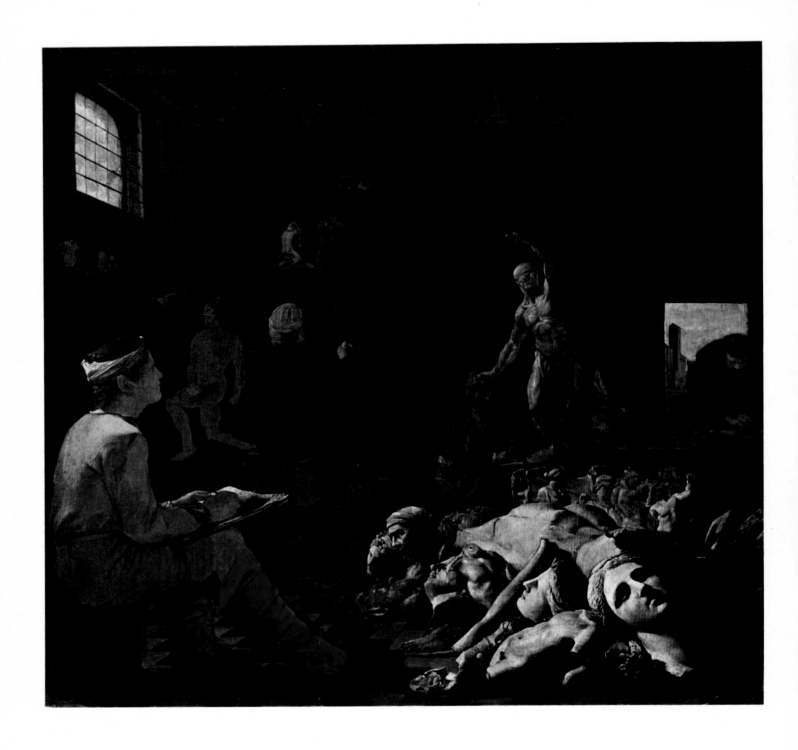

PAULUS POTTER. *Horses in a Field.*
Pupil of his father, Pieter Potter, at Amsterdam, Paulus is famous as the
greatest Dutch animal painter of the 17th century. Among the many "little
masters" who worked in this genre, he stands out and seems very modern to
us because he often eliminated all narrative elements. We have inherited
this formalist view from the work of some late-19th-century artists who were

MICHIEL SWEERTS
A Painter's Studio
Oil on canvas; 28″ × 29 1/4″.
Painted around 1650.
From a Russian private collection, it
entered the Bredius collection,
The Hague. Acquired in 1901.

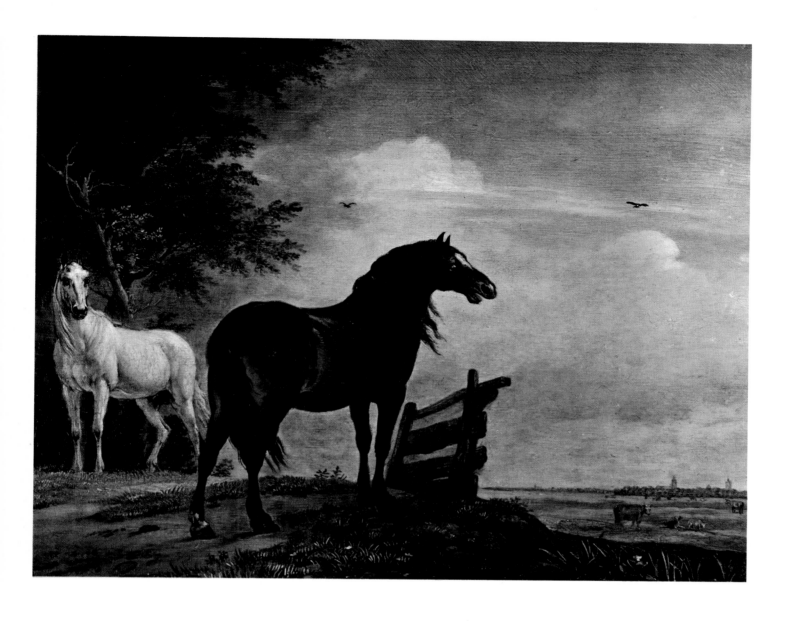

PAULUS POTTER
Enkhuizen 1625 — Amsterdam 1654
Horses in a Field
Oil on panel; 9 1/4" × 11 3/4".
Signed and dated: "Paulus
Potter f. 1649."
Jonkheer J. Goll van Frankenstein sale,
Amsterdam, 1833. It belonged to the van
der Hoop collection. Bequest to the City of
Amsterdam in 1854. On loan since 1885.

influenced by this period in Dutch painting, and from the indestructible but erroneous legend that Potter and others anticipated the Barbizon School by two centuries and worked from nature, in the open air. The subject of horses in a field figures among Potter's best-known works. In its apparently free composition, it lends itself to the confusion mentioned above. But in fact the work is carefully and methodically built up on a system of tensions and contrasts, heightened by the light and dark color contrast of the two animals.

JAN VAN DE CAPPELLE. *Winter Landscape.*   *p. 104*
The artist, an Amsterdam painter, specialized in marine views and winter landscapes. His seascapes were influenced by Simon de Vlieger, to whom

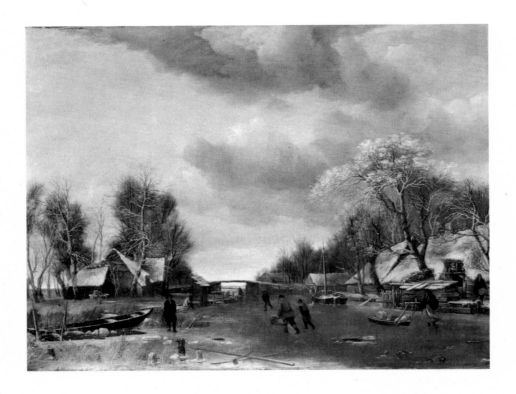

JAN VAN DE CAPPELLE
Amsterdam circa 1626 — Amsterdam 1679
Winter Landscape
Oil on panel; 20 1/4″ × 26 1/4″.
J. Pekstank sale, Amsterdam, 1793. Collections of Graf. Lottum; Fürst Puttbus; Dr. A. Pauli, Amsterdam, 1925. Recently acquired by the Rijksmuseum.

some of his paintings have been erroneously ascribed. In his mature work, he rendered calm seas and fleecy clouds in crystalline colors, with a sensitive play of light. In this wintry landscape the uncertain sky seems ready to go dark with the threatening clouds or turn light with a ray of sunshine. The changeable nature of the season is rendered with feeling.

JAN VAN DE CAPPELLE.   *The State Barge Saluted by the Fleet.*
A salute is being fired by two of the ships floating on a sea so calm that it mirrors their hulls and sails. In the foreground, the barge is full of dignitaries, including Prince Frederick Henry of Orange. Reflecting the importance of the sea and waterways in the life and prosperity of the Netherlands, marine views are one of the most exalted subjects in Dutch painting. Here, the "official" aspect of the picture is apparent only in the theme. The painting itself is very free, with sensitive and vibrant brushwork whose total effect anticipates the atmospherics of Turner's seascapes.

104

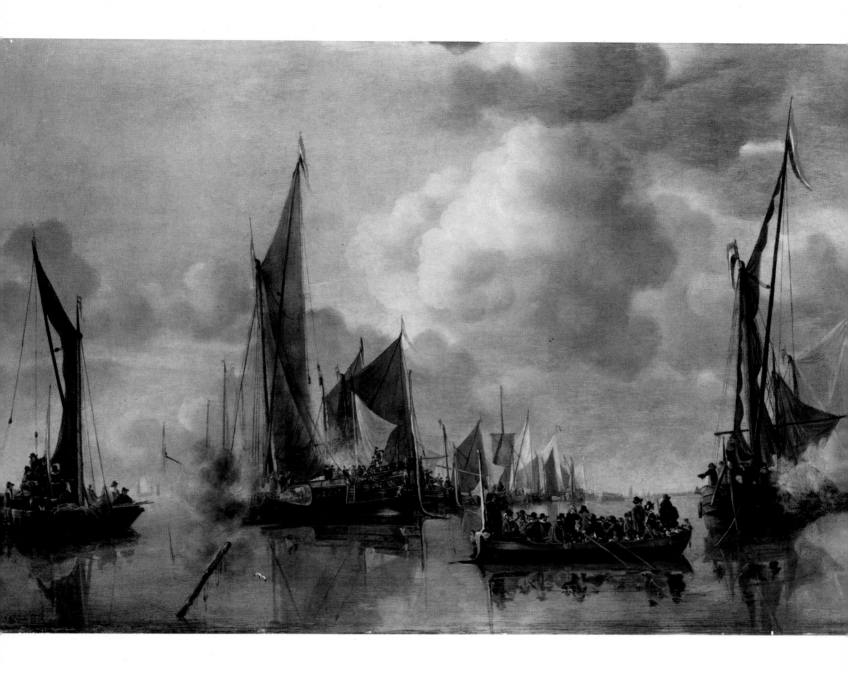

JAN VAN DE CAPPELLE
The State Barge Saluted by the Fleet
Oil on panel; 25 1/4" × 36 1/2".
Signed and dated: "JVCapel 1650."
In the past, the signature had been
altered to that of Simon de Vlieger,
the artist's master.
From the National Museum of The Hague.

JAN STEEN. *The Sick Lady.*   *p. 106*
Steen is often considered the most observant and the liveliest of the great
Dutch interior painters. Everything represented in his work is warm and
alive, and he recreates the intimacy of snug rooms in the long Northern eve-
nings. It becomes clear here that the compositional conventions are only the   **105**

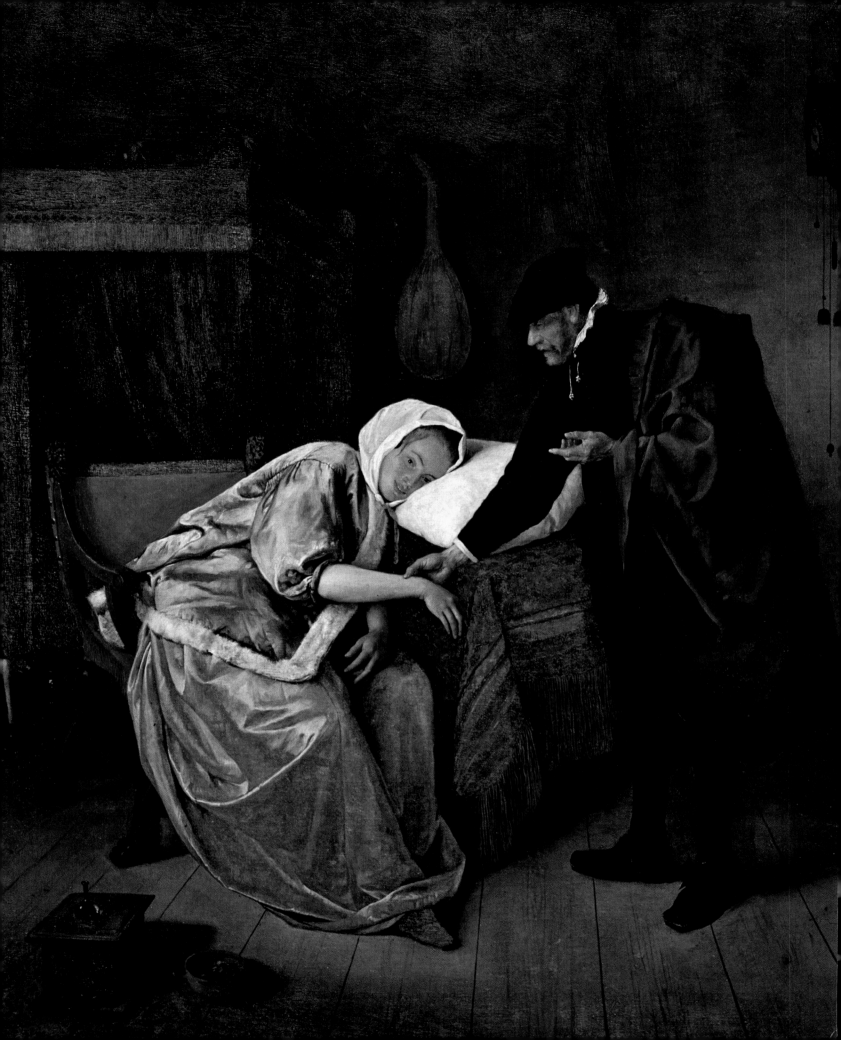

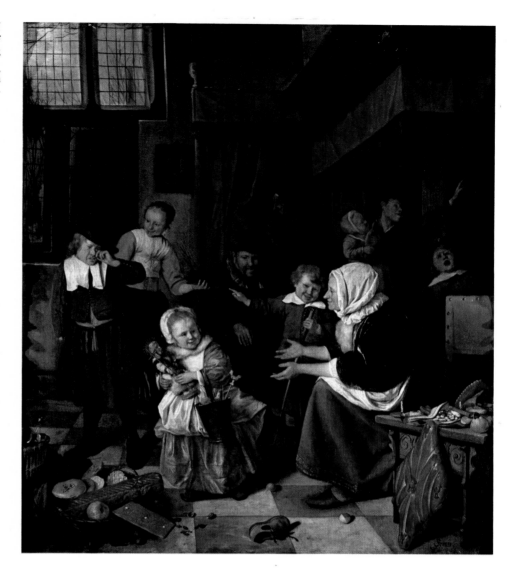

framework for a poetic effect. The big bed on the left is not just a means of measuring out the space, but another more intimate "room" inside the one we are looking into. The lute, besides marking the central axis of the picture with its swelling volume, provides a domestic touch, like the clock placed to show the perspective recession of the side wall. In the midst of all the objects of everyday use, stands a doctor, conventional in dress and pose, expressing uncertainty in his face and hands. The psychology of the patient is ambiguous. Her eyes and mouth look concerned, but this is expressed somewhat ironically. It is almost as if the illness were occasion for a holiday. The drooping arms and cushioned head are full of sensuality.

JAN STEEN. *The Feast of St. Nicholas.*

It is hard to imagine a subject more suited to Steen's imagination than this children's holiday. Some have been given toys and candy and are happy; another is crying because he has been punished. The family has been caught at a lively moment that sums up the ordinary, but most genuine, states of mind. In this canvas, too, the rendering of the place and the objects is exceptionally sharp in focus. The windows in the background convey the exact feeling of a winter's day, and the contrast with the warm interior is vivid. The old people are enjoying the pleasure of the children — a theme dear to Steen. He often portrayed this reciprocal play of pleased expressions. In the figure of the child clutching the statuette of a saint and holding a pail as she looks back at her grandmother, a rare poetic tone is achieved. Because of the blithe atmosphere of works like this, it has been suggested that their authors were oblivious to pictorial problems. But the mind of the cheerful Steen may have been as complex and vital as that of artists principally concerned with theory.

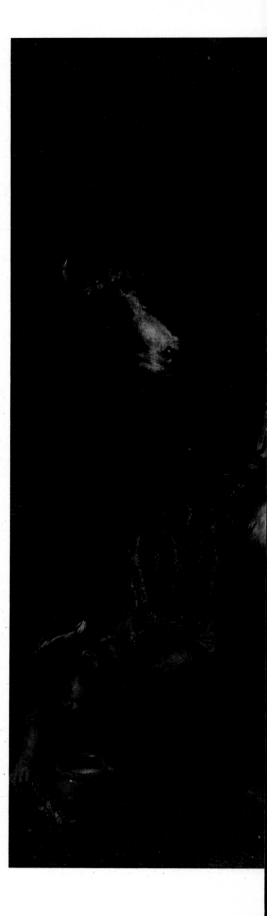

JAN STEEN
Adoration of the Shepherds
Oil on canvas; 20 3/4″ × 25 1/4″.
Signed: "JSteen."
From the English art market it entered the collection of D. A. Hoogendijk, Amsterdam, and then that of A. A. van Sandick, Rotterdam. Purchased in 1947. There is a replica in Wavel Castle, Cracow.

JAN STEEN. *Adoration of the Shepherds.*
Religious subjects were rare in Protestant Holland of the 17th century. Altarpieces were banned from churches; the religious pictures that were executed were done for private clients and were small in format. Only in Rembrandt's work are religious subjects frequently found, and his mainly are Old Testament scenes with didactic or symbolic allusions. Steen was a Catholic, however, and he often turned to religious themes. Here the interpretation is unusual, for the subject is represented as a family party, except for the figure of the Madonna which follows official iconography. Note the old woman offering Joseph a dish of eggs, as well as the festive visitors bringing presents as if at a village celebration. Unlike the faces and expressions in Brouwer and van Ostade, which have something of the grotesque, these are warmly human and individualized. Indeed Steen's art is suffused with an individual warmth of feeling; its roots may lie in 17th-century Dutch civilization, but his expression is creative and unique.

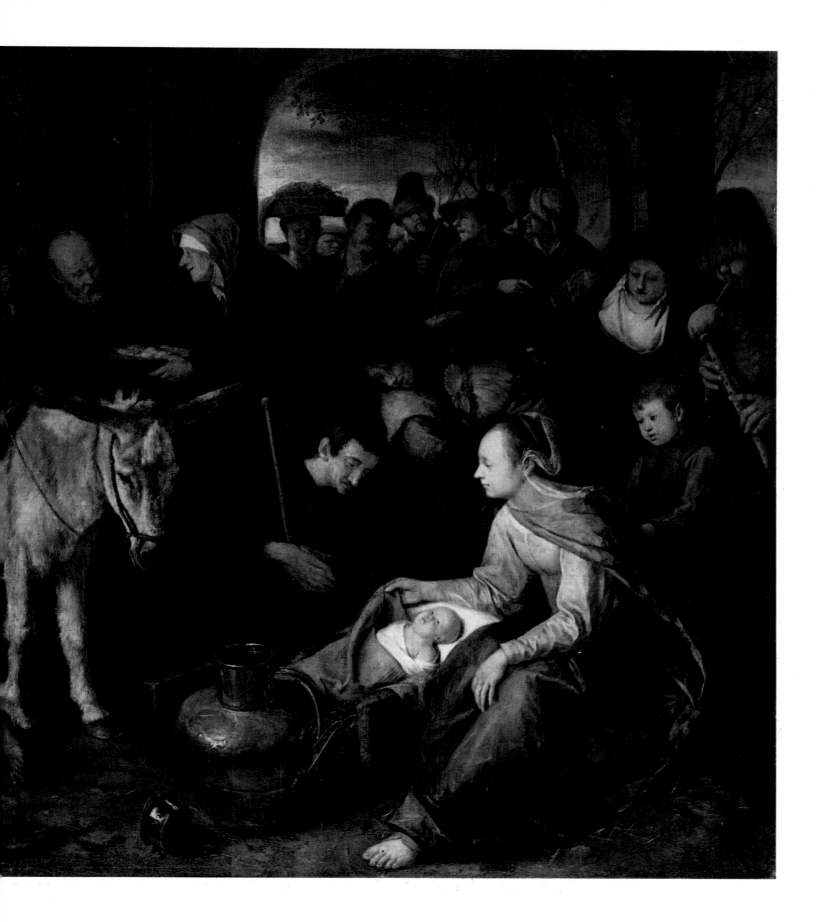

JAN STEEN. *The Toilet.*

Steen has the reputation of being the most "libertine" of the 17th-century Dutch painters. He owes this particular fame to the hostility aroused by his being a Catholic and his exuberant career combining painting, brewing and tavern-keeping. The main cause, however, was his occasional choice of intimate subjects: scenes that give the spectator a feeling of involvement and that would have been classed by the Dutch burghers as too private for public view. This picture is a case in point. There might be something suggestive in the uncovered bed with the sleeping dog, the woman in her nightdress with her legs crossed so that her thighs show and in such details as the slippers and chamber-pot. Steen, however, as in all his work, here creates a warm feeling of human sympathy that negates any suggestion of vulgarity.

JAN STEEN. *The Merry Family.* *p. 112*

Hilarity reigns in the family dining room. There is food on the table, and the convivial family is engaged in singing, drinking and smoking. The man playing the bagpipes (left, rear) is a self-portrait of the artist. On the mantelpiece is a sheet of paper that bears Steen's comment on the scene, a Dutch proverb: "While the old sing, the young twitter."

Steen is perhaps best known, especially outside of Holland, for interiors such as this, but he was also important as a painter of mythological and religious subjects, generally medium or large in size. In these it is much clearer than in the smaller works how much he owed to the 16th-century tradition of Leyden. The influence of Italian Mannerism, filtered through Lucas van Leyden, Scorel and Heemskerck, is evident in the iconography, the bold foreshortening, the light and subtle palette, and in the St. Andrew's-cross compositions. Some of the more complex family scenes are close to his more formal works.

The Merry Family is a subject the artist painted a number of times. In the tavern scenes some descriptions tend toward the squalid, but here the individual figures are portrayed with sympathy. The cheerful movement of the group turns on the singing woman in the center. Each actor in the scene is given the character appropriate to his age and sex.

GABRIEL METSU. *The Sick Child.* *p. 113*

Metsu was probably a pupil of Gerard Dou, and at least during his formative years he was influenced by Rembrandt. In this painting, which is one of

JAN STEEN
The Toilet
Oil on arched panel; 14 1/2″ × 10 3/4″.
Signed: "JSteen."
G. Braamcamp collection, Amsterdam. H. A. Baner sale, Amsterdam, 1820. Hargreaves collection, Liverpool. E. Secrétan sale, Paris, 1889. Collections of R. Kann, Paris; M. Bromberg, Hamburg; Dr. A. Pauli, Amsterdam, 1929.

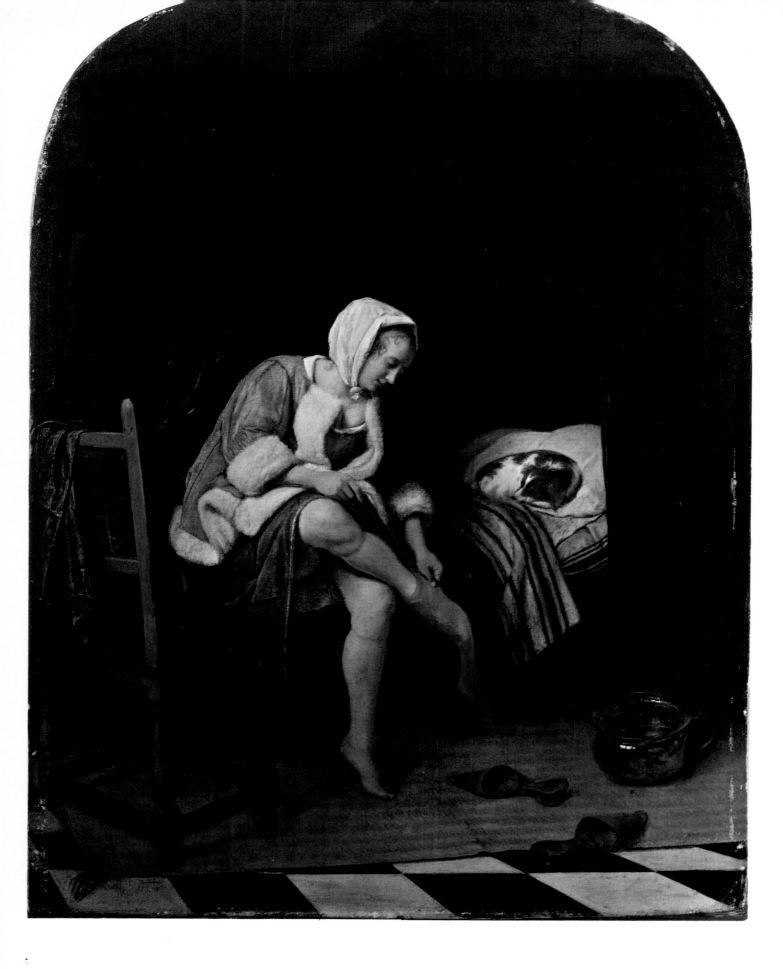

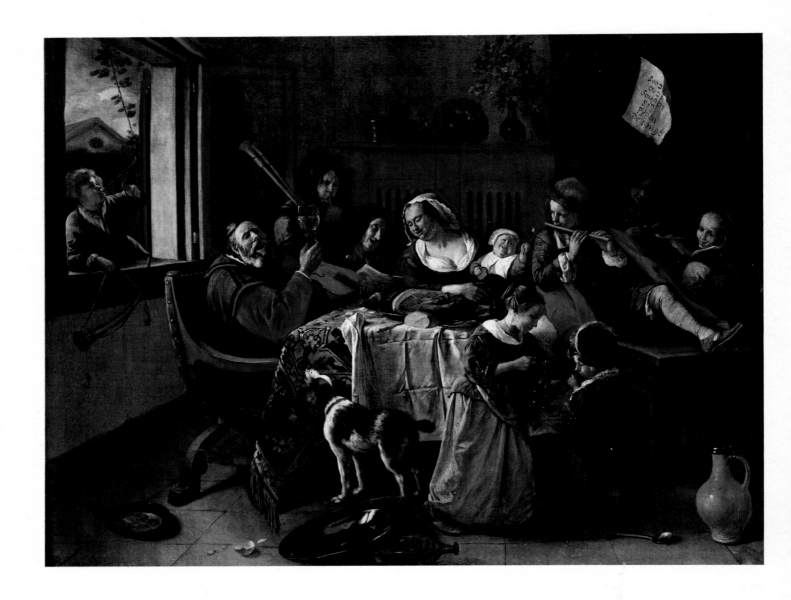

JAN STEEN
The Merry Family
Oil on canvas; 43 1/2" × 55 1/2".
Signed and dated: "JSteen 1668."
In a sale in Amsterdam, 1712. Owned by
J. H. van Heemskerck, The Hague, 1770.
Sold in Amsterdam in 1796. In the O'Neil
collection, 1828. Belonged to Charles Brind
in 1833. Bought by A. van der Hoop from
John Smith, London, in 1833. Bequest to the
City of Amsterdam, 1854. On loan since
1885.

his best and most famous works, he comes close to Vermeer in composition and feeling. The figures are vividly set forth in the foreground and the objects around them are arranged so as to define the space. In the background a painting of the Crucifixion and a map are not utilized to open up new spaces, but to return the interest to the foreground: note how the woman's head is tilted forward. A firm structure has been created, with the geometrical objects countering the tensions of the two figures, which extend in contrasting directions. The narrative is just as carefully calculated. The foreshortening of the woman's face avoids distracting attention from the main actor, the child. Her listlessness is contrasted with the mother's solicitude.

GABRIEL METSU
Leyden 1629 — Amsterdam 1667
The Sick Child
Oil on canvas; 13" × 10 3/4".
Signed: "G. Metsue."

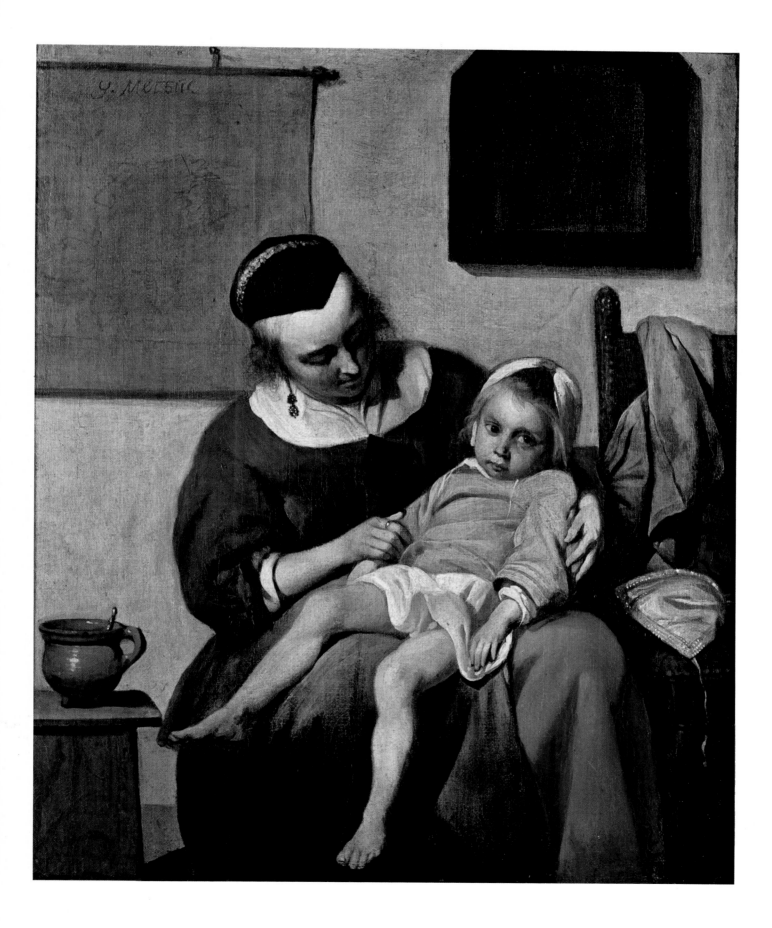

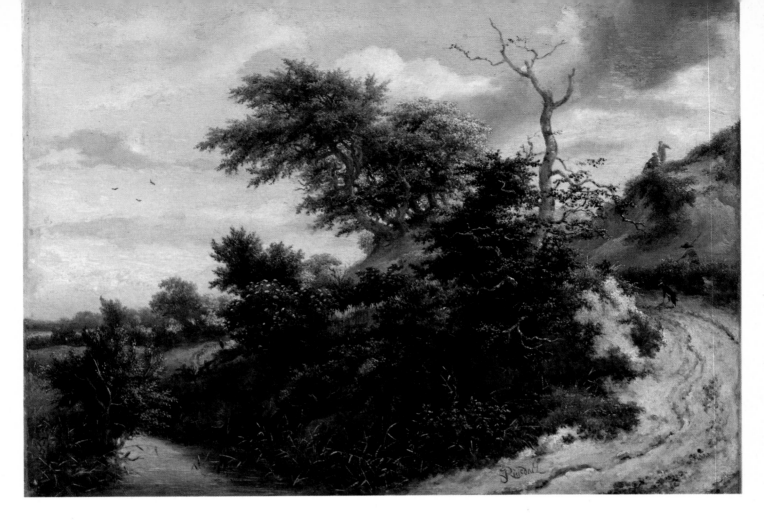

JACOB VAN RUISDAEL
Haarlem 1628 — Amsterdam(?) 1682
Sandy Path along the Dunes
Oil on panel; 12 1/2 × 16 3/4".
Signed: 'JVRuisdael.''
It belonged to the P. van Lennep collection
in Amsterdam. Donated to the City of
Amsterdam. On loan to the Rijksmuseum
since 1892.

JACOB VAN RUISDAEL.   *Sandy Path along the Dunes.*

An early work by Jacob van Ruisdael, this painting is variously dated between 1647 and 1649 or around 1652. Very likely the artist was a pupil of
his father, a painter and cabinetmaker, and of his uncle, the great Salomon
van Ruysdael. The best landscapist of his generation, Jacob in his youthful
paintings seems to want to leave the great examples even of the immediate
past behind him and create more freely structured images. The new aspect
in these landscapes is a new feeling about the subject itself. Whereas in Salomon, to take an immediate example, the sentiment and the structure of the
work are always harmonized, Jacob's early works suggest a high emotional
charge even in his technique of painting. Composition and viewpoint, the
relationship of the path to the trees and the sky, have a dynamics that seem
to come from an emotional exaltation in front of nature. A legend has
grown up around Jacob van Ruisdael as a painter of landscape impressions
with a pre-Romantic flavor. The most famous example of this phase is his
Jewish Cemetery in Dresden, which was so admired by Goethe. But this
vein is absent from most of his mature works in which synthesis and organization were re-established.

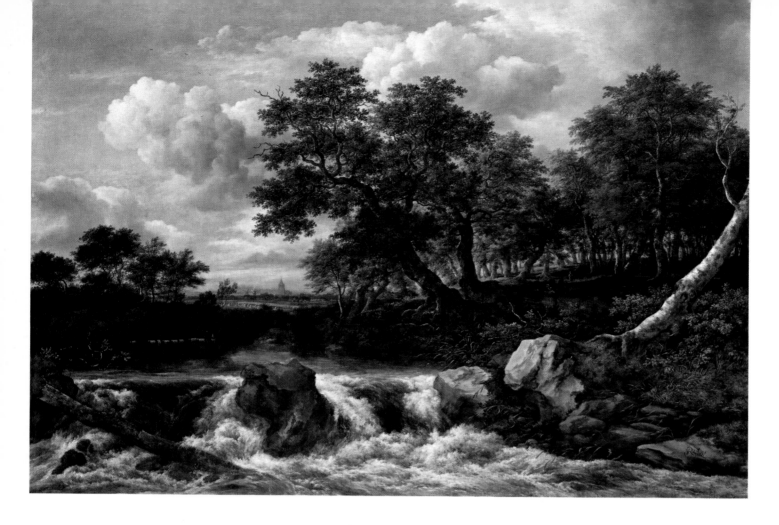

JACOB VAN RUISDAEL
Landscape
Oil on canvas; 4'8" × 6'4 3/4".
Signed: "JVRuisdael."
In the Sir Charles Blount collection, London, until 1836; in that of A. van der Hoop, until 1854. Gift to the City of Amsterdam. On loan since 1885.

JACOB VAN RUISDAEL. *Landscape*.
Rapids, almost a waterfall, occupy the foreground. Behind is an oak woods, and in the background a spire and windmills are set against a sky with white clouds. Painted probably around 1670, this is one of the landscapes of the artist's maturity that still show a strong emotional impact. Although van Ruisdael's desire to "paint the real" is apparent, every descriptive detail has an additional element of vitality and feeling.

JACOB VAN RUISDAEL. *The Windmill at Wijk bij Duurstede. p. 116*
The mill stands on the right bank of the Rhine, towering over the dense brush. In the background lies the town of Wijk bij Duurstede, with the Bishop's Palace on the left and the church tower on the right. The center of interest is the mill, whose cylindrical volume is emphasized by the way the light falls across it. Its vanes stand out against the cloudy sky. The prominence of the mill alters the spirit and meaning of the traditional Dutch view of a waterway. Other architectural details are diminished and merge into the landscape. The ship and the barely roiled water of the river seem motionless in the evening light. On the right the little figures are also immobile and the sails of the mill are like a giant's arms holding up the passage of time.

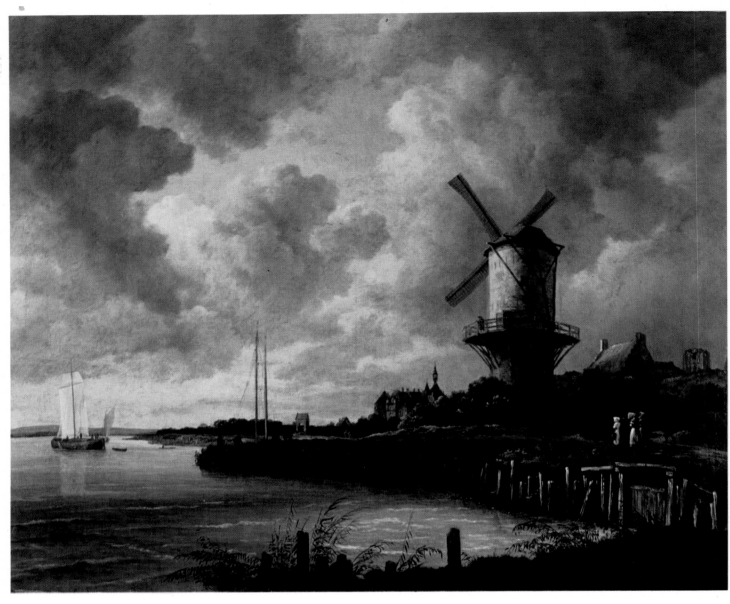

JACOB VAN RUISDAEL. *View of Haarlem.*

To obtain this panorama of the city, which he painted dozens of times, Ruisdael utilized the vantage point of the high ground near Overveen, on the west. The spacing of the elements and the recession in depth is carefully structured, and is enhanced by an adroit play of light and shade. The distant townscape is precisely detailed, and shows a number of recognizable landmarks. Realistic descriptions also provide picturesque notes, as in the windmills that dot the scene and the lengths of linen laid out in the foreground. Haarlem was known for the linen-bleaching establishments that operated in its environs.

JACOB VAN RUISDAEL
The Windmill at Wijk bij Duurstede
Oil on canvas; 32 1/2″ × 39 3/4″.
Signed: "JVRuisdael."
Collections of J. Smith, London, and A. van der Hoop, Amsterdam. Donated to the City of Amsterdam in 1854. On loan since 1885. The old mill still existing in this neighborhood is not the one represented in the canvas.

JACOB VAN RUISDAEL
View of Haarlem
Oil on canvas; 17″ × 15″.
Signed: "JVRuisdael."
Van Nagell van Ampsen sale, The Hague, 1851. Bequest of L. Dupper Wz. of Dordrecht, 1870. The canvas was painted about 1670. Numerous versions exist in various collections, including the Mauritshuis and the National Museum, Berlin.

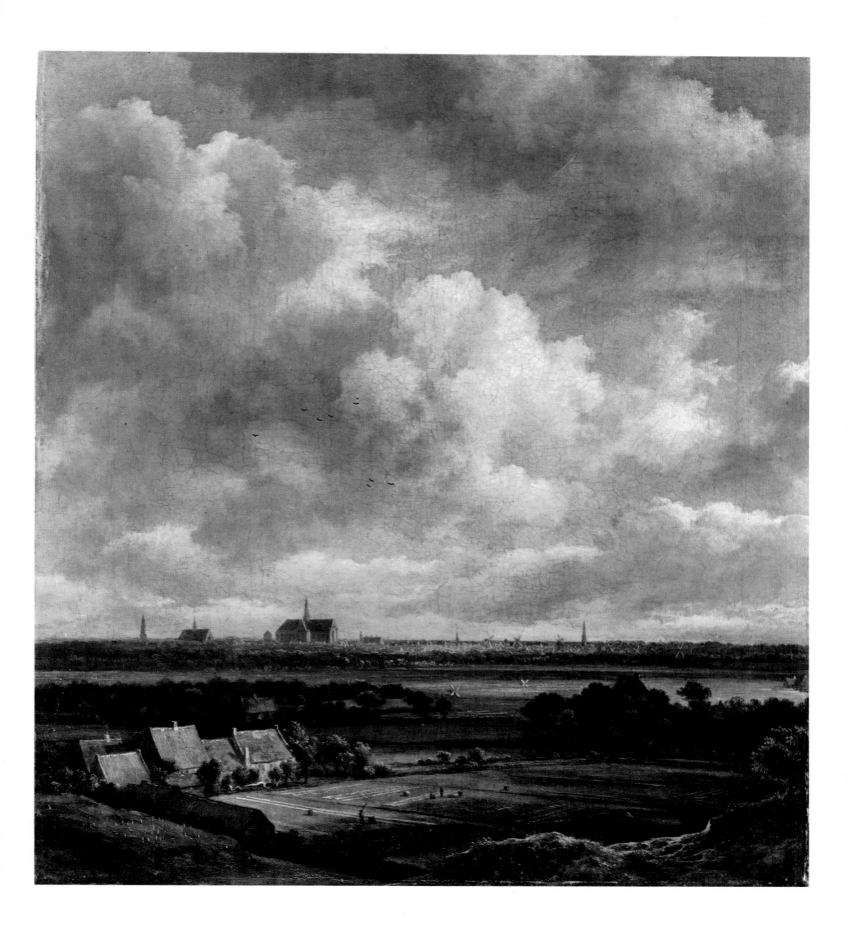

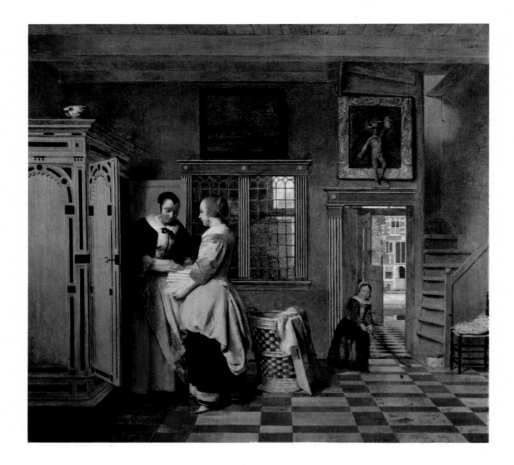

PIETER DE HOOCH
Rotterdam 1629 — Amsterdam circa 1683
At the Linen Closet
Oil on canvas; 28 1/4″ × 30 1/2″.
Signed and dated: "P D Hooch 1663."
In the sales of Baron Lockhorst, Rotterdam, 1726, and of Joachim Rendorp, Amsterdam, 1793 and 1794. In the Smith, Stanley and J. Six (Amsterdam) collections. Donated to the City of Amsterdam by the *Vereeniging Rembrandt* in 1928. On loan to the Rijksmuseum since that year.

PIETER DE HOOCH. *At the Linen Closet.*

The picture shows a tidy Dutch housewife putting linen away in a tall closet decorated with inlay. A maid has brought in the freshly ironed sheets or pillowcases and holds them out for her mistress. In the doorway a little child is playing *kolf* (the ancestor of golf). Typical of de Hooch is the sequential view from one room to another, and then beyond to the out-of-doors. The depth of perspective is reinforced by the change in pattern of the tiles in the second room. During the artist's early career in Delft, he must have known Vermeer, and like him he was fond of painting interiors with two or three figures engaged in some household task. A favorite effect of his was to keep the foreground room relatively dark, and to create areas of bright light in the succeeding spaces. Ultimately this play of light derives from Caravaggio, via the Utrecht School.

PIETER DE HOOCH. *A Country Cottage.*

The foreground again is in shadow, while the light strikes beyond in the middle ground and background. At a shady table a lady, squeezing lemon into a glass of white wine, converses with a gentleman. The lady, a plainly dressed woman, perhaps a servant, stands holding another drink, while another woman scours a brass pan. Still in the spirit of the artist's Delft style, the picture must have been painted around 1665, some two or three years after he moved to Amsterdam.

PIETER DE HOOCH
A Country Cottage (circa 1665)
Oil on canvas; 24″ × 18 1/2″.
Signed: "P. D. Hoog."
O'Neil sale, 1832. Collection of A. van der Hoop, Amsterdam. Donated to the City of Amsterdam in 1854. On loan since 1885.

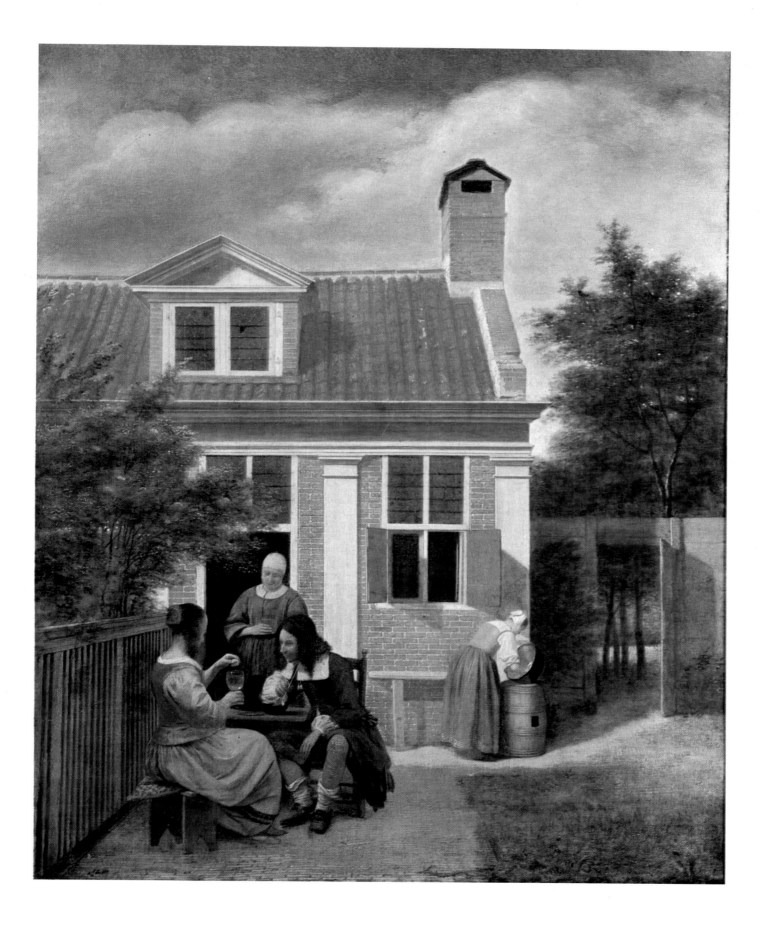

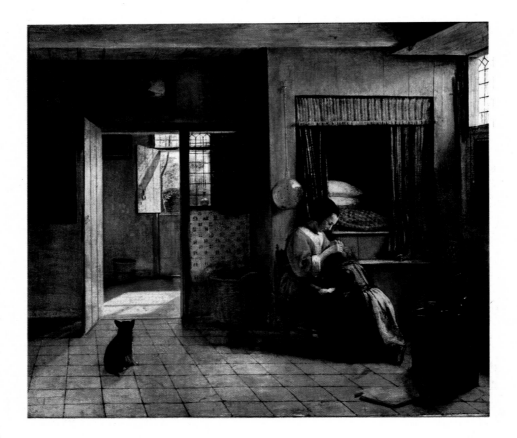

PIETER DE HOOCH
Maternal Duty (circa 1660)
Oil on canvas; 20 1/2″ × 24″.
Signed: "P. d. hooch."
In the Braamcamp sale, 1771. It belonged
to the A. van der Hoop collection, Amsterdam, and was bequeathed to the City of
Amsterdam in 1854. On loan to the Rijksmuseum since 1885.

PIETER DE HOOCH. *Maternal Duty*.

In another typical sequence of spaces, the foreground scene shows a mother inspecting her child's hair. The room contains a bed with partially drawn curtains, a brass bed-warmer and a baby's chair — on the last is the artist's signature. On the left there is a little dog sitting by the door, through which can be seen another room and a sunny garden. This is one of the most intimate of de Hooch's interiors, with the feeling of snug domesticity concentrated on the mother intent on her work.

PIETER DE HOOCH. *The Pantry*.

A particularly subtle play of perspective and light and shade in the tiled floors creates the magically ample spaces in this intimate interior. The actors in this domestic scene of a mother handing a jug to her child are probably the painter's wife, Annetje van der Burch, and their eldest son, Pieter, who was born in 1655. (In 17th-century Holland boys wore skirts until they were six years old.) It has been suggested that the portrait just visible on the far wall of the adjoining room is that of de Hooch's father, and that the artist's intention was to make *The Pantry* a sort of family genealogy.

120

PIETER DE HOOCH
The Pantry (circa 1658)
Oil on canvas; 25 1/2″ × 23 3/4″.
Monogrammed: "P.D.H."
In the sale of Pieter van der Lip, Amsterdam 1712. Then in sales of Walraven, Amsterdam, 1765; de Bruyn, Amsterdam, 1798; de Smeth, Amsterdam, 1810; and Mrs. Hogguer, Amsterdam, 1817.

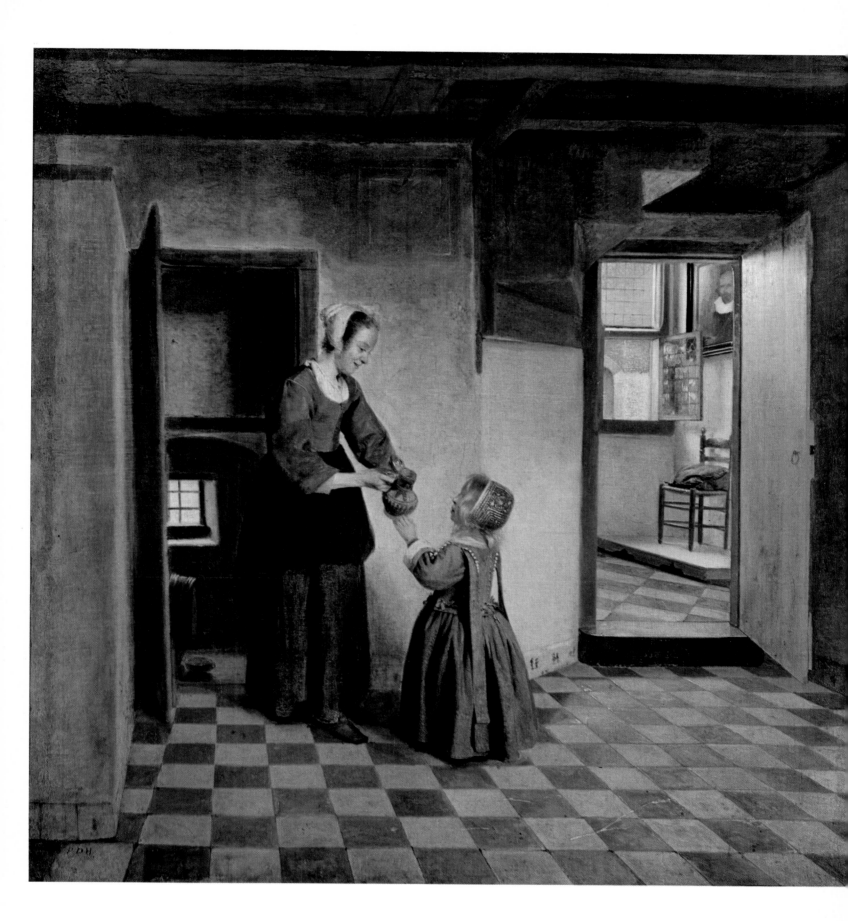

JAN VERMEER. *The Kitchen Maid.*

Sir Joshua Reynolds' admiration for this masterpiece initiated the modern rediscovery of Vermeer's work. The 18th-century English painter was thus instrumental in reviving the name of the master of Delft, which had been forgotten since his death a century earlier. To the few who had been aware of his existence, he was merely a follower of Carel Fabritius.

This picture is generally dated around 1658 and thus is contemporary with *The Soldier and the Girl* and the two views of Delft. Fabritius' influence is apparent in the relationship between foreground and background, although the emphasis is more on the closeup view of figure and objects than on the perspective structure. The color, feeling and texture of things are remarkably expressed. Each object and substance is rendered with unerring skill and understanding, whether it is a pot, bread, milk, cloth, flesh or a flaw in the wall. The construction of the composition, the relationship of the objects to one another and the position of the figure have the same air of inevitability. Slow, painstaking effort went into the creation of the sober simplicity of the forms and the still, golden atmosphere. The striking affinity with the work of Chardin, the 18th-century French painter, was pointed out by the Goncourt brothers in their *Journal*. The paths of the two artists to the peak of painting, in still life and domestic scenes, were entirely independent, however, as Chardin never knew Vermeer's work.

JAN VERMEER. *The Letter.*   *p. 124*

In composition this is one of the most unusual of the some forty paintings by Vermeer that are left (others may have been destroyed in the great explosion at Delft in 1654). It is laid out like a triptych, with the middle wing occupied by the domestic scene. A lady is seated by a fireplace in a room that we see through an open door. She has been interrupted in her lute playing by the arrival of a letter, which she holds in her raised right hand. She looks inquiringly at the smiling serving girl who is standing behind her. In the foreground a tapestry curtain is looped up over the doorway. To the right is a chair with sheets of music on it; to the left, a map of northern Holland. Like other paintings by Vermeer, this one shows part of the interior of the artist's own house.

The feeling of abstract geometry underlying the work is very strong. The brightly lighted group is set back in depth by the darker wings of the fore-

JAN VERMEER
Delft 1632 — Delft 1675
The Kitchen Maid (circa 1658)
Oil on canvas; 18″ × 16 1/4″.
At the end of the 17th and throughout the 18th century, the painting appeared at numerous sales in Amsterdam, where it fetched fairly high but not exceptional prices. From the J. Six collection, to which it belonged from the early 19th century, it went to the Rijksmuseum in 1908, having been acquired with the aid of the *Vereeniging Rembrandt.*

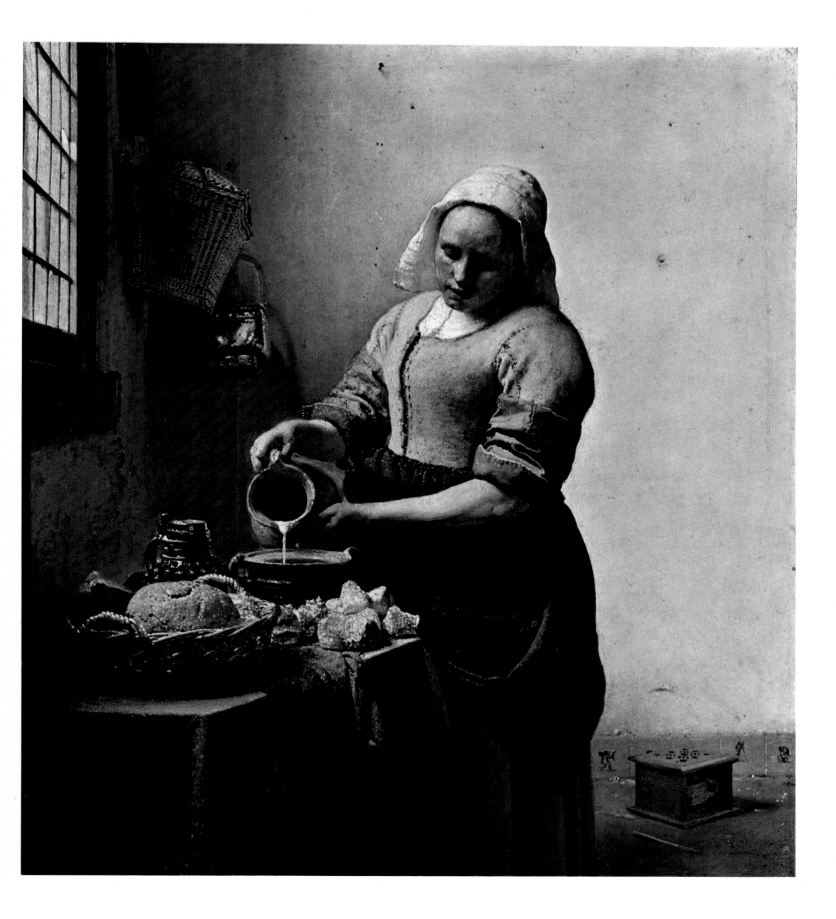

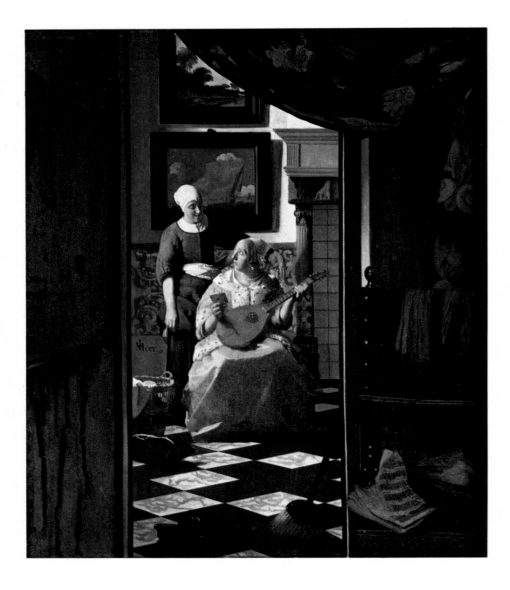

JAN VERMEER
The Letter
Oil on canvas; 17 1/4" × 15 1/4".
Signed: "I. V. Meer."
The painting belonged to the Y. F. van
Lennep collection, in Amsterdam. In 1892
it was in the Messchert van Vollenhoven
sale, Amsterdam, and the following year it
was bought by the Rijksmuseum.

ground. The perspective system focuses on the meeting of the ermine edges
of the lady's jacket. Dense and tactile color, limpid light, are rendered with
magical skill.

JAN VERMEER. *Street in Delft*.

A much appreciated work to which Proust devoted a famous passage in his
novel, this has been called the most beautiful easel painting in the world.
The view is from the back of Vermeer's house in Delft, looking toward the
Old Women's Home on the Voldersgrachte, which was demolished about

JAN VERMEER
Street in Delft
Oil on canvas; 21 1/4" × 17 1/4".
Signed: "I. V. Meer."
At various sales in Amsterdam during the
17th and 18th centuries, it then belonged to
the van Winter and Six collections during
the 19th. It was bought in 1921 by Sir
Henry Deterding, who presented it to the
Rijksmuseum.

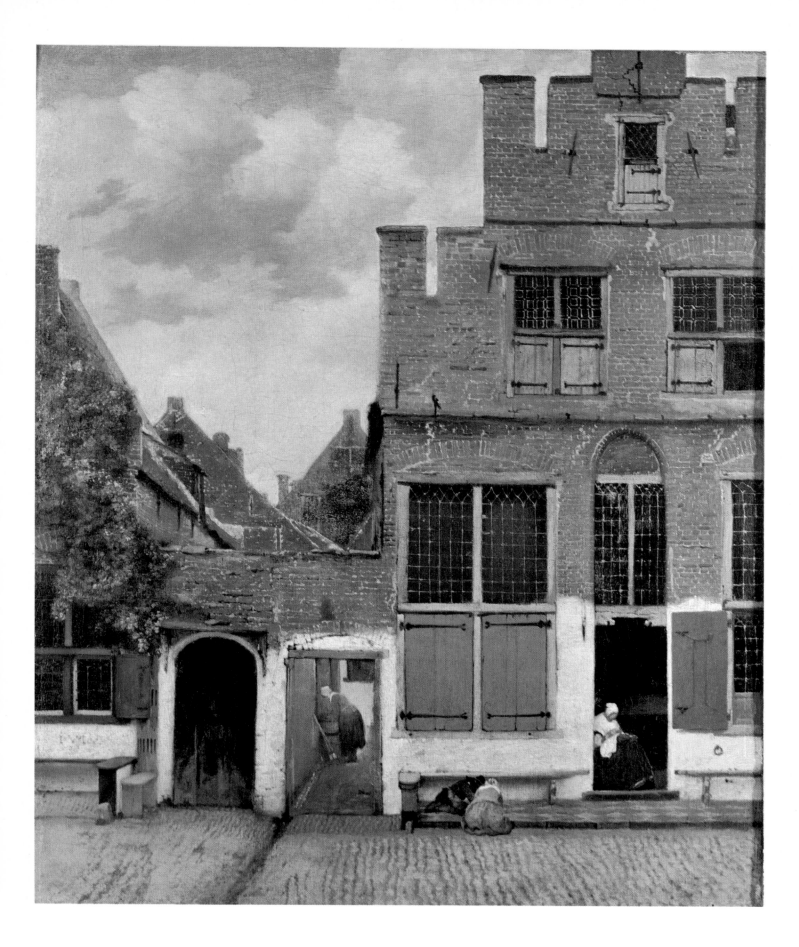

1660 to build the house of the Guild of St. Luke. On the far left is the Old Men's Home. The point of view of the meticulous perspective construction is from a ground floor window of the painter's house, about six feet from the ground. A unique example of structural balance, all of its minutely realistic details are contained in the breadth of the construction in depth, with no feeling of dispersion. What distinguishes this Dutch view from innumerable others is the "elegiac clarity" described by Huizinga: Vermeer's genius for turning an everyday image into an immutable lyric vision.

JAN VERMEER. *Young Woman Reading a Letter.*
A work of Vermeer's full maturity, this painting differs from an earlier one in Dresden not only in detail but in the change from evening to morning light. The map of Holland in the background also appeared in *The Soldier and the Girl.* Vermeer's wife may have been the model for the subject, who is shown as pregnant. In the play of geometric forms composing the picture, the draped table subtly repeats the motif of the figure. Van Gogh commented on the "infallible sense" of composition in this "strange artist," and praised his pearl gray, black and white, lemon yellow and silvery blue colors. Vermeer again has taken a simple, domestic subject and made of it an enduring image that once seen continues to hold its place in the mind's eye.

126

JAN VERMEER
Young Woman Reading a Letter
Oil on canvas; 18 1/4" × 15 1/4".
This work also went through many sales during the 18th century, was taken to France and then appeared in London at J. Smith & Sons, in 1839. It was bought by A. van der Hoop of Amsterdam, who donated it to the city in 1854. On loan since 1885.

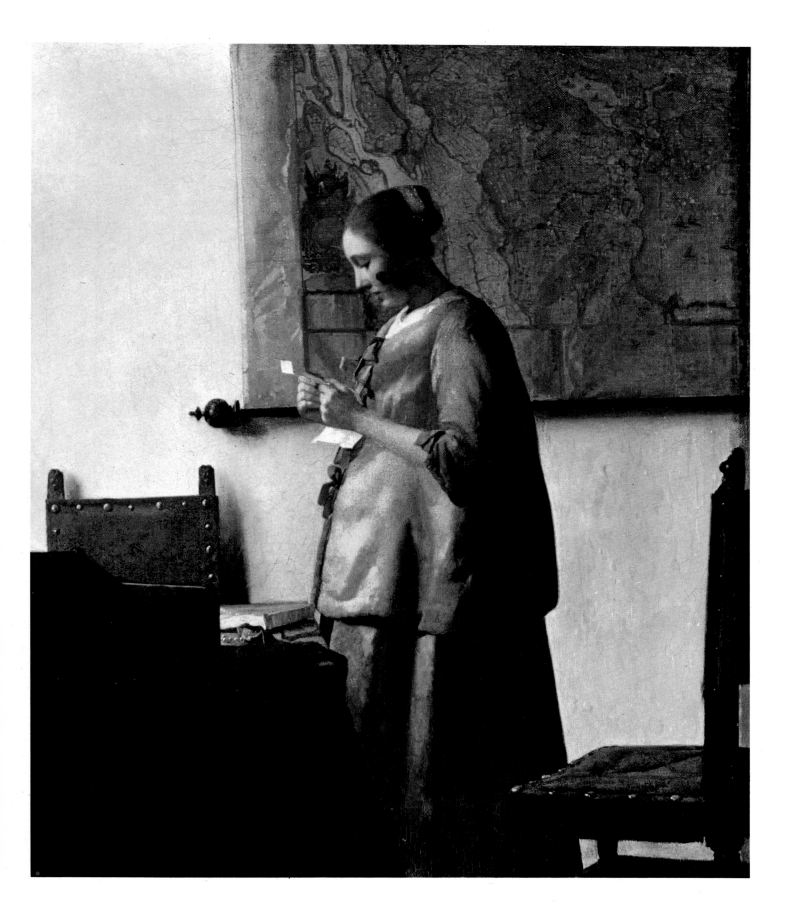

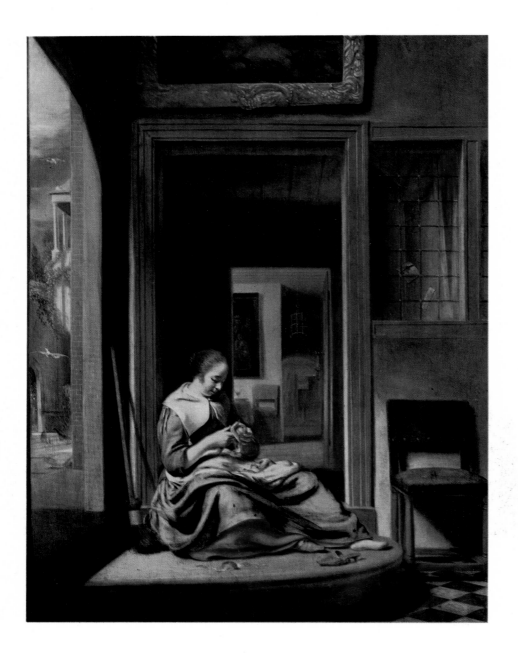

CORNELIS BISSCHOP.   *Woman Peeling Apples.*
The complex composition of this work shows three divisions, like a triptych,
and is similar to the one we have seen in Vermeer's *The Letter* (page 124),
which was painted in the same year (1667). Here, however, the inter-rela-
tionships are very different. On the left, the view opens onto a garden, while
on the right a precise rendering of a window starts a succession of planes in
depth, which are emphasized by the play of light. The figure, seen in three-
quarter view, appears to alter the balance established by the tri-partite structure. But the compact mass of the figure — as in Mabuse's *Danae* (see *Pina-
kothek/Munich,* page 69) — is the center around which the architectural
128 elements of the composition turn.

CORNELIS BISSCHOP
Dordrecht 1630 — Dordrecht 1674
Woman Peeling Apples
Oil on panel; 28 1/2″ × 22″.
Signed and dated:
"C. Bvsschop: Fecit: 1667."
In the Hartford collection, Paris,
until 1903.

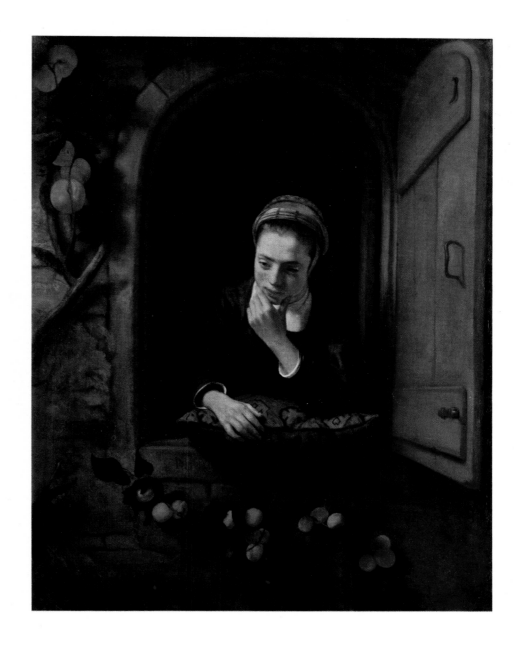

NICOLAES MAES
Dordrecht 1634 — Amsterdam 1693
Dreaming
Oil on canvas; 48 1/2″ × 37 3/4″.
Signed: "N MAES."
From De Lelie and Hulswit,
Groningen, 1829.

NICOLAES MAES. *Dreaming.*

The picture of a young girl at a window recalls the composition of Gerard Dou's celebrated *Self-Portrait,* which is also in the Rijksmuseum. Like Dou, Nicolaes Maes was a pupil of Rembrandt, whose influence is more apparent in Maes's numerous official and group portraits than it is here. The artist had been back in his native town of Dordrecht for about two years — that is, around 1655 — when he painted this simply dressed peasant or serving girl. Light from the left gives relief to the woman leaning on a figured cushion in the open, arched window. The flat wall is relieved by the bricks showing through patches of broken plaster, and by espaliered peaches and apricots.

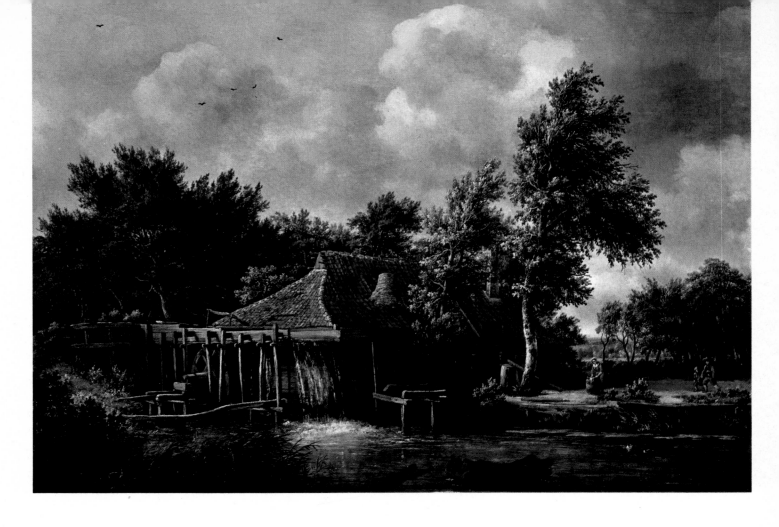

MEINDERT HOBBEMA
Amsterdam 1638 — Amsterdam 1709
Watermill
Oil on panel; 24 1/2″ × 33 1/2″.
Signed: "M. Hobbema."
It belonged to the collections of William
Smith, London; Lafontaine, Paris: Allan,
Edinburgh; A. van der Hoop, Amsterdam.
Bequest to the City of Amsterdam, 1854.
On loan since 1885.

MEINDERT HOBBEMA. *Watermill.*

A friend and pupil of Jacob van Ruisdael, Meindert Hobbema often painted
the same subjects in a similar manner. But the differences are marked. In
Hobbema the trees usually form a screen blocking the horizon. Where Ruisdael was dramatic, throwing bright and somber areas into strong contrast,
Hobbema created serene and lyric effects of diffused sunlight and subtle nuances of color. His quieter tone makes his views seem more "real" than those
of Ruisdael. Although he lived in Amsterdam, like Ruisdael he went into
the countryside to find his subjects. He often painted the same scene several
times, from different angles and in different light. The watermill represented
here appears again, but at a greater distance, in paintings in the Wallace
Collection, London, and in the Chicago Art Institute.

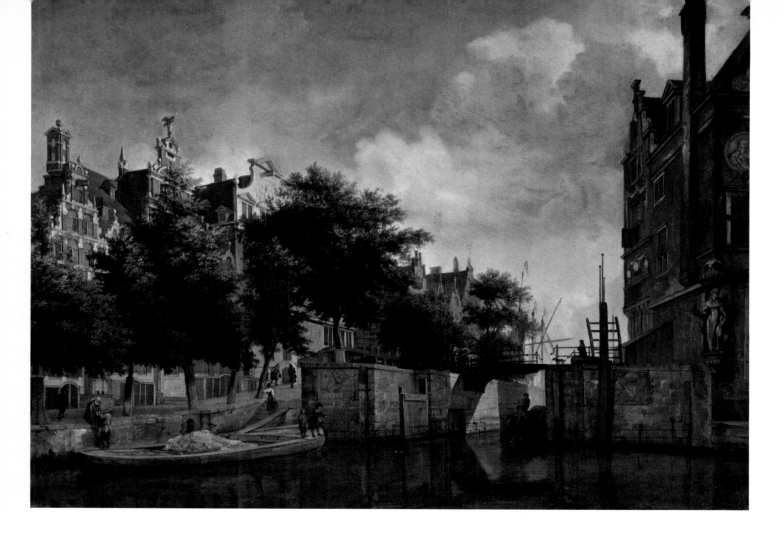

JAN VAN DER HEYDEN
Gorinchem 1637 — Amsterdam 1712
View of the
Martelaarsgracht in Amsterdam
Oil on panel; 17 1/4" × 22 1/2".
Signed: "VHeyde."
From the Cabinet van Heteren,
The Hague, 1809.

JAN VAN DER HEYDEN. *View of the Martelaarsgracht in*
Amsterdam.

Known by his contemporaries for his "mechanical curiosity," Jan van der
Heyden was an engineer and certainly familiar with the camera obscura. As
an artist, he devoted himself to urban scenes in which buildings have the major role or to landscapes with important architectural elements. His compositions follow the classical Dutch rules. Consequently there is no question that
he might have attained his rigorous results only by passive, mechanical
means, such as the camera obscura. This view of a canal in Amsterdam is a
major example of the artist's ability to make a monumental image out of an
ordinary scene.

131

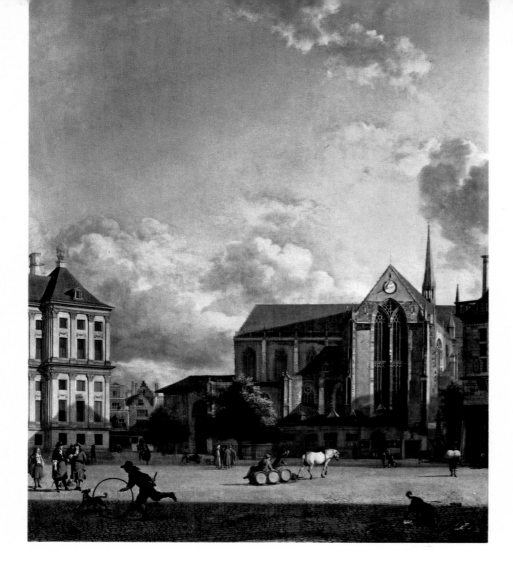

JAN VAN DER HEYDEN
View of the Dam at Amsterdam
Oil on panel; 26 3/4″ × 21 3/4″.
Signed: "VHeyde."
In the sales of W Lormier, The Hague, 1763;
C. S. Roos, Amsterdam, 1820; A. de Haas,
Amsterdam; C. J. Nieuwenhuis, London,
1833. J. F. van Lennep collection, Amsterdam. Bequest to the City of Amsterdam,
1893. On loan to the Rijksmuseum since
1893.

JAN VAN DER HEYDEN.   *View of the Dam at Amsterdam.*
The intense afternoon light strikes the Nieuwe Kerk and the right wing of
the Town Hall, two of Amsterdam's principal landmarks. The broad foreground space is not coldly monumental, but animated by people working,
strolling and playing. Unfortunately this little panel does not show us the
original composition in its entirety. The left side and the upper part have
been cut down. As the artist gave great weight to his modular systems, the
rhythm of the work as conceived has been impaired. The measure of the
lyric side of his art is that even without the complete intellectual framework,
this luminous townscape makes a strikingly poetic impression.

GERRIT BERCKHEYDE.   *The Spaarne at Haarlem.*
"Architectural beauty was an excellent guide for the men of the 17th century. It helped them to understand the environment in which they lived.
. . . the 17th century saw this beauty plainly, even if it did not seek for
words to define it. Otherwise, how could so many painters and draftsmen
represent views of cities and villages with that love . . . shown . . . in the
clear precision of a van der Heyden or a Berckheyde?" The picture is illu-
minated by these words of Huizinga, from his famous essays on 17th-century

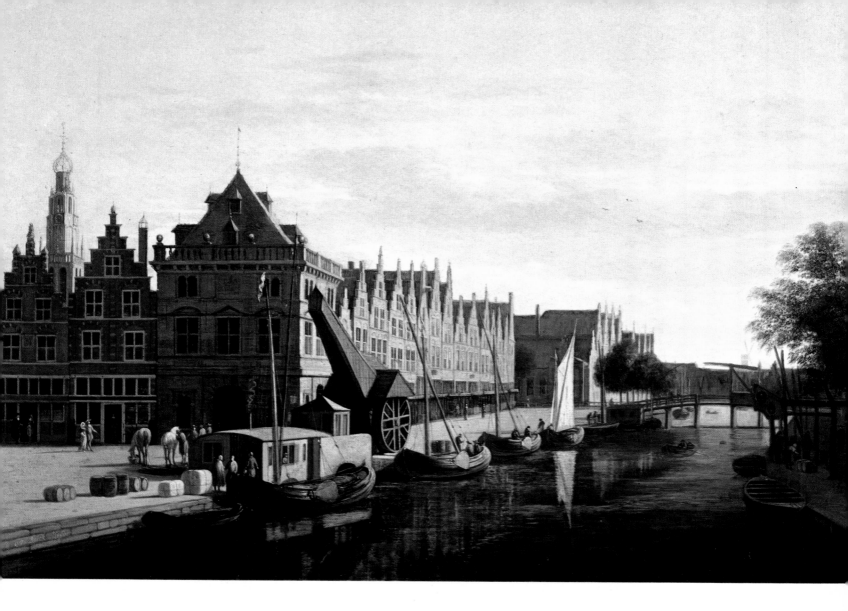

GERRIT BERCKHEYDE
Haarlem 1638 — Haarlem 1698
The Spaarne at Haarlem
Oil on panel; 12 1/2″ × 18″.
Signed: "g Berck Heyde."
Sale of Ad. La Coste, Dordrecht, 1832.
In the Cabinet J. Rombouts, Dordrecht,
1850. Bequest of L. Dupper Wz.,
Dordrecht, 1870.

On page 134:
CORNELIS TROOST
Amsterdam 1697 — Amsterdam 1750
The Garden of a Town House
Oil on canvas; 26″ × 22″.
Signed: "C. Troost."
Gift of C. Hoogendijk, The Hague, 1912.

Dutch civilization. Van der Heyden, as we have seen, went beyond "clear precision." Here Berckheyde's special atmosphere overtakes objective representation. In the limpid stillness of the broad spaces and the regular rhythms of the architecture, a mood of steady contemplation is invoked.

CORNELIS TROOST.   *The Garden of a Town House.*   *p. 134*

The most notable 18th-century Dutch painter, Troost was famous as a portraitist and an illustrator of manners and customs. In the structure of his interiors, an emphasis on the decorative details (middle-class taste had rapidly changed) may distract one from grasping the compositional metrics, which are close to those of Metsu and Gerard Dou. This scene, however, is a clear demonstration of Troost's use of a centrally focused structure with symmetrical halves. The scheme is perhaps even too apparent, but the mirror effect suggests a sort of magic game perfectly in keeping with the gallantry of the figures and objects. The seated woman in the foreground can trace her ancestry, historically if not stylistically, to the figure conversing in the foreground of Pieter de Hooch's *A Country Cottage* (page 119).

133

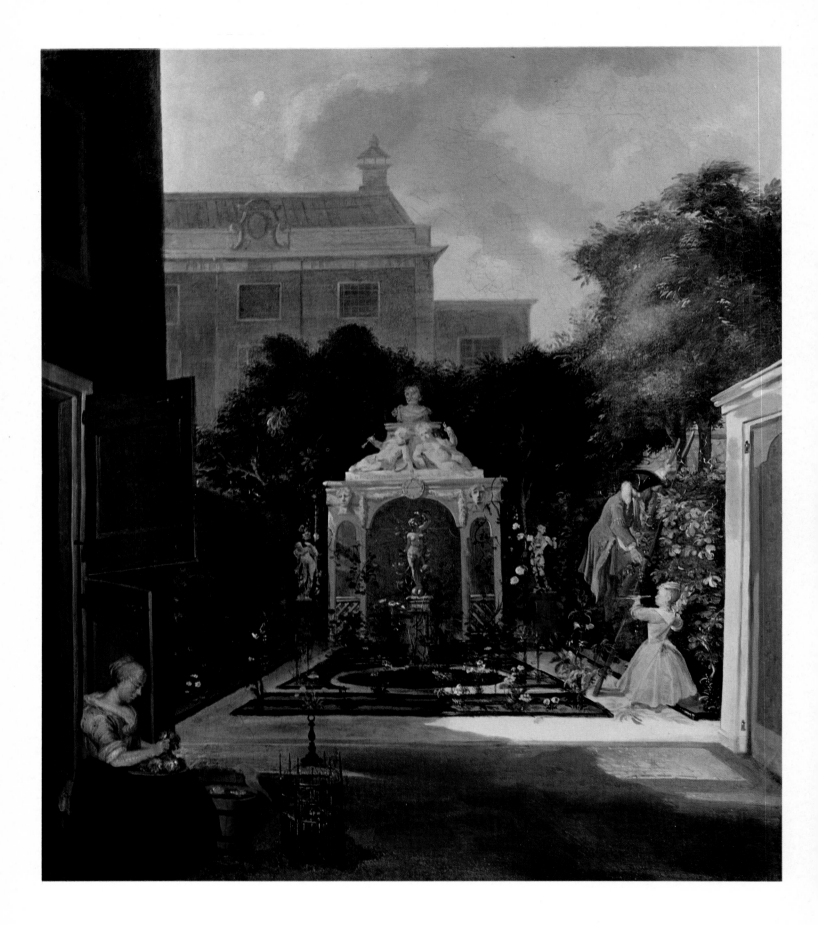

ITALY
SPAIN
FLANDERS
FRANCE

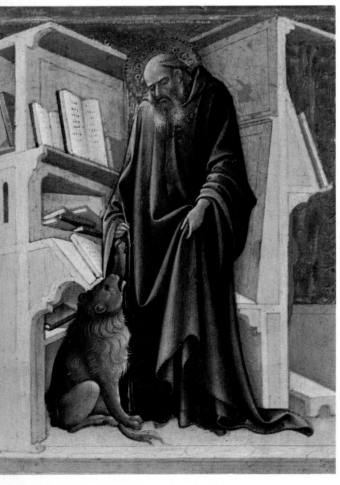

136

LORENZO MONACO.   *St. Jerome in His Study*.

A rather late work of Pietro di Giovanni, who is better known by his 19th-century appellation of Lorenzo Monaco, Lorenzo the Monk. Certainly it follows the *Coronation of the Virgin,* 1414 — executed for his monastery of Santa Maria degli Angeli and now in the Uffizi — which was fundamental in Lorenzo's career; and it is probably contemporary with the decoration of the Bartolini-Saltimbeni Chapel at Santa Trinità and the *Adoration of the Magi* panel, also in the Uffizi (see *Uffizi/Florence,* page 28). The artist's early work was marked by exuberant ornamentation. Subsequently, under the influence of Ghiberti his painting became more composed and classicizing. Yet in this *St. Jerome,* the bent toward linear simplification is expressed in the sharp wedging of the figure between the walls of his study. It is also seen in the verticality of the squarely constructed group and in the rhythmic cadence of the drapery set off against a gold ground.

CARLO CRIVELLI.   *Mary Magdalene*.

Despite appearances, the panel was conceived as a complete composition and not as the right wing of a polyptych. This is shown by the inscription at the bottom (not included in the detail produced), for Crivelli had the habit of signing the central panel of his polyptychs, sometimes on the crowning element of the composition. Modeled on the *Mary Magdalene* of the dismembered and fragmentary polyptych at Montefiori and akin to an arbitrarily reconstructed work in the National Gallery, London, this painting must have been executed around 1475–80, during the full maturity of the artist. This variation on a frequently repeated theme indicates that Crivelli progressively reassessed the results of his previous efforts. Here he lucidly intensified the refined elegance of the line, which derived from the master's Paduan experience — shared with Mantegna. With great virtuosity the subtle linear development defines the areas of color and culminates in the whirlpool of tresses.

PIERO DI COSIMO.   *Portrait of Giuliano da Sangallo* and *Portrait of Francesco Giamberti.*   pp. 138–139

These paintings, formerly ascribed to Dürer and Lucas van Leyden, were evidently conceived as a diptych, and are securely datable through documents to the beginning of the 16th century. In them the artist, originally called Piero di Lorenzo but named Piero di Cosimo after his master Cosimo Rosselli, radically revised the current approach in Florentine portraiture.

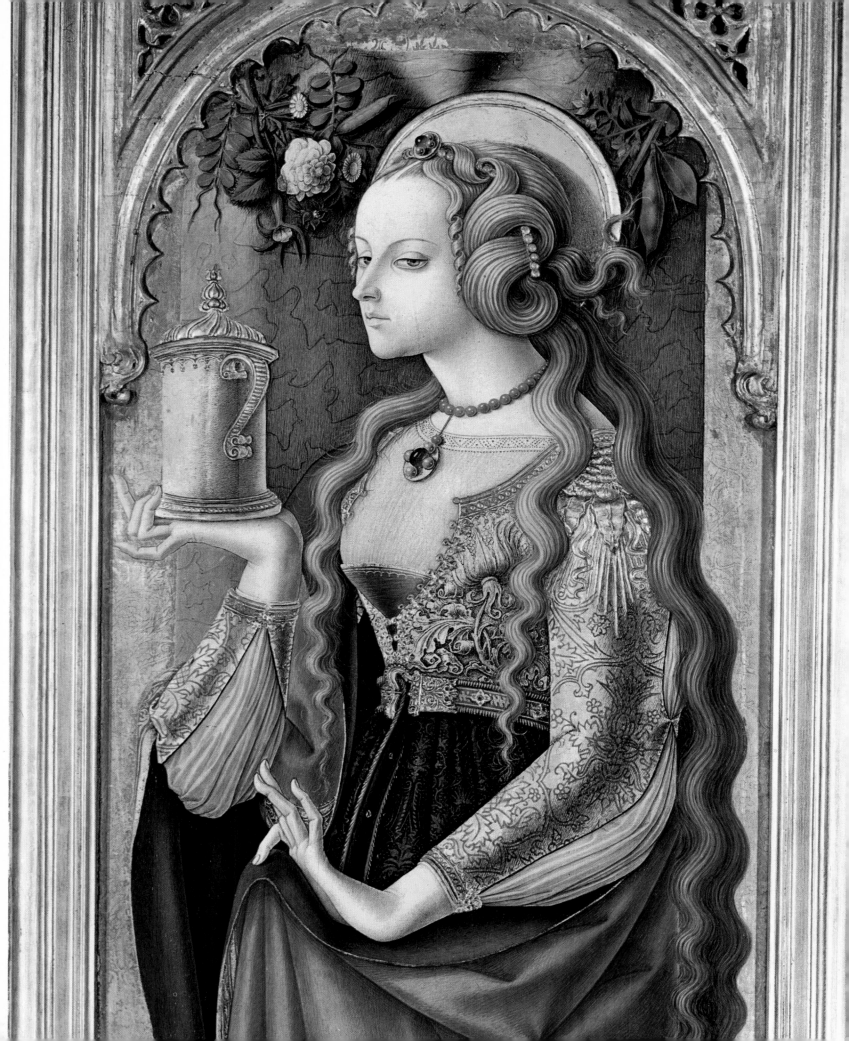

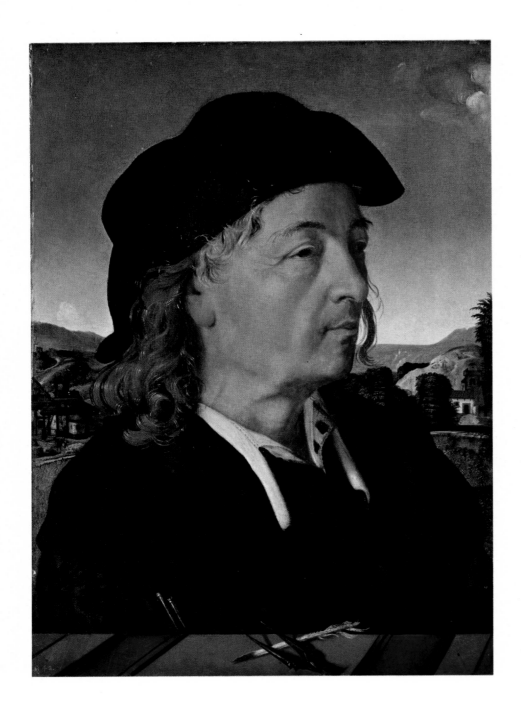

Minute description and anecdotal detail are avoided, while emphasis is placed on the firm structure of the two interrelated compositions, in which the perspective systems meet at the center and the two figures confront each other. Space is created in part by the foreground "parapets," whose three-dimensional extension is emphasized by the symbolic objects lying on them. These indicate that Giuliano da Sangallo (1443–1517) was an architect and Francesco Giamberti (1405–80), a musician. Space is developed fur-

138

PIERO DI COSIMO
(PIERO DI LORENZO)
Florence circa 1461–62 — Florence 1521
Studied with Cosimo Rosselli; his presence in the master's studio in 1480 is documented. He may have followed Rosselli to Rome in 1481. In 1498 he was consulted, with others, on the placing of Michelangelo's *David*. He joined the doctors' and druggists' guild as a painter in Florence in 1504.
Portrait of Giuliano da Sangallo
(circa 1500–1504)
Panel; 18 3/4″ × 13 1/4″.
Formerly in the possession of Francesco da Sangallo; subsequently in the Dutch royal collection. On loan since 1948 from the Mauritshuis at The Hague.

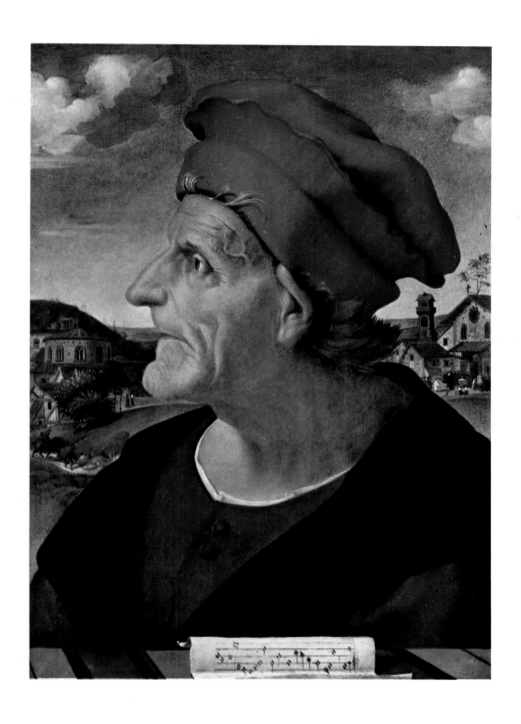

PIERO DI COSIMO
Portrait of Francesco Giamberti
(circa 1500–1504)
Panel; 18 3/4″ × 13 1/4″.
The companion piece of the preceding
work, it has the same history.

ther through the torsion of the figures seen in three-quarter view. From broad effects in the bodies the painting passes to greater detail in the faces, especially in the *Portrait of Francesco Giamberti*. As the subject had died in 1480, the painting was not done from life; the sharp contours suggest that it was drawn from a portrait medal. The cauliflower ear and swollen vein are perhaps more conventional than the rest, and are reminiscent of Leonardo's caricatural drawings.

139

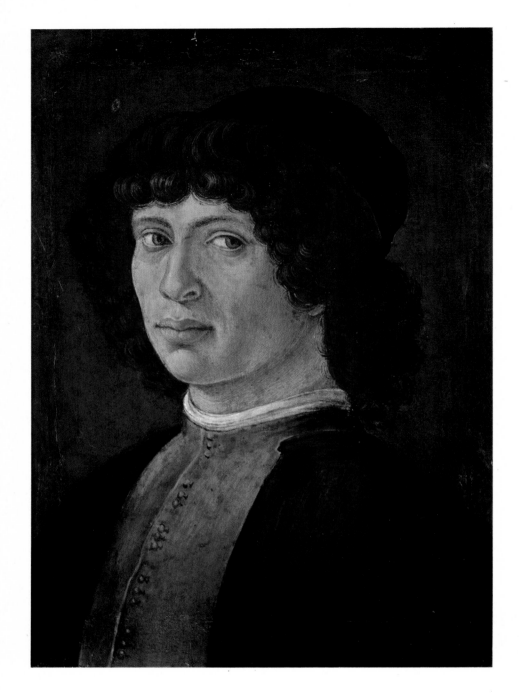

ANTONIO POLLAIOLO. *Portrait of a Man.*
The figure is set on a diagonal directed toward the left, which is balanced by
the torsion of the head, creating a system of opposed and balancing forces.
The composition is animated mainly, however, by the subject's glance,
which creates a psychological connection with the observer. In contrast to
the simple volume of the bust, there are the linear tension of the contours
and the play of light and dark that emphasizes the vitality of the face framed
by the hair.

140

ANTONIO POLLAIOLO
(ANTONIO BENCI DA JACOPO)
Florence circa 1431 — Rome 1498
Trained as a goldsmith, perhaps in the
workshop of Vittorio Ghiberti, he left his
father's house in 1459 to open his own
studio in Florence. Probably journeyed to
Rome in 1469. Except for intervals in Tuscany, where he also practiced as an archi-
tect, he was permanently in Rome after
1480, working on the tomb of Sixtus IV and
then on the tomb of Innocent VIII.
Portrait of a Man (1475)
Panel; 16″ × 11 3/4″.
Attributed by Bode to Filippino Lippi —
the name under which it still appears in the
Rijksmuseum — or to Sandro Botticelli.
Berenson ascribed it to Francesco Botticini.
Bredius, van Marle and Ragghianti attribute it to Pollaiolo. Formerly in the collections Robiano, Brussels, and Bartels, Berlin.
Acquired for the Augusteum in Oldenburg in
1869; in the Rijksmuseum since 1925.

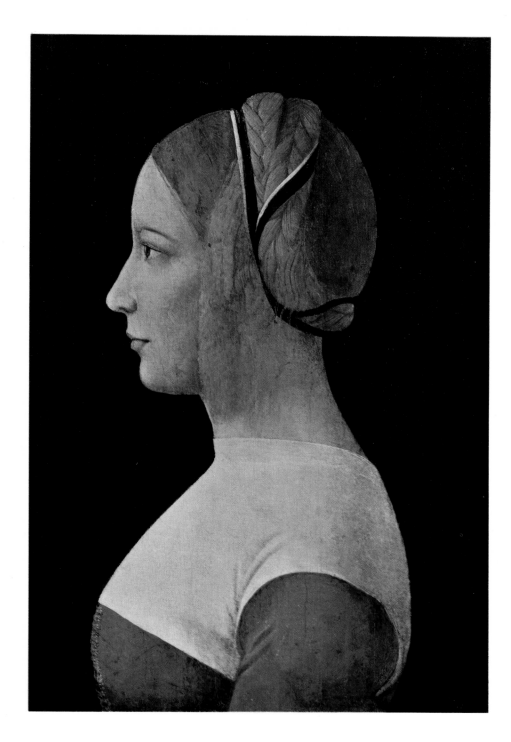

VINCENZO FOPPA
Brescia (?) circa 1427–30 — Brescia circa
1515–16
From 1456 to 1458, domiciled in Pavia; in
1461, at Genova. A citizen of Pavia from
1467 to 1489, with sojourns in Milan, Ge-
nova and Brescia. He settled definitively in
Brescia in 1490, and was official painter of
the city until 1496. Documented as being in
Pavia in 1499.
Portrait of a Young Woman (circa 1465–70)
Panel; 17 3/4″ × 12 1/4″.
Early provenance from Brescia. It was ac-
quired, as a work by Boltraffio, for the
Augusteum of Oldenburg in 1869. In the
Rijksmuseum since 1923, with attribution to
Ambrogio de' Predis. Identified by Rag-
ghianti in 1954 as a Foppa, an attribution
accepted by Arslan (1958), who, however,
dates it around 1490.

VINCENZO FOPPA. *Portrait of a Young Woman.*
Attributed by some scholars to Ambrogio De' Predis, this exquisite profile
of an unknown woman is one of the key works in Foppa's occasional activity as a portraitist. The figure is shown bust length. The linear development
is agile and continual, defining the profile, the close-fitting crimson and
white bodice and the red-blond braided hair through which a black and
white velvet ribbon is threaded.

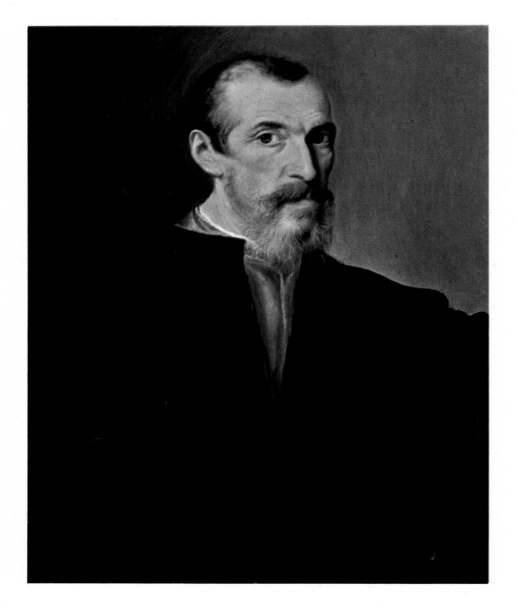

GIOVANNI GEROLAMO SAVOLDO
Brescia circa 1480–85 — Milan 1548(?)
In 1508 he registered as a painter with the
doctors' and druggists' guild in Florence,
but was again in Brescia in 1509. From
1511 he stayed permanently in Venice, ex-
cept for occasional visits to Brescia and a
period in Milan around 1530, working for
Duke Francesco II Sforza.
Portrait of a Man (circa 1540)
Oil on canvas; 27 1/4" × 22 1/4".
Attributed by Suida to G. B. Moroni, and
by Creighton Gilbert to the Master of the
Sala Portrait. Savoldo was the author for
Berenson. It appeared at the Sedelmeyer
sale in Paris, 1907, as a *Self-Portrait* by
Bassano; at the Trotti sale, Paris, as a work
by Lotto. As a Lotto it entered the A. van
Buuren collection, Amsterdam, in 1925.
Donated to the Rijksmuseum in 1937.

GIOVANNI GEROLAMO SAVOLDO. *Portrait of a Man.*

Various places of origin have been proposed for this work, but they all
point to the hinterland of the Venetian Republic which reached at the time
as far as Bergamo and Brescia. Brescia is a probable choice, and the attribution to Savoldo, suggested by Berenson, is plausible. It would be a late
work by Savoldo, datable around 1540, as shown by a comparison with his
Nativity in San Giobbe, Venice. The St. Joseph in the latter is the precedent
for the position of the half-length figure, with its sharp foreshortening, and
for the bright tones of the face emerging strongly from the neutral wall.

JACOPO TINTORETTO. *Portrait of Ottavio Strada.*

This portrait was executed during Tintoretto's full maturity, on the occasion
of Ottavio Strada's visit to Venice with his father, the Mantuan painter and
antique dealer, Jacopo Strada. They were there to collect antiques for Al-

JACOPO TINTORETTO
(JACOPO ROBUSTI)
Venice 1518 — Venice 1594
Already active as a Master in 1539. Probably visited Rome in 1547. In contact with
Ercole Gonzaga in 1562. Visited Mantua in
1579–80.
Portrait of Ottavio Strada (1576)
Detail. Oil on canvas; 50 1/2" × 39 3/4".
The inscription in the upper left of the picture, probably added later, gives the name
and age of the subject (18), the date (1567)
and the name of the artist. Probably a companion piece to the portrait of Ottavio's
father, which is now in Vienna. Formerly in
the collections of Kaufmann, Berlin; Gold-
farb; Tjetje, Amsterdam; Wolff, Wassenaar.
Acquired by the Rijksmuseum in 1956.

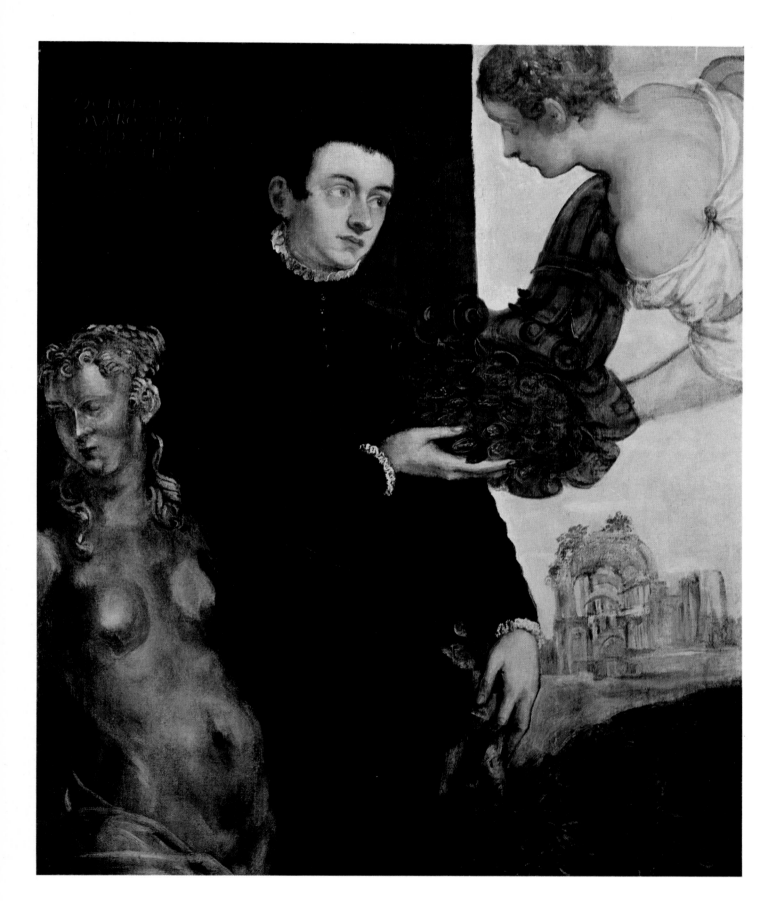

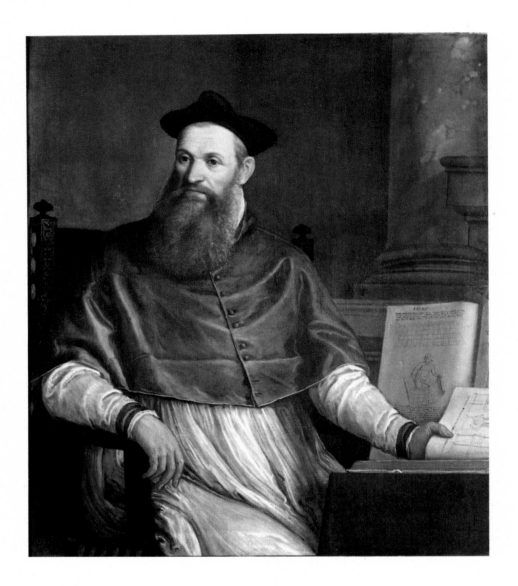

bert V of Bavaria. The painting is one of the most expressive of Tintoretto's numerous, splendid portraits, and combines Venetian experience with the Tuscan and Roman novelties introduced to Venice by Vasari and Salviati. This is felt in the subtle correspondence between the figure of the youth and the female statue, emphasized by the introduction of the Goddess of Plenty hovering over ancient ruins in the background — source of Strada's prosperity. Descending from the sky, the goddess offers him a cornucopia filled with gold coins.

PAOLO VERONESE. *Portrait of Daniele Barbaro.*
The artist was in touch with the Barbaro brothers, Daniele and Marcantonio, from the time when he decorated their villa at Maser (Treviso) in 1561. Daniele Barbaro, humanist and translator of Vitruvius, probably was the author of the allegorical and mythological themes of that fresco cycle, which is the impressive culmination of Veronese's youthful period. The portrait is later and much more severe in structure than the frescoes. Returning

PAOLO VERONESE
(PAOLO CALIARI)
Verona 1528 — Venice 1588
Pupil and assistant of Antonio Badile at Verona in 1541. In 1555 acquired a studio in Venice, where he settled permanently in 1557. He is mentioned as residing with his brother, Benedetto Caliari, in Padua in 1575, though registered as a painter in Venice.
Portrait of Daniele Barbaro
(circa 1565–70)
Oil on canvas; 47 1/2″ × 41 1/2″.
Formerly in a private collection in Basel, then in the Lanz collection, Amsterdam. It was acquired by the Rijksmuseum in 1952.

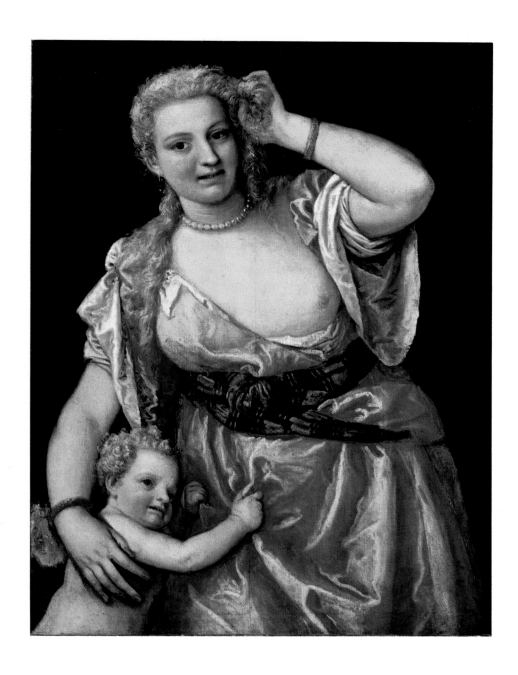

to Raphael as a model, it shows the figure three-quarter length, seated in an armchair. The relationships are architectural, the mass of the figure playing systematically against the other compositional elements — column, book and chair. Barbaro is shown opening his translation of Vitruvius' *De Architectura,* published in 1566.

PAOLO VERONESE. *Venus and Cupid.*
A late work executed with considerable assistance from Paolo's brother, Benedetto Caliari, the painting shows the full development of color of Veronese's final period. There is a clear relationship here with the allegorical and

PAOLO VERONESE
Venus and Cupid (circa 1580)
Oil on canvas; 38 1/4″ × 28″.
Mainly from the hand of Benedetto Caliari, according to Pallucchini. For Berenson and Fiocco it is an autograph Paolo Veronese. Formerly in the collection of the Comte d'Espagnac. Acquired for the Augusteum of Oldenburg in 1869. In the Rijksmuseum since 1923.

mythological series the painter did for Rudolph II, but the connection between group and surroundings is canceled by the introduction of a dark ground, which heightens the effect of the bright colors. The composition is built up on a system of curves and ellipses, interrupted only by the diagonal movement of the Cupid and Venus's raised arm.

ALESSANDRO MAGNASCO. *Monks in a Landscape.*
Absorbed in religious exercises, three Carthusian monks are seen in a fantastic landscape. The artist did a number of compositions with similar themes. Virtuoso brushwork defines the volumes, and the masterful technique recalls 16th-century Venetian art on the one hand and the work of the Bolognese painter, Giuseppe Maria Crespi, on the other. Magnasco, however, transformed these elements by adopting a more emphatic rhythm and more explicit structure, as seen in the space created by the figures within the rocky cavern.

ALESSANDRO MAGNASCO. *Massacre of the Innocents.* p. 148
The dating of this picture is disputed, with some critics calling it a youthful work and others attributing it to late in Magnasco's career. In any case, this expressive painting has a strongly organized structure beneath its crackling colors. Horizontally braked by the column and arcades, the slaughter in the foreground is developed in two converging diagonal directions. These connect at center in the figure of the man on the rearing horse, making a broad-based pyramid. Convergence toward the center comes from all sides, and especially in the fantastic ballet of the three cutthroats on the left. In the repetition of their convulsive gestures, they are like a sequence of stills from a film. Beyond the pivotal central group, the unexpected movement of the horseman wielding a saber on the right makes a sharp contrast with the general structure of the composition.

In highly effective passages like this, Magnasco showed his descent from a tradition that owed something to the mediocre Filippo Abbiati, his Milanese master, but much more to Rubens' influence in Genoa as seen in the work of Grechetto and Valerio Castello. These two painters provide the immediate point of departure for the dense color and rapid brush strokes characteristic of Magnasco.

GIOVANNI BATTISTA TIEPOLO. *Telemachus and Mentor.* p. 149
Almost certainly this painting is a fragment, the right-hand part of a much larger composition devoted to one of the adventures of Telemachus, son of Ulysses, and Minerva under the guise of Mentor. Stylistically it is close to

ALESSANDRO MAGNASCO
(IL LISSANDRINO)
Genoa 1667 — Genoa 1742
In the last decade of the 17th century he worked with Abbiate in Milan; subsequently he returned to Genoa. Traveled in Lombardy, Emilia and Tuscany. In Florence from 1703 to about 1711; Milan, 1711 to 1735.
Monks in a Landscape (circa 1720–30) Oil on canvas; 21 1/2" × 15 1/4". Companion piece to *Capucin Monks in Prayer,* which is also in the Rijksmuseum. Acquired at Antwerp in 1822. On loan from the Mauritshuis, The Hague, since 1948.

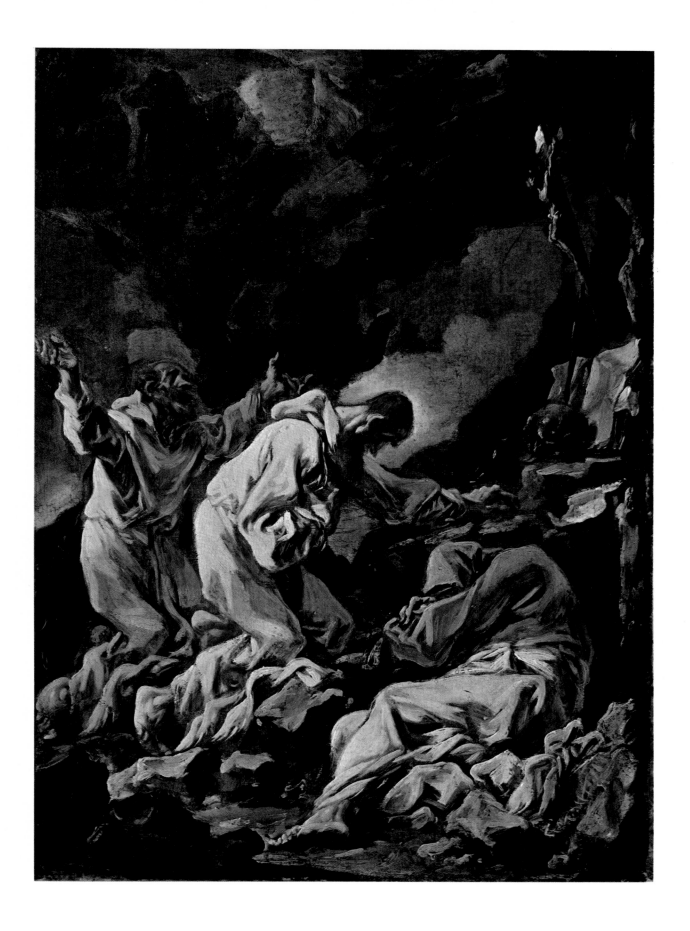

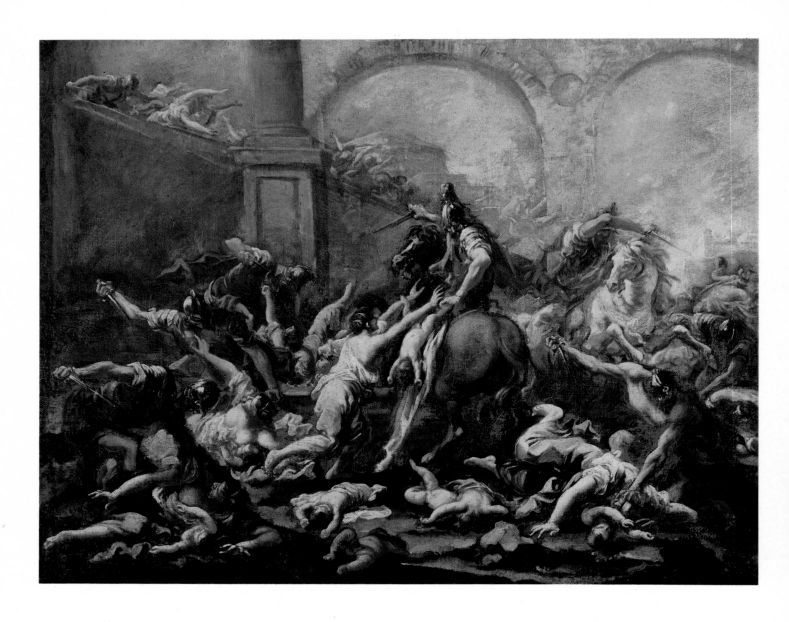

ALESSANDRO MAGNASCO
Massacre of the Innocents
(circa 1735–42)
Oil on canvas; 25 3/4″ × 32 3/4″.

Tiepolo's works of around 1740, like the two canvases in the parish church of Verolanuova (Brescia), the *Way to Calvary* in Sant'Alvise, Venice, and the ceiling of Palazzo Clerici in Milan. This was a time when the artist was wavering between a plastic conception of form, derived from his closeness to Piazzetta in youth, and an emphasis on effects of atmosphere and color. The latter comes from Veronese via Sebastiano Ricci, but is directed toward scenic and decorative uses and occasionally toward a frank and sunny sensuality, as in the Milanese cycle. Here, the youthful emphasis on form is apparent. Although sensitively executed, it is prosy in tone and does not extend the master's repertory.

148

GIOVANNI BATTISTA TIEPOLO
Venice 1696 — Madrid 1770
Appears on the register of Venetian painters in 1717. Married Cecilia, sister of Gianantonio and Francesco Guardi, in 1719. At Milan in 1731; Bergamo, in 1732 and 1733; Milan, 1737; Würzburg, 1750–53. In 1762 in Spain with his two sons, Giandomenico and Lorenzo, on the invitation of Charles III. *Telemachus and Mentor* (circa 1740) Oil on canvas; 43 1/4″ × 28 1/4″. Probably a fragment.

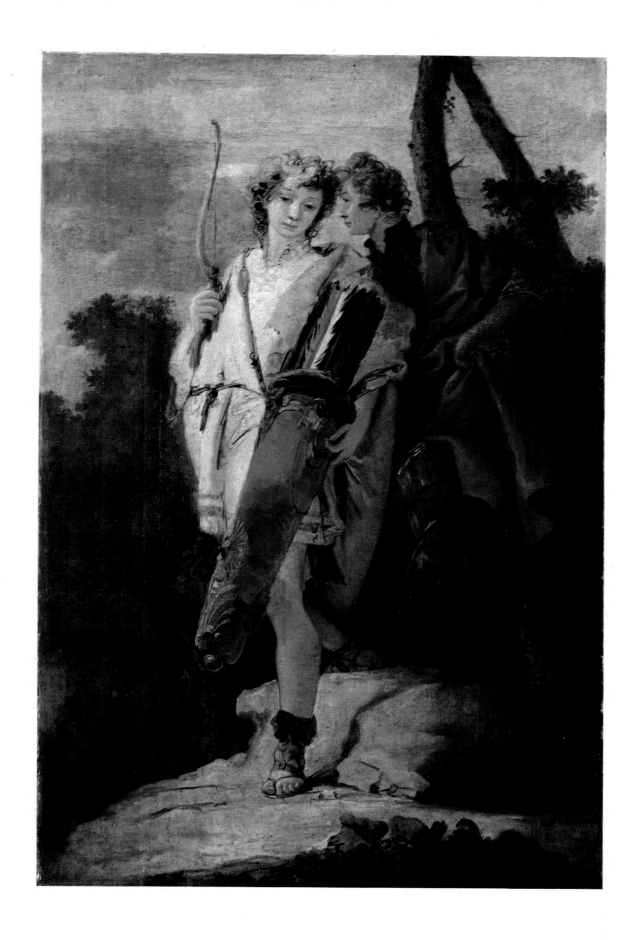

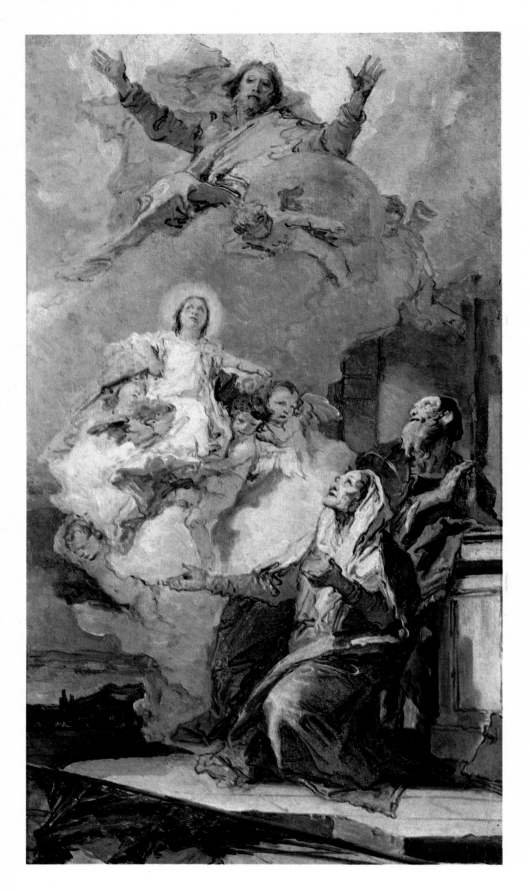

GIOVANNI BATTISTA TIEPOLO
The Vision of St. Anne (circa 1759)
Oil on canvas; 19 1/4″ × 10 1/4″.
Formerly in the Galleria Barlese Tiepolo, 1808. Subsequently in the collections of Benigno Crespi, Milan; Cassirer, Berlin; Tjetje, Amsterdam. Acquired by the Rijksmuseum in 1948.

FRANCESCO GUARDI
Venice 1712 — Venice 1793
Entered the studio of his brother, Gianantonio, with whom he collaborated, but soon was active on his own. From 1761 he was on the register of Venetian painters. Lived permanently in Venice, except for two brief stays in the Trentino area (1778 and 1782). Elected member of the Academy of Venice in 1784.
Regata on the Grand Canal (circa 1765) Oil on canvas; 22 1/4″ × 12 3/4″. Donated to the Rijksmuseum in 1936 by Sir Henry Deterding.

GIOVANNI BATTISTA TIEPOLO. *The Vision of St. Anne.*

The sketch for a convent altarpiece now in Dresden's museum, this work represents St. Anne and Joachim (right foreground) in the act of consecrating Mary (in the clouds) to God the Father (above). Grandiose in conception, the pomp and rhetoric of the composition, built up on a system of diagonal tensions, is pushed to the limit. The figure of God the Father giving His benediction crowns and completes the system of movements. In this sketch, more than in the Dresden painting, the mechanical aspect of the structure is softened by the freshness of the brushwork. With rapid precision, the faces have been given sharp, somewhat humorous, psychological definition. The broadness and freedom of the color go beyond Tiepolo's official "grand manner."

FRANCESCO GUARDI. *Regata on the Grand Canal.*

This work is probably an early example of the master's view painting, showing similarities to the *View of Rialto and the Palazzo dei Camerlenghi* in the Metropolitan Museum, New York (circa 1764), and to a series on the Doge's festivals (1766). In layout and visual approach, the influence of Canaletto is most evident, but the execution is completely in the Guardi manner, showing vibrant and agitated brushwork, sureness of rhythm and limpidity of tone and texture.

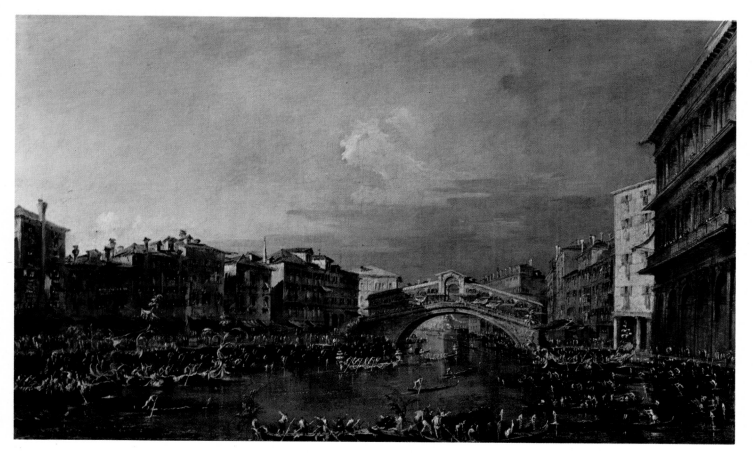

EL GRECO. *Crucifixion.*

Produced during the master's last years, like the variant by his own hand in the Museo de Santa Cruz, Toledo, this painting is the concluding high point in the stylistically somewhat discontinuous career of the Cretan painter. This discontinuity has been complicated by pseudo-critical interpretations, like that of Jean Cocteau, for whom Greco was a demigod. These have made it difficult to understand the paintings, by imposing on them mystical and religious values for which there is no evidence in the work. What the work does show is a knowledge of 16th-century Venetian paintings — from Titian to Jacopo Bassano — and especially of Tintoretto. Indirectly, a vein of Tuscan and Roman influence is also felt. In the paintings of the Toledo period, this background also emerges, but always, as in this picture, stripped down and reinterpreted in linear and vertical terms and in twisting forms. This is seen in the ashen flame of Christ's body, tormented by the wind. Any systematic perspective is rejected in favor of a fabric of lights and darks that make up the desolate landscape and the ominous wall of clouds. The violence of this vision is expressed in unreal color, like a damped down fire, without any suggestion of sunlight. As Giulio Clovio, Greco's companion during his Roman years, testified: "Daylight disturbed his inner light."

EL GRECO
(DOMENICO THEOTOKOPOULOS)
Candia 1541 — Toledo 1614
At Venice from 1566 to about 1574, with a stay at Rome in 1570–71. He may have been at Madrid in 1575–76. Settled permanently at Toledo in 1577.
Crucifixion (circa 1600–1611)
Oil on canvas; 22 1/4″ × 12 3/4″.
Numerous variants exist, including one in the Museo de Santa Cruz, Toledo. It entered the van Beuningen collection, Rotterdam, in 1930. Donated to the Rijksmuseum in 1933.

PETER PAUL RUBENS. *Portrait of Helena Fourment.*   *p. 154*

The artist's second wife is shown in her wedding dress. Boldly framed, the half-length figure is presented full face. The central axis is crossed and balanced by a left-to-right diagonal along which the chiaroscuro is graded toward the dark on the right. This considered composition structure is not immediately apparent as it is fused with the rich color that Rubens acquired from studying the Venetian painters, as well as Correggio and Barocci.

PETER PAUL RUBENS. *The Procession to Calvary.*   *p. 155*

In execution, this sketch for one of Rubens' numerous large altarpieces is typical of the master's hand, showing the rapid blocking out of the color and the sensuality of the paint. Most important of the many differences between the sketch and the finished version, now in Brussels, is the absence of the horseman behind the fallen Christ. But in each of his several preparatory sketches for the final work, the artist varied the positions and attitudes of his figures. The traditional theme is stamped with Rubens' personality in each figure and in the composition as a whole. Christ is shown as having

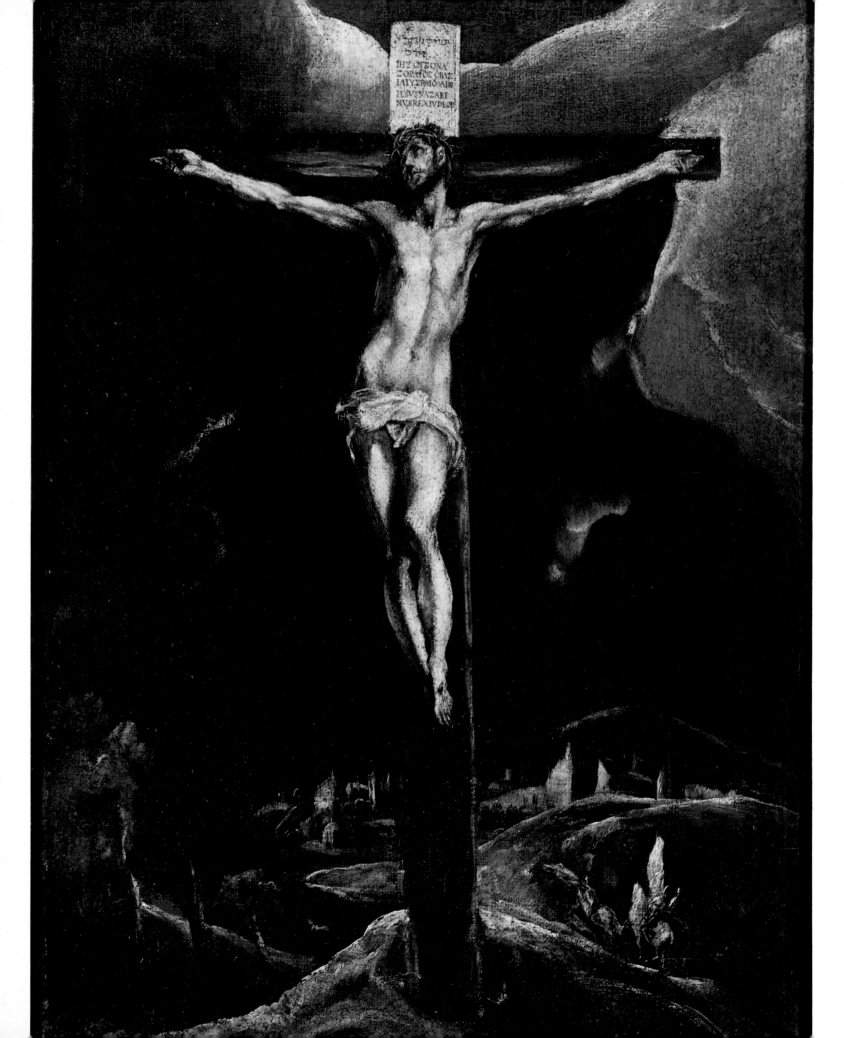

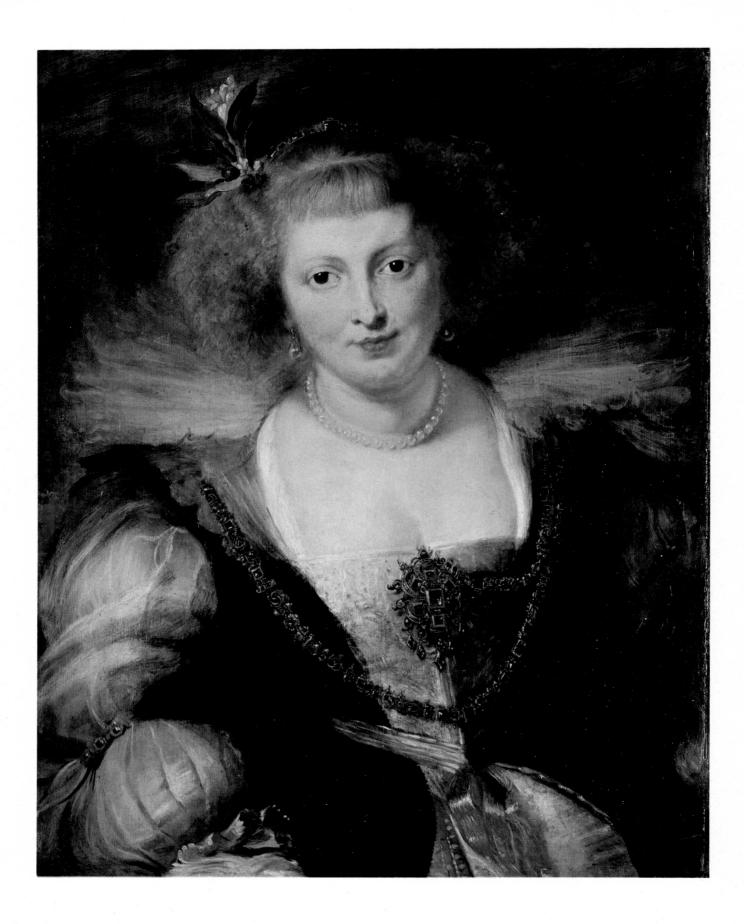

PETER PAUL RUBENS
Siegen 1577 — Antwerp 1640
From 1591 to 1598 he studied with Adam van Noort and Otto van Veen. Master in 1598. Worked in Italy from 1600 to 1608, in the service of the Duke of Mantua; also in Venice, Rome, Genoa, and in Spain (1603). He settled in Antwerp in 1608 and subsequently traveled to Paris (between 1621 and 1627), Madrid (1628–29) and London (1629–30) as ambassador. He returned to Antwerp in 1630.

The Procession to Calvary (circa 1634)
Oil on panel; 29″ × 21 3/4″.
Perhaps cut down on the right.
Sketch for the altarpiece now in the Musée Royal des Beaux Arts, Brussels, which was commissioned in 1634 and completed in 1637. It appeared at the Meyers sale, Rotterdam, in 1722. Subsequently owned by Jac. de Roore, The Hague, 1737; Thérèse van Halen, Antwerp, 1749; Van der Marck, Amsterdam, 1773. Reynolds saw it in 1781 at Van Heteren's in The Hague, and from that collection it entered the Rijksmuseum in 1809.

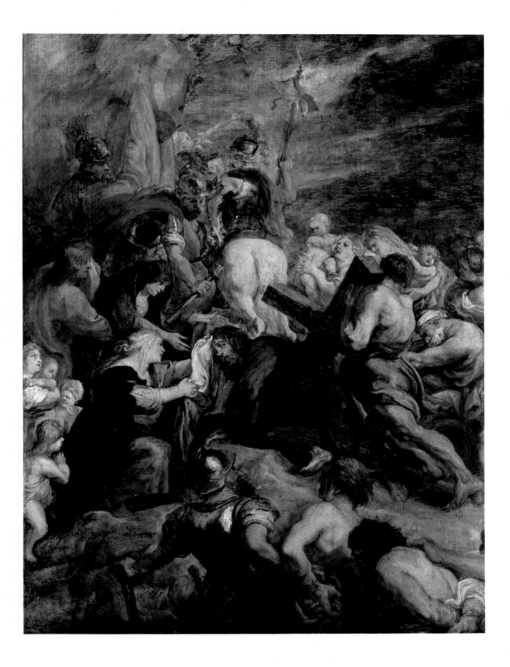

PETER PAUL RUBENS
Portrait of Helena Fourment
(circa 1630–35)
Oil on panel; 29 1/2″ × 22″.
A variant of the portrait of the same subject, shown full length, which was painted in 1630–31, and is now in the Alte Pinakothek, Munich. It appeared at the Du Tartre sale in Paris, 1804, then was in the possession of Lucien Bonaparte. Acquired by A. van De Hoop from John Smith, London, in 1833. Given to the City of Amsterdam in 1684; lent to the Rijksmuseum in 1855.

fallen under the weight of the cross, which is being held up by two powerful figures, one of which is probably Simon of Cyrene, as stated in St. Luke. St. Veronica wipes Christ's face with her "veil." Amidst the unruly crowd of soldiers and bystanders, Mary and John are seen, just behind Veronica. In compositional structure and organization of the space, the work is skillfully constructed for dramatic effect. The religious theme is transformed, in fact, into an exaltation of "fiery and pulsing life," as Burckhardt put it.

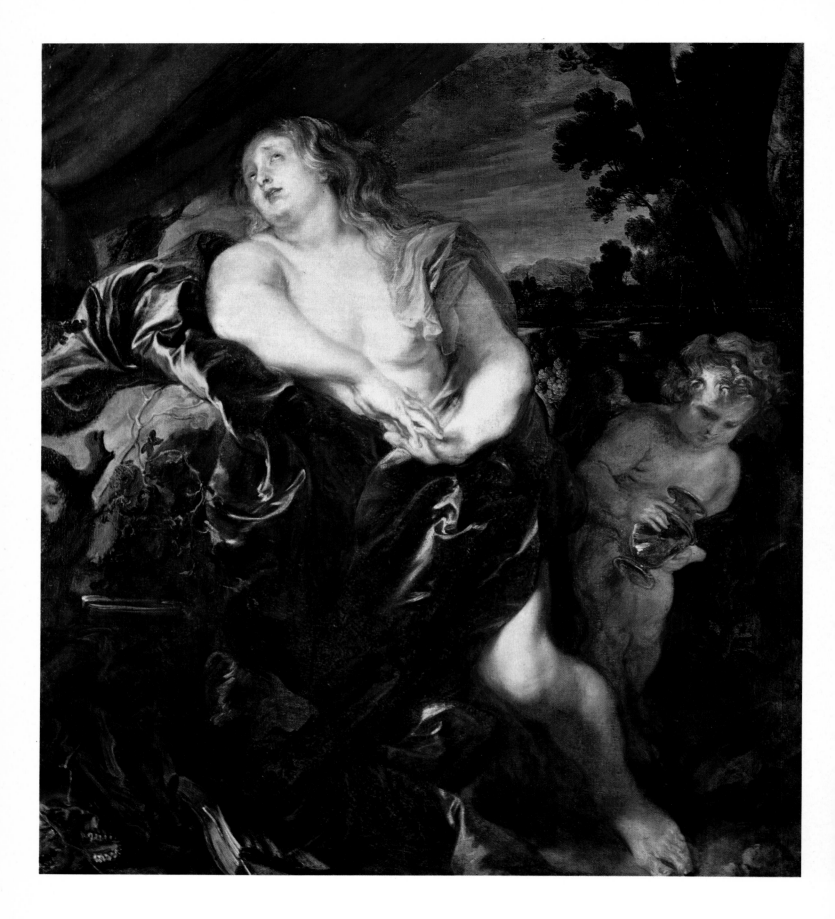

ANTHONY VAN DYCK
Prince William II and His Young Wife,
Princess Mary Stuart (1641)
Oil on canvas; 71 3/4″ × 56″.
In 1667 in the possession of Princess Amalia
van Solms, from whom it passed to the
Frisian branch of the Nassaus. In the Na-
tional Museum, The Hague, in 1808, and
from there to the Rijksmuseum.

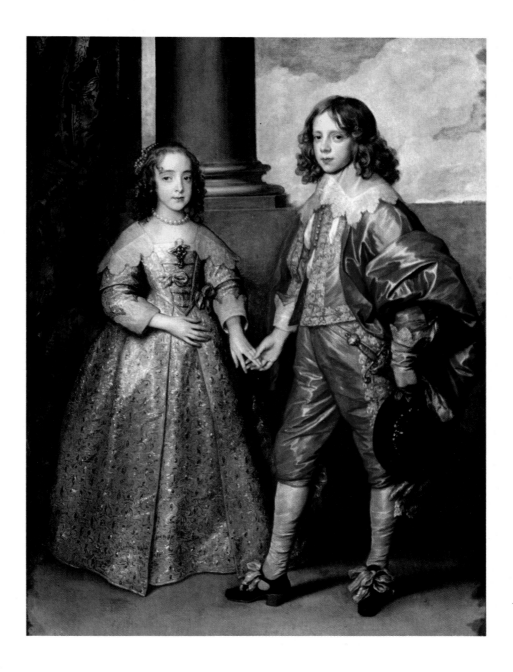

ANTHONY VAN DYCK
Antwerp 1589 — Blackfriars
(London) 1641
Pupil of Hendrik van Balen in 1609 and
later of Rubens, whose assistant he re-
mained after qualifying as a master painter
in 1618. Active in England from 1620 to
1621, in Italy until 1627, mainly in Venice
and Genoa; subsequently, in Antwerp. In
1632, he became court painter to Charles I,
in London, but worked for short periods in
Brussels (1634–35) and Paris (1640–41).
The Penitent Magdalene (circa 1620)
Oil on canvas; 66 1/2″ × 58 1/2″.
Three other versions are known.
From the National Museum of
The Hague, 1908.

ANTHONY VAN DYCK.   *The Penitent Magdalene.*
This youthful work was painted around 1620, when the artist was closest to
Rubens in style, although the sensuality of the modeling and the exuberant
color are more tempered. Van Dyck at this time was not strictly imitative
but had mastered the program he was following, and was seeking his own
direction while in the process of assimilating Rubens' repertory. This painting shows originality of decision in its structure and command of a rich palette. The sumptuous figure is represented full length and almost nude, weep-   157

MATHEIU LE NAIN
Laon 1607 — Paris 1677
Worked with his brothers Antoine and Louis
for a year in Laon, then settled in Paris
(1630), where he became an official painter
of the municipality (1633). All three broth-
ers were elected to the Academy on its
foundation in 1648.
The Gamblers (circa 1745–50)
Oil on canvas; 36 1/2″ × 47 1/4″.
In the sale of the Hôtel de l'Aligre, 1776.
Subsequently in the collections of Ch. Brun-
ner, Paris; J. W. Nienhuys, Bloemendaal.
Donated to the Rijksmuseum in 1929.

ing and wringing her hands. Her eyes are raised to heaven. An angel with a vase of ointment appears behind her. Landscape and drapery provide deep color effects that contrast with the pearly skin of the Magdalene.

ANTHONY VAN DYCK. *Prince William II and His Young Wife, Princess Mary Stuart.* p. 157

Painted in 1641, the last year of Van Dyck's life, this portrait perhaps was finished by Peter Lely, as another hand appears to have worked on the canvas. Van Dyck had been living in London since 1632, as court painter to Charles I. Princess Mary, the King's daughter, was married to Prince William of the Netherlands in London. She is portrayed here with the jewels the prince gave her on the day after the wedding. His splendid lace-trimmed, gold-embroidered suit was made by a London tailor. The young couple is shown full length, ceremoniously holding hands. A subtle balance has been created in the composition, between the two figures on the one hand, and the curtain, column and rectangle of sky on the other. An equally fine adjustment determines the stance of the figures and the inclination of their heads, with the glances directed toward the spectator. The sumptuous variety of textures is rendered with meticulous skill.

MATHIEU LE NAIN. *The Gamblers.*

The issue of Antoine and Louis Le Nain's artistic development is still controversial, but their much younger brother Mathieu served his apprenticeship in their studio, and in this painting he is very close to Louis' style. Three men in a stage-like setting are shown gambling at a round table. Looking on are a young boy, on the right, and a manservant holding a purse, on the left. In the right foreground are two greyhounds, and in the right background there is a glimpse of a landscape. This is probably a youthful work, as it shows the kind of Caravaggesque influence on the brothers Le Nain that is apparent in Mathieu's early painting. In the diagonal composition and in the hieratic poses and gestures, the picture reflects the main elements of Louis Le Nain's *Peasant Meal* (1642) in the Louvre. But here Mathieu follows painters like Pieter van Laer in giving Caravaggio's style an anecdotal interpretation.

On page 160:
PIERRE PAUL PRUD'HON
Cluny 1758 — Paris 1823
Pupil of Devesges at Dijon and of Pierre in
Paris. Won the Prix de Rome in 1748. He
returned to France in 1789, showed at the
Salon of 1797 and obtained a studio at the
Louvre. In 1800, with his *Allegory of Peace*,
he attracted the attention of Napoleon and
subsequently received official commissions.
*Rutger Jan Schimmelpenninck and
His Family* (1801 or 1802)
Oil on canvas; 8′7 3/4″ × 6′6 3/4″.
In the possession of descendants of the fam-
ily until 1929, when it came to the Rijks-
museum.

PIERRE PAUL PRUD'HON. *Rutger Jan Schimmelpenninck and His Family.* p. 160

As unlike David, with his cold, modular constructions, as Ingres with his bold archaism, Prud'hon is also considered an exponent of Neoclassicism, which demonstrates how loose a term that is. In this portrait, the deliberateness of the vertical scansion and the triangular disposition in plan do not

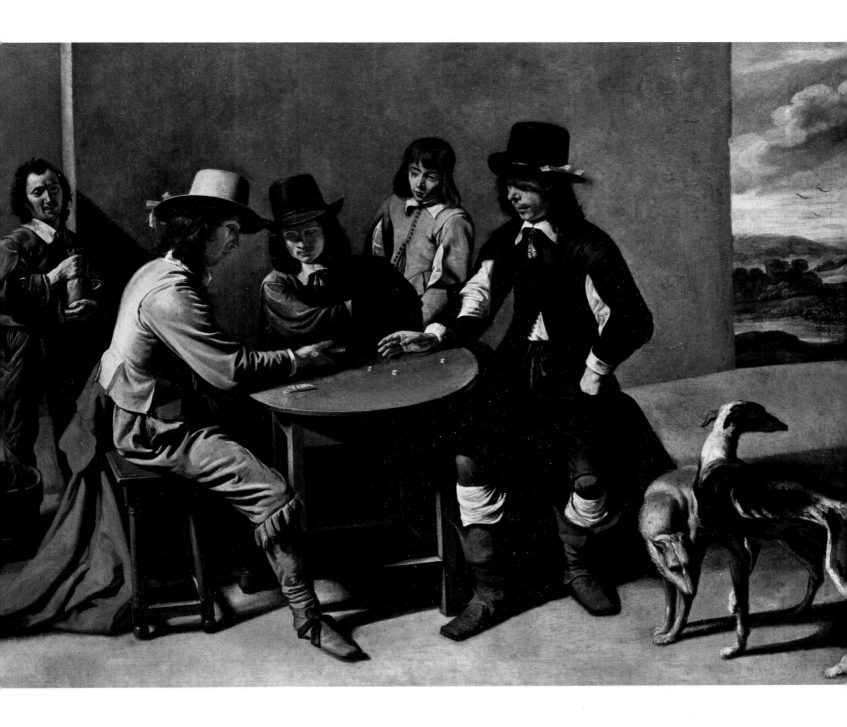

create that "austerity of the ancients" that is a fundamental of Neoclassical aspiration, but rather an atmosphere of lyrical surprise and suspension. The soft, sensual light derives from the influence of Boucher and Correggio on the artist. Schimmelpenninck, who held important ambassadorial posts and was President of the Batavian Republic from 1805 to 1806, is shown with his wife, his daughter and his son.

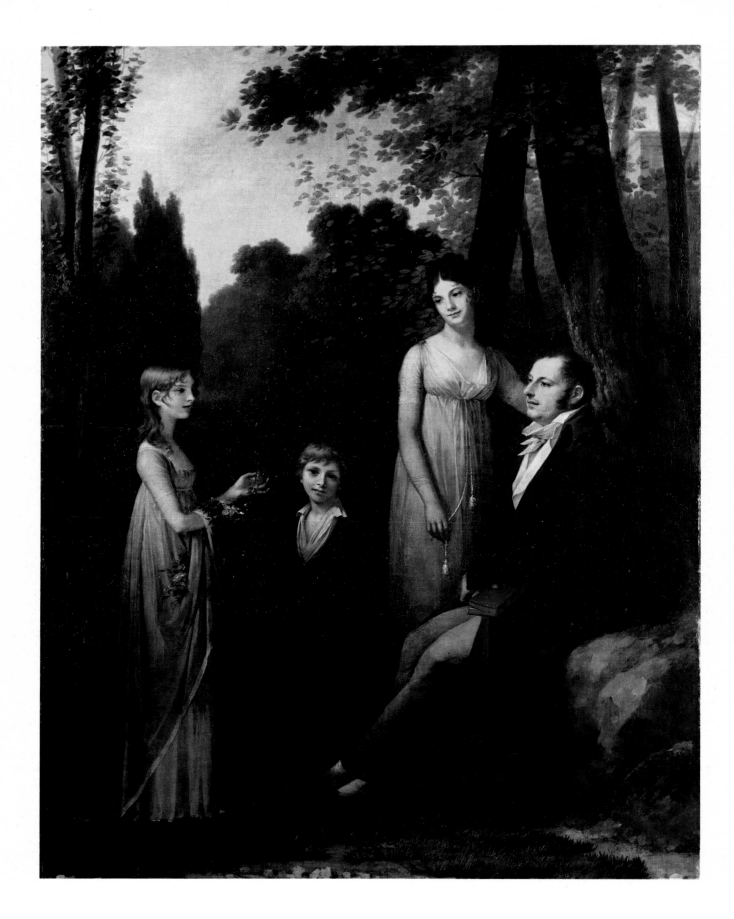

HISTORY OF THE MUSEUM
AND ITS BUILDING

The birth of the Rijksmuseum in Amsterdam opens an important chapter in the history of the modern museum. Its story is parallel to that of the Louvre: both were founded at the end of the 18th century, but neither was organized systematically until Napoleon's reign. Although the nucleus of the Rijksmuseum's first possessions came from the private collection of Prince William V, the museum did not develop, as had the Louvre, under the influence of a royal and aristocratic tradition. The Dutch museum rather got its impetus from the municipal organizations typical of Dutch mercantile society. This civic spirit is seen in the character of the collections, to which a fundamental coherency is given by a group of local masterpieces from the 17th century — the Golden Age of Dutch painting.

In 1800, at The Hague, a National Art Gallery with 225 paintings — mostly from William V's collection — was established. Eight years later, as soon as he had moved his court to Amsterdam, Louis Bonaparte, King of Holland, decreed the foundation of a "collection of paintings, drawings, sculptures, bronzes, gems, antiquities, works of art and curiosities of every kind." The existing collection at The Hague was increased by sixty-five canvases acquired at the van der Pot van Groeneveld sale, and by the City of Amsterdam's gift of *The Night Watch* and *The Syndics of the Cloth Guild* by Rembrandt, Bartholomeus van der Helst's *Banquet of the Civic Guard* and Willem van de Velde's *The Harbor of Amsterdam*. In the same year, through the intervention of the King, the museum bought the van Heteren Grevers collection, which included works by Berchem, Brouwer, Rubens, Metsu, Ter Borch and others. The old Town Hall, built by van Campen in 1648, was chosen to house the museum. Cornelis Apostool, an amateur artist and connoisseur, was named director, and he published the first catalogue, which listed 583 pieces. This felicitous start to the story of the Rijksmuseum ended a few years later with the abdication of Louis Bonaparte and the annexation of the state of Holland by France. Difficult times followed, and it was not until 1815 that the old plan to move the museum to more adequate quarters in the 17th-century Trippenhuis could be carried out. In 1816 the Gael collection, including numerous Rembrandt etchings, which had been bought in 1807 by Louis Bonaparte, was arranged as a Prints and Drawings Cabinet. The following year, the renovated museum was inaugurated, now including several notable acquisitions, such as Frans Hals's *The Merry Toper,* Jan Steen's *Self-Portrait* and Pieter de Hooch's *The Pantry.*

In the third decade of the 19th century, the directors of the Rijksmuseum were mainly interested, it seems, in establishing a collection of contemporary art. To this end, in 1828 they sold twenty-five pictures to make room and raise money for purchases in this field. The same year, following an old plan proposed by Louis Bonaparte, it was decided to exhibit the contemporary paintings in the 18th-century Welgelegen Pavilion at Haarlem, and to add a permanent exhibition of works lent by living painters. The plan was not realized, however, until 1838, when the first series of pictures transferred from The Hague and Amsterdam was installed at Haarlem.

Unfortunately the separation of the states of Holland and Belgium in 1830 was followed by a period of economic depression, which also limited the development of the museum. In the ensuing thirty years the only important work that the museum was able to buy was Frans Hals's *Portrait of a Married Couple.* Subsequently, however, the museum was enriched by two lavish bequests: in 1870, that of L. Dupper Wz., comprising sixty-three paintings (Hobbema, Ruisdael, van Goyen, Steen, Maes, etc.); and in 1875, that of M. A. Liotard, which consisted of fifteen pastels by the Swiss painter, J. E. Liotard. The acquisition of the Liotards created an interest in foreign works, and with the subsequent donation by Professor Tilanus of six more pastels by the same artist, the collection of Liotards was now second only to the one in Geneva. It was also in the second half of the 19th century that the policy was begun of regularly buying contemporary paintings, and in 1878 some of these were lent to public offices for the first time. In the meantime the position of director was abolished, and a board of trustees was established to run the museum.

In the 1870s the museum benefited not only from the bequests already mentioned, but also from the establishment of a State Advisory Board in 1874 and of a Department of Arts and Science in 1875, which facilitated the task of enlarging the museum building. Work was begun in 1876, and in 1885 the new museum, in a Neo-Gothic style, was inaugurated. With its additional space, the museum was now able to house, among other acquisitions, the fifty-two Dutch paintings of the recent van de Poll bequests; the van der Hoop collection, bequeathed to the municipality in 1854 and including Rembrandt's *The Jewish Bride* and Vermeer's *Young Woman Reading a Letter;* and several works from public buildings and guilds, on loan from the municipality. In addition to these there were thirty-four works lent by the Royal Society of Antiquarians, several bequests from private families and the collection of contemporary pictures formerly exhibited at the Welgelegen Pavilion. This phase of expansion ended with the opening in 1887 of the Nederlands Museum, a collection of sculpture, decorative arts and objects of historical interest that was installed in the same building.

By now the collection was very extensive, and the major concern of the trustees at the end of the 19th century was to round it out and fill in gaps. A group of art lovers called the *Vereeniging Rembrandt,* was founded in 1883; it supplied the funds for the acquisition of some fundamental works. Furthermore, the collection of French art was enriched by bequests of modern masters from R. Baron van Lynden (1889) and the family of Mr. C. Hoogendijk (1912). Meanwhile the building was modernized to improve the space for exhibitions and to arrange for further donations, such as that of the Drucker collection in 1916. Between the two World Wars, under the directorship of Dr. F. Schmidt Degener, the museum acquired a number of foreign masterpieces, including G. B. Tiepolo's *Portrait of a Senator* and *Telemachus and Mentor* and Goya's *Portrait of a Man.* With the addition of Italian paintings from the museum of the Grand Duke of Oldenburg (in 1923–25), a department of foreign art was opened. The department adopted a policy of representing various schools and currents by a few, select works.

Although the museum virtually had to mark time during World War II and move its collection to safe hiding places, it continued to receive donations, the most important of which were the Kessler-Hülsmann bequest of eighty-seven paintings (Rembrandt, Pieter Bruegel the Elder, etc.) and the Edwin vom Rath bequest of seventy-four Italian pictures. After the war, most of the post-1850 paintings were transferred on loan to the municipal Stedlijk Museum of Amsterdam. In recent years the collection of Dutch 15th- and 16th-century art was rounded out with the acquisition of works by Geertgen tot Sint Jans, Mostaert, Lucas van Leyden, Jan van Scorel, Bloemaert, etc. New departments were created for ancient and Asian art, for the applied arts of the 18th century and for Dutch history. Since 1946, the Rijksmuseum has held annual summer loan exhibitions of important Old Masters and subjects of art-historical interest.

THE BUILDING

The Rijksmuseum's original home, the 18th-century Trippenhuis, was already too small and inadequately lighted when it was opened to the public in 1817. It was not until 1862, however, that a committee was organized to discuss plans for a new structure. A competition was held, with the participation of twenty-one architects, but a decade went by before the winning plan was chosen. P. J. H. Cuypers was the architect, and he designed the present edifice. The Rijksmuseum of Amsterdam was officially opened on July 13, 1885.

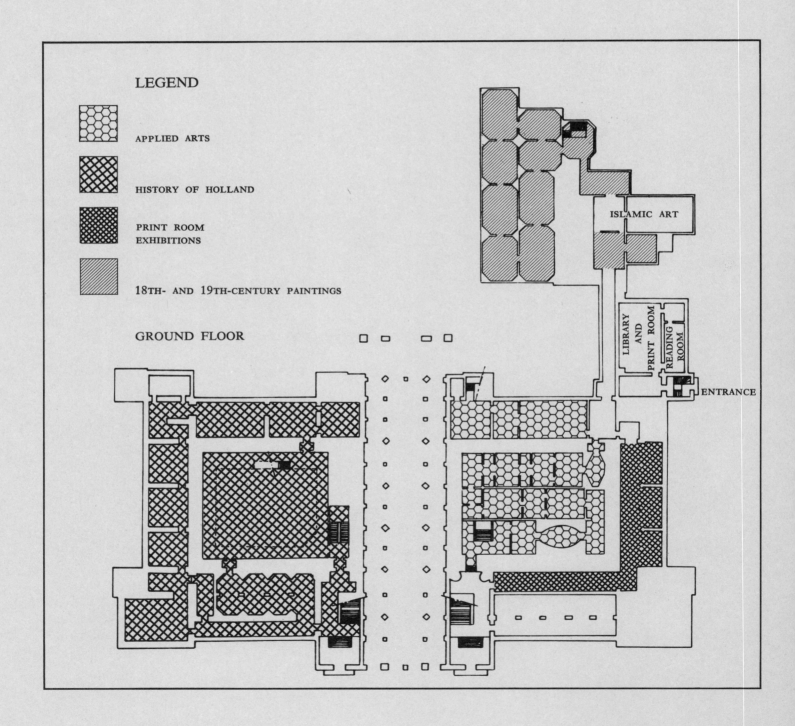

LEGEND

APPLIED ARTS

HISTORY OF HOLLAND

PRINT ROOM
EXHIBITIONS

18TH- AND 19TH-CENTURY PAINTINGS

GROUND FLOOR

ISLAMIC ART

LIBRARY AND PRINT ROOM

READING ROOM

ENTRANCE

Cuypers (1827–1921), the most important Dutch architect of the 19th century, was a faithful follower of Eugène Emmanuel Viollet-le-Duc's archaeological approach to buildings. He restored historic structures and adopted the Neo-Gothic style in his designs for the railroad station and the church of the Magdalene, as well as the Rijksmuseum, in Amsterdam. The type of revival to which Cuypers subscribed was based on local architecture of the 16th century, which itself was a modification of the earlier Gothic though it still continued the tradition. Again, from its inauguration the museum was overcrowded. After World War I a radical thinning out of the collections was undertaken and new criteria for the exhibition of the material were applied.

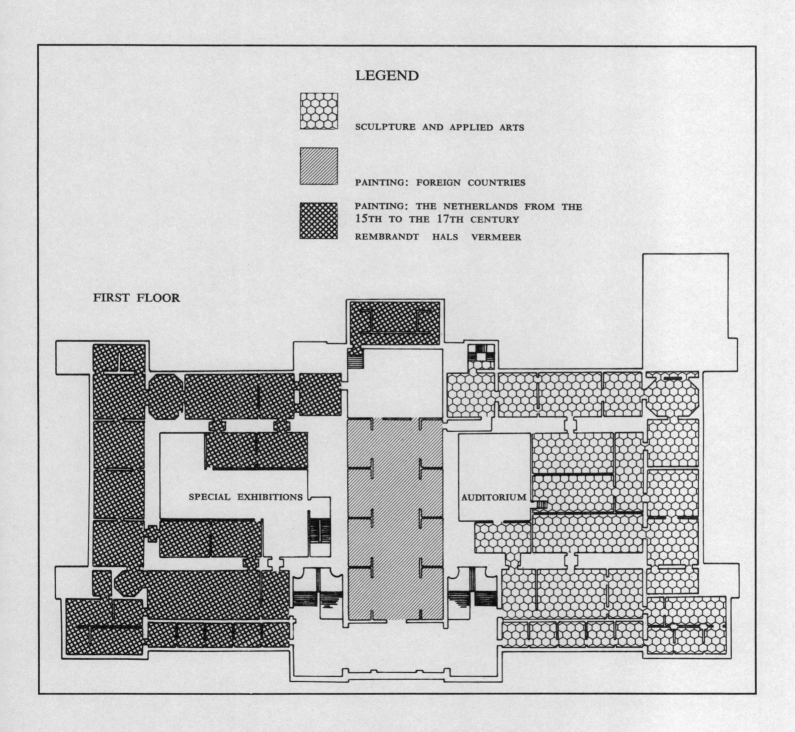

LEGEND

SCULPTURE AND APPLIED ARTS

PAINTING: FOREIGN COUNTRIES

PAINTING: THE NETHERLANDS FROM THE
15TH TO THE 17TH CENTURY
REMBRANDT HALS VERMEER

FIRST FLOOR

SPECIAL EXHIBITIONS

AUDITORIUM

SELECTED BIBLIOGRAPHY

BERGSTRÖM, INGVARD. *Dutch Still Life Painting*. tr. by Christine Hedström and Gerald Taylor. (P. Joseloff, New York, 1956).

BOON, K. G. *Rembrandt: The Complete Etchings*. (Abrams, New York, n.d.).

CLARK, KENNETH. *Rembrandt and the Italian Renaissance*. (N.Y.U. Press, New York, 1964).

DESCARGUES, PIERRE. *Hals*. tr. by James Emmons. (Skira, Geneva, 1968).

DUPONT, J. and MATHEY, F. *The 17th Century: From Caravaggio to Vermeer*. (Skira, Geneva, 1951).

FRIEDLANDER, MAX J. *Early Netherlandish Painting*. tr. by H. Norden. (Praeger, New York, 1967).

FROMENTIN, EUGENE. *The Masks of Past Time: Dutch and Flemish Painting from Van Eyck to Rembrandt*. tr. by A. Boyle. (Phaidon, London, 1948).

GERSON, H. K. *Rembrandt Paintings*. (Reynal, New York, 1968).

GOWING, LAWRENCE. *Vermeer*. (The Beechhurst Press, New York, 1953).

LASSAIGNE, JACQUES and DELEVOY, ROBERT L. *Flemish Painting*. (Skira, New York, 1957).

LEYMARIE, JEAN. *Dutch Painting*. (Skira, Geneva, 1956).

MEIJER, EMIL R. *Dutch Painting: 17th Century*. (McGraw-Hill & Co., New York, 1962).

MUNZ, LUDWIG. *Rembrandt*. (Abrams, New York, 1954).

ROSENBERG, JAKOB, et al. *Dutch Art and Architecture 1600–1800*. (Penguin, Baltimore, 1966).

SLIVE, S. *Drawings of Rembrandt*. 2 vols. (New York, 1965).

STECHOW, WOLFGANG. *Dutch Landscape Painting of the 17th Century*. (Phaidon, New York, 1966).

WILENSKI, REGINALD H. *Dutch Painting*. (Faber, London, 1955).

Paintings of Vermeer. Phaidon ed. (Oxford University Press, N.Y., 1940).

For their courtesy in furnishing information for this publication, the editors wish to thank Professor A. van Schendel, Director General of the Rijksmuseum, and Dr. Gerard van der Hoek, Head of the Educational Section of the Rijksmuseum.

INDEX OF ILLUSTRATIONS

169

INDEX OF NAMES

GENERAL INDEX